Arab Media

Arab Media

Globalization and Emerging Media Industries

NOHA MELLOR, MUHAMMAD AYISH,
NABIL DAJANI AND KHALIL RINNAWI

polity

The right of Noha Mellor, Khalil Rinnawi, Nabil Dajani, Muhammad I. Ayish to be identified as Author of this Work has been asserted in accordance with the UK Copyright, Designs and Patents Act 1988.

First published in 2011 by Polity Press

Polity Press
65 Bridge Street
Cambridge CB2 1UR, UK

Polity Press
350 Main Street
Malden, MA 02148, USA

ISBN-13: 978–0–7456–4534–6
ISBN-13: 978–0–7456–4535–3(pb)

A catalogue record for this book is available from the British Library.

Typeset in 11 on 13 pt Adobe Garamond Pro
by Servis Filmsetting Ltd, Stockport, Cheshire
Printed and bound in Great Britain by MPG Books Group Limited, Bodmin, Cornwall

The publisher has used its best endeavours to ensure that the URLs for external websites referred to in this book are correct and active at the time of going to press. However, the publisher has no responsibility for the websites and can make no guarantee that a site will remain live or that the content is or will remain appropriate.

Every effort has been made to trace all copyright holders, but if any have been inadvertently overlooked the publisher will be pleased to include any necessary credits in any subsequent reprint or edition.

For further information on Polity, visit our website: www.politybooks.com

Contents

Contents

Contents

Tables and Figures

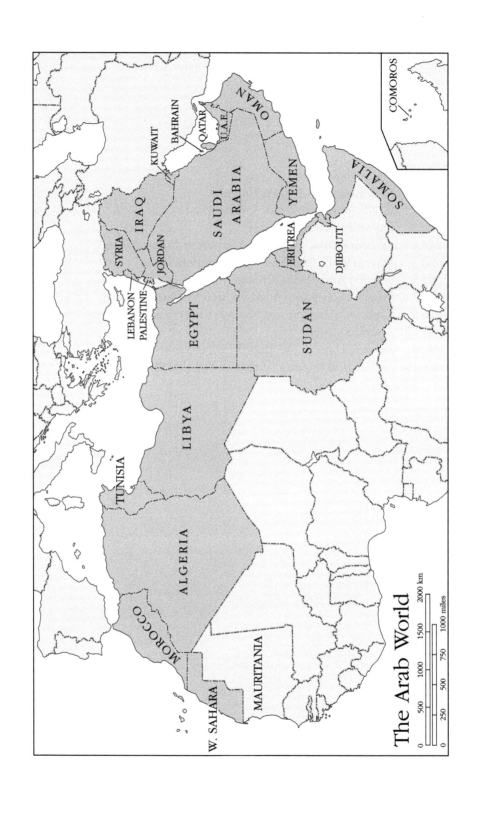

The Arab World

COMOROS

OMAN
BAHRAIN
QATAR
KUWAIT
U.A.E.
IRAQ
SYRIA
JORDAN
LEBANON
PALESTINE
SAUDI ARABIA
YEMEN
ERITREA
DJIBOUTI
SOMALIA
EGYPT
SUDAN
LIBYA
TUNISIA
ALGERIA
MOROCCO
W. SAHARA
MAURITANIA

0   500   1000   1500   2000 km
0   250   500   750   1000 miles

Introduction

Noha Mellor

Boundaries of the region

This book focuses on the media industries in the Arab-speaking countries in the Middle East, the region that is usually referred to as the Arab homeland or the Arab world (Hopkins & Ibrahim, 2003). What are the cultural unifiers and diversifiers among Arab populations across the region?

The Arab region is part of a geopolitical entity called the Middle East, which was a British term created during the Second World War (Smith 1968, 4). The military used this name when referring to Persia and eastern Arabia in particular, while the western part of the Middle East was called the Levant. Thus, the British military at that time "never thought of the Middle East as a single or distinctive region possessing any particular unity, except in so far as it was but a portion of the Muslim world" (Smith 1968, 4). The name was originally used by the Royal Air Force, which amalgamated its Iraq and Cairo units, retaining the name Middle East for the new unit. The term spread after that in other communiqués, and perhaps one reason for its success is its vagueness. As the phrase "Middle East" is only an invented geopolitical label, it "should not lead to assumptions about similarities between these countries" (Sreberny-Mohammadi 1998,180). The Middle East, as a geographical area, was later expanded to include Libya, Sudan, the Maghreb countries, and even Afghanistan. This expansion increased the confusion resulting from mixing "separate and distinct concepts of Arab Asia, the Arab world, the Islamic world, and the Middle East" (Smith 1968, 8).

Arabs are usually defined as those "who speak the Arabic language, identify themselves as 'Arabs' and are nationals or residents of member countries of the League of Arab States." (Hopkins & Ibrahim 2003, 1). The word "Arab" does not refer to a particular race, as Arabs are of diverse religions and ethnic origins. Various ethnic groups such as Nubians, Bedouins, Kurds, and Berbers are encompassed by the term, as well as other religious groups including Christians (of various denominations), Muslims (Sunni, Shiite, Bahhai, Druze), and Jews. Several terms denote Arab identity: Arab, Arabic, Arabian. These are used interchangeably.

The Arab region referred to in this book includes the following countries: Algeria, Bahrain, Egypt, Iraq, Jordan, Kuwait, Lebanon, Libya, Morocco,

Oman, Palestine, Qatar, Saudi Arabia, Sudan, Syria, Tunisia, the UAE, and Yemen. This limitation is in line with other scholars (Amin 2001), and it confines itself to countries where Arabic is the official language. Other countries, such as the Comoros, Mauritania, and Somalia, are also members of the League of Arab States (LAS), and thus are seen – at least officially – as part of the Arab world. The Arabs are not a homogenous group. "Their world, cultural unity, and political division have been evolving throughout history. Even the cultural boundaries, let alone the political borders, have continued to change" (Hopkins & Ibrahim 2003, 4). This is seen, for instance, in the joining of Mauritania, Somalia, and Djibouti to the LAS in the 1970s, followed by the Comoros Islands in the 1990s.

These newcomers are not included here because they have unique historical backgrounds that distinguish them from other Arab countries. This is reflected in the several other official languages (particularly French and Somali) that form part of their unique identities. The Comoros, for instance, has three official languages: Comorian, Arabic, and French. The country has been a member of four different organizations, each of which represents a part of the Comoros history and identity: the African Union, La Francophonie, Organization of the Islamic Conference, and the Arab League. This reflects the impact of French, Arab, African, and Islamic cultures on the shaping of the Comoros. The Arab cultural influence has been evident since the sixteenth and seventeenth centuries, with the Omani rule of Zanzibar, and several Omani intellectuals spreading their Arabic publications in Zanzibar, such as the Omani newspaper *Al Falaq* (al-Kindi 2001). The unique relationships the Comoros, Somalia, and Mauritania have with other members of the LAS, and their cultural similarities and differences, have yet to be analyzed.

Language, culture and traditions are among the similarities connecting the Arab countries; they share a history of being subordinated to first Ottoman and then European colonial powers. The Ottoman Empire was challenged by the new colonial powers in Europe who sought "to colonize whatever territories they could reach overseas" and the "intensity of colonial competition over the Arab world was due not only to the quest for markets and raw materials, but also for its many strategic advantages. The Arab homeland is geographically situated at the center of the 'Old World' of Asia, Africa and Europe" (Hopkins & Ibrahim 2003, 3). The dominance was mainly French or British, as shown in Table 1.

In addition, several other Arab countries were British protectorates, such as Bahrain, Jordan, Kuwait, Lebanon, Oman, Qatar, and the UAE. Morocco was a French protectorate (Abdelali, 2004). Following their independence, Arab governments established large bureaucracies, which in turn encouraged

Table 1: Arab Regions as Former Colonies

Country	Control	Dates
Algeria	France	1830–1962
Egypt	Britain	1882–1952
Iraq	Britain	1917–1932
Libya	Italy	1929–1949
Sudan	Britain	1873–1954
Syria	France	1922–1946
Tunisia	France	1881–1956
Yemen	Britain	1839–1965

(Source, Abdelali 2004, p. 24)

the population to move to the capitals (Ibrahim 1975). This relates urbanization to modernization, as Lerner described this process in his 1958 study.

Since the nineteenth century, the Arab countries have increased their exports, particularly to Europe. This increase encouraged the growth of coastal cities and seaports (Ibrahim 1975). The proportion of Arab city dwellers has grown immensely in the course of the first half of the twentieth century, compared to the Western world, where it took two centuries to achieve a similar growth (Ibrahim 1975). Urbanization was driven by population increases as well as migration from rural areas to cities. During the first half of the twentieth century, Arab states' urbanization differed widely. Egypt, Lebanon, Syria, Jordan, Tunisia, Kuwait, and Iraq were among the most urbanized compared to Yemen, Sudan, or Saudi Arabia (Ibrahim 1975). Saudi Arabia has since undergone a significant urbanization process, with the percentage of its city dwellers jumping from less than 10 percent in 1902 to 84 percent in 1999 (Assad 2007).

Cultural unifiers

The most important cultural unifiers for Arab states are language (Modern Standard Arabic: MSA), religion (Islam remains the dominant religion in the region, with over 90 percent of the population Muslims) and common history (Hopkins & Ibrahim 2003, 2). This has prompted several countries to seek a unified Arab identity, particularly following independence. Egypt and Syria formed the United Arab Republic in 1958; it was disbanded in 1961. Arab nationalism was seen as a political reaction to both Turkish nationalism and European colonialism during the late nineteenth and early twentieth century (Haddad 1994, 217). Even in states where Arabic was not the only official language, such as Algeria, Tunisia, and Morocco, the decision to enforce Arabization in the post-independence era was a political decision par excellence. It was the political regime that determined the success or failure of the Arabization process (Al-Thawadi 1990). For instance, in Algeria, Arabization was aimed at enforcing a new Arab identity to counteract the French identity enforced during colonization (Al-Thawadi 1990).

Despite the existence of distinct dialects in each Arab state, the spread of one shared written language, or MSA, has contributed to the spread of pan-Arab media and publications. The spread of Islam has resulted in written Arabic's prevalence across the region. The classical language of the Koran, however, is different from MSA, which has been simplified to suit media and educational purposes. Moreover, Islam's migration from Arabia to other Arab countries, and the conquest of several of these countries, played a major role in spreading the Arabic language at the expense of indigenous languages such as Coptic, Aramaic, and Greek (Mellor 2005). In fact, early pan-Arab nationalist movements in the nineteenth century were inspired by Muslim modernists, such as those in Syria who "felt that educational reform should be pursued through Arabic, the language of the land of Islam" particularly when faced with Turkification in education (Haddad 1994, 202). Thus, among Syrian Christians, Arabic replaced Greek as the language of the church at the end of the nineteenth century, particularly with the appointment of an Arab patriarch to replace the Greek one (Haddad 1994).

Arab leaders propagate this pan-Arab discourse and indeed, "no Arab regime . . . has dared formally to go against the proclaimed national self-identification" (Hopkins & Ibrahim 2003, 4). However, those leaders tend to diffuse Arabism with other discourses that bind Arab populations with non-Arabic speaking Islamic countries as well. Former Egyptian president Gamal Abdel Nasser (1952–1970), the father of pan-Arabism, who linked Egyptian identity with "Arabism, Islam and Africa" (Smith 1968, 8). Undoubtedly, the pan-Arab discourse glosses over the ethnic and religious diversity that characterize the Arab populations, and this "diversity . . . reflects the ebb and flow of empires, and the spread of cultures and religions in the past – thus the concentration of Berber-speakers in the Maghreb, the inclusion of Nuer, Dinka, Azande, Fur, and others in Sudan, and the combination of Christians and Druze in Lebanon" (Hopkins & Ibrahim 2003, 2).

Some scholars do not see the Arab region as part of one unified Arab society. Tibi, for instance, argues, "With a few exceptions, such as Egypt and Morocco, most of these newly established nation-states lack historical legitimacy and thus are historically questionable . . . the post-colonial Arab states are nominal nation-states" (1997, 23). Thus the Arab states would be seen here as "a regional subsystem." The defeat following the 1967 war (between Israel and Egypt, Jordan, and Syria, which ended with Israel seizing the Gaza Strip, the Sinai Peninsula, the West Bank, and the Golan Heights) was seen as the first serious blow to Arab unity (Mellor 2007). The Iraqi invasion of Kuwait came as a second blow (Hopkins & Ibrahim 2003), with the future option being "a system of regional cooperation based on the national sovereignty of the participating states" (Tibi 1997, 24). There were indeed attempts among several Arab states to group in separate political and economic unions, such as the Gulf Cooperation Council (GCC) formed in 1981, comprising Saudi Arabia, Kuwait, Bahrain, Qatar, Oman and UAE. The Arab Cooperation Council (ACC) comprising Egypt, Jordan, Iraq, and Yemen, was formed in 1989 as a response to the GCC. The ACC, however, did not survive the political division following the Iraqi invasion of Kuwait and the tensions between Egypt and Iraq in the wake of the invasion. Another example is the Arab Maghreb Union (AMU) founded in 1989 and comprising Mauritania, Morocco, Algeria, Tunisia, and Libya. This alliance aimed to strengthen the economic partnership among its member states. Indeed, scholars tend to divide the Arab world into the Mashreq, Maghreb, and Gulf regions (e.g. Boughanmi 2008; Fargues 2006; Page 2006), and some of the data presented in this chapter will reflect this particular regional division.

Socioeconomic diversifiers

There are also remarkable differences among Arab states in terms of their political, economic, and demographic situations. For instance, while Algeria had an estimated population of 33 million in 2007, Bahrain had less than one million inhabitants. Table 2 shows these economic and demographic differences across the region.

Poverty figures differ from one country to another, so in Egypt the percentage of population under the poverty line was estimated at 20 percent in 2005, compared to 25 percent in Algeria, 7 percent in Libya, 11 percent in Syria, and 45 percent in Yemen in the same year (CIA World Factbook).

Some Arab states depend on industry (UAE, Qatar, and Libya), particularly in the Gulf oil region. The economy in other states, such as Jordan, Lebanon, Syria, and the Palestinian territories, depends more on services. In addition, as shown in Table 2, some states struggle with poverty while others (such as the oil-rich Gulf States) are more prosperous. The Gulf States countries enjoy higher literacy rates, more globalised economies, higher Gross Domestic Product (GDP) and living standards; they have embraced new technologies more quickly than other Arab states. Although the region

Table 2: GDP and Demographic Indicators

	Population in 000s in 2009	Nominal GDP in $US bn in 2009
Algeria	34,178*	125*
Bahrain	795	19
Egypt	76,704	188
Iraq	28,945*	70**
Jordan	5,898	23
Kuwait	3,536	115
Lebanon	3,857	33
Libya	6,324*	60*
Morocco	31,879	91
Oman	2,796	52
Palestine	4,008	6
Qatar	1,218	93
Saudi Arabia	25,519	380
Sudan	39,117	54
Syria	20,368	54
Tunisia	10,429	40
UAE	4,907	229
Yemen	23,687	26

*figures are estimate for 2005, extracted from CIA World Factbook
** estimate for 2009 by CIA World Factbook

currently has the largest growth in internet users in the world (Dutta et al. 2007), there are remarkable differences among the Arab states. Some are advanced while other countries still lag far behind. While the UAE has nearly 34 users per 100 inhabitants, Syria has only 4, and while the former has 117 personal computers per 1,000 inhabitants, the latter has only 19 (Dutta et al. 2007).

These conditions combine to make the Gulf States suitable candidates to lead the region in the twenty-first century. Some commentators, however, see this role as likely to be modest, mainly because the Gulf States rest on factors that reduce their appeal to the Arab masses, such as dependence on the USA for security and an abundance of resources absent in other countries (Springborg 2008).

Recent economic reforms in several Arab states have increased their exports. Table 3 shows export increase as percentage of GDP in several Arab countries, including the resource-poor countries such as Egypt and Jordan.

Economic and demographic indicators are not the only diversifiers among Arab states. There are also cultural diversifiers that give each Arab state its own distinct national identity: local dialects and religious denominations that exist side-by-side with the unifiers (Hopkins & Ibrahim 2003). Some

Table 3: Export Percentage of GDP

Country	1996–99	2006
Egypt	18.1	31.4
Jordan	48.5	52
Lebanon	12.7	19.9
Morocco	28	36.7
Algeria	23.6	42.3
Syria	35.1	41.4
Yemen	35.8	44.2

(Source, UNESCO, 2005)

language scholars argue that the differences among dialects can be so great as to be mutually unintelligible, say for Moroccans and Omanis (Mellor 2005). Even in the written variety of Arabic or MSA, there are differences in spelling and usage and adoption, as manifested in the language of Arab newspapers (Abdelali 2004).

Arab leaders draw on the unifiers and diversifiers according to their political interests, so "times of Arab strength and glory are those in which the 'unifiers' are invoked. Periods of weakness or decline are those in which the "diversifiers" are manipulated by indigenous or external factors to divide the Arabs" (Hopkins & Ibrahim 2003, 6). However, diversifiers and unifiers are diffused in times of crisis, such as the civil wars in Lebanon (1975–1985), and Sudan (1956–1973 and 1983–1996). This also includes the recent crisis in Darfur, the turmoil in Iraq in the 1960s and 1970s, and the recent tensions in Iraq (Hopkins & Ibrahim 2003). Arabs may feel united and/or divided by crisis.

The political situation has influenced development plans in the region and the intensification, or conversely the downplaying, of Arab nationalist discourse. In one example, the region experienced more than 20 parliamentary elections between 1985 and 1996, or only twice the number of elections that took place over the preceding twenty years, following the independence of Arab states (Sadiki 2000). There were other political crises, particularly the second Gulf war in 1991, the Iraq war in 2003, and the recent turmoil in Lebanon in 2006. These crises have also had an impact on the pattern of media consumption. For instance, during the Israeli attack on Lebanon in 2006, news circulation (print and broadcasting) increased across the region (Arab Media Outlook 2007). The alternative discourse of pan-Islamism has gained tremendous importance particularly since the Islamic Revolution in Iran in 1978, and "pan-Islamism has emerged as a competing paradigm contending for public space with other paradigms" (Hopkins & Ibrahim 2003, 7).

Arab media in the age of globalization

The main argument of this book is that Arab media has undergone a series of changes over the past two decades as a direct result of the acceleration of the globalization process. Thus, the book acknowledges the interplay between local and global cultures, seeing globalization as a process (Robertson 1992; Waters 2001). Globalization as a phenomenon has been at the centre of several Arab publications and at the centre of debate among Arab scholars over the past decade. Several Arab scholars see in globalization a celebration of capitalistic values and a threat to native cultural identity. To back this argument, such scholars point at the increasing consumerism and imitation of Western lifestyles among Arab youth, thereby focusing on the cultural exchange of the globalization process rather than the economic or political exchanges.

For instance, Abdel Rahman (2002) argues that globalization has resulted in the accentuation of the gap between the North or Developed World and the South or Developing World. In so doing, the South has become more and more dependent on the North, which only uses the South as a market for cultural products. Such views usually accuse the West (particularly the USA) of spreading their cultural values at the expense of indigenous cultural heritage. Increasing consumption of American media products among Arab youth is seen as escapism, rather than as a means of encouraging them to participate in public debates (see e.g. Al Kahtani 2000).

Likewise, Al Yasin (cited in Hindkær 2001, 61) fears that the increasing consumption of Western cultural products may be the most immediate threat to local cultures. Such scholars then equate globalization (at least at the cultural level) with dependency on the West and hegemony of the latter in setting up new values and norms. Such views usually refer to the global statistics on cultural flow, showing, for instance how the Arab states' import of cultural products (from the USA and UK in particular) exceeds its export. One such state is Egypt: its cultural exports were reduced by one-third from 1994 to 2002, with the rest of Arab countries as major importer of Egyptian cultural exports. Core cultural goods are defined as those including heritage goods, books, newspapers and periodicals, printed matter, recorded media, visual arts, audiovisual media.

On the other hand, the expansion of Arab satellite channels during the past decade has prompted several scholars to claim that this is a sign of the so-called "contra-flow of culture" from the Arab region to the rest of the world. For instance, Wessler & Adolphsen (2008) show that leading Western channels such as the BBC World Service, CNN, and Deutsche Welle relied on Arab satellite channels such as Al Jazeera during the Iraq war 2003, which helped to highlight the "Arab perspective" on the war.

Table 4: Arab Countries' Import and Export of Cultural Goods, 2009

	Exports in thousands USD	Imports in thousands USD
Bahrain	337.5	15,156
Egypt	10,7717	33,330
Jordan	4,417	23,737
Lebanon	55,453	54,912
Oman	1,141	18,959
Qatar	139	16,263
Saudi Arabia	6,102	94,335
Sudan	432	8,943
Syria	2,327	1,724
Tunisia	5,249	42,334

Moreover, Arab leaders now support international initiatives to spread Arab culture in the world. One such initiative is The Sharjah Prize for Arab Culture, established in 1998 on the initiative of the United Arab Emirates. The prize is given to nationals of Arab states who have contributed, through their artistic or intellectual work, to the diffusion of Arab culture in the world. In addition, Arab states, as we shall see in Chapter One, now compete in profiling their cities as "global" cities, as a result of recent economic reforms in the region.

In the Arab context, globalization can be seen as a positive force in certain aspects, such as economic prosperity and development. At the cultural level, however, there are ambivalent attitudes as to how globalization may prove beneficial for the native culture. For instance, while the Americanization of certain (serious) genres, that is, news and debate programs, has been hailed as a sign of *progressive* and democratic revolution in the region, the Americanization of the (popular) genres such as music videos and soap operas has been regarded as a *regression* from the authentic heritage of the region (Mellor 2005, 5). Thus, globalization can be seen as a medium that may threaten the "authentic" culture: traditions and customs. Changes at economic or political levels usually take place voluntarily, going top-down, that is, enforced from the more privileged elites and circulated to laypeople. The cultural changes, on the other hand, are seen as going from the bottom up, that is, the changes are incorporated by ordinary people who, thanks to technical advances, can access global media such as transnational media, Internet, books, and so on. Moreover, the impact of globalization on cultural heritage may indeed vary from one Arab state to another. Suleiman (2003), for instance, argues that the Lebanese people tend to see themselves as a liaison between East and West, while in Saudi Arabia, due to the existence of holy places there, it is tradition and customs that form the national identity. Saudi

Arabia, moreover, has long opened the door for economic and technical expertise from the West while attempting to maintain traditional core values (Yamani 2000). Seen against this backdrop, different discourses may prevail in Arabic discussions regarding the impact of globalization. Resistance to this globalization process, however, may arise if it is seen to tarnish the "authentic," or if the changes are seen to be imposed by – rather than sought or even bought from – the West.

The following chapters will pick up on this theme of globalization and its impact on the development of local as well as pan-Arab media industries. It is the view of the authors that the recent changes in Arab media have been the outcome of this globalization process. Thus, the political, technological, and cultural changes on the global media scene have resulted in the reorganization of the Arab media field in terms of media policies, media technology, and the content and genre developed for the new generation of media consumers.

Structure of the book

We begin with an overview of the modern Arab media landscape and particularly the change in the role of media from a tool for mobilizing the public to a tool of commercial and symbolic profit. The first chapter also reviews some of the pressing changes in the region that have affected the media scene, such as increasing immigration within and outside the region. The subsequent chapters deal with the impact of these changes on a selected media industry.

Chapter 2 deals with the printing and publishing industry. A large part of the chapter reviews the historical evolution of this industry in the region in order to understand the contemporary changes. The main argument is that Arab printing has been subject to immense technological developments that seem to undermine the development of the human component of this industry and instead to center on copying Western technology.

Chapter 3 deals with the press, and it too begins with a historical overview of the development of press in the Arab region. The chapter also discusses the role of the press as a watchdog, and how the press has failed to play that crucial role because of its orientation to the interests of the political and financial elites rather than the general public.

Chapter 4 surveys the Arab radio broadcasting industry, paying particular attention to recent developments since the 1990s. The chapter also sheds light on the role of radio in the age of media convergence and multimedia environments. These changes offer both opportunities and threats to radio broadcasters.

Chapter 5 surveys the television industry, which has been subject to state monopoly since its inception, reviewing recent developments and the launch of privately owned satellite channels. The main argument here is that despite the major cultural transformations in the region over the past two decades, changes were induced by global rather than local developments and hence were not sustainable. They thus had little impact on the television industry and its role in ensuring pluralistic public space.

Chapter 6 focuses on cinema, paying great attention to Egyptian film as the pioneer in the region. The chapter discusses the changing role of the cinema as an industry, becoming part of the progressive image of Arab states, particularly those in the Gulf regions. The chapter reviews current challenges that face the cinema industry, as well as its function as a space to expose and debate social ills. The chapter argues that this role is likely to continue in the future, where joint Arab-European production will be more common.

Chapter 7 surveys internet spread and usage in the Arab region and discusses the role of the internet in the Arab public sphere. Despite state censorship and filtering of internet sites, states still strive to update their telecommunication and internet development as an element in their economic development plans. This reflects governments' ambivalent attitude toward internet usage, which is increasing rapidly in comparison to other regions, particularly with the this region's changing demographics.

Chapter 8 sums up the recent trends in the Arab media industries, reflecting, for instance, on the role of the Arab Diaspora as media audiences as well as the role of Arabic-speaking transnational media in enforcing a sense of pan-Arab national identity among Arab audiences inside and outside the Arab world.

We conclude this book with brief remarks on the outlook of Arab media industries (particularly printing, press, radio, TV, cinema, and internet) and their expected role in the twenty-first century.

1   Arab Media: An Overview of Recent Trends

Noha Mellor

Most Arab media industries (particularly print, broadcasting, cinema, and New Media) are controlled by totalitarian governments that exercise great powers over media organizations. This is in sharp contrast to democratic societies, where the media are largely independent and attempts to reflect diverse voices in these societies. Although it is hard to envisage Arab totalitarian societies as a nurturing environment for commercially vibrant media systems, the Arab region represents an unusual case: commercialization and liberalization of selected media industries has gone hand-in-hand with continuous state intervention and an increasing self-censorship.

This chapter looks at the factors that have contributed to recent changes on the Arab media scene. It provides a brief overview of these changes and discusses the use of media first for mobilization purposes and later for commercial purposes. It argues that the recent local changes – whether political, demographic, cultural, or economic – have been very much influenced by wider global changes, such as the increasing immigration within and outside the region. It also argues that pan-Arab media have grown into large industries operating under state control, and self-censorship is widely practiced by media owners and producers to save their advertising revenues.

We will first review the main factors behind the rise of pan-Arab media industries and then discuss the role of Arab media in mobilizing the Arab nation.

The rise of media industries

Following their independence, Arab states sought to use the media as a means of mobilizing Arab public opinion. Journalists were regarded as new mouthpieces for Arab regimes. Political turmoil in the region halted this mobilization, first with the defeat in the 1967 war and later with the 1991 Gulf war, intended to end the Iraqi invasion of Kuwait. Indeed, the 1991 Gulf war was seen as the catalyst of media reforms in the Arab region, with many Arab states launching their own satellite channels and opening the market for privately owned outlets.

There are several factors behind the rise of private media outlets. One of these factors was the emergence of a new generation of Arab politicians and heads of state wishing to modernize their states' image through modernizing their media institutions. For instance, the Jordanian King Abdullah II has introduced several amendments to the press laws since his succession to power in 1999, and the young Bashar Al Asad has made several media reforms since his accession to power in 2000 (Mellor 2005, 9). Also, Colonel Qadhafi's son, Saif Al Islam Qadhafi, has expressed interest in allowing new private media in the Libyan market (IREX 2005, 39) and the Egyptian president's son, Gamal Mubarak, has promised a series of reforms. This change of power has also been accompanied by the rise of a new generation of Arab journalists, who have trained in Western media institutions or have been educated in Western-oriented schools and colleges in their home countries. This new generation has introduced new genres such as political debates and talk shows, and uses more sophisticated interview techniques, new to Arab media (Ayish 2001a).

Economic reforms adopted by several Arab states have resulted in massive privatization programs: "Economic privatization in the Arab world seems to have spilled over to the communication sector . . . with the expansion of privately owned print media and book publishing outlets and the launch of commercial broadcast operations inside and outside the Arab region"(Ayish 2001, 123).

Another important factor is the external competition that currently faces the Arab media. CNN launched a website in Arabic in 2002; CNBC Arabiya was inaugurated on July 27, 2003; and BBC Arabic launched its TV channel on March 11, 2008. The last two decades have seen an increase in access to new information technologies and telecommunication among Arab audiences: Internet access, mobile telephony, and satellite television are all now on the menu. Although several Arab countries filter websites, Arab audiences can still access vast amounts of information and entertainment on the World Wide Web. Arab broadcasters have therefore been compelled to diversify their programming in order to maintain their audience shares.

This privatization has stirred a harsh competition among Arab media outlets. The Arab press has witnessed the launch of more specialized newspapers and magazines: the Egyptian Akhbar al-Youm Publishing House issues a newspaper dedicated to crime news, another to celebrity news, and another again to literature. The size of newspapers has also increased tremendously: the average number of pages in a daily newspaper increased from 4 to 6 pages during the 1940s to 8 to 10 pages during the 1980s (Rugh 1987, 16), and has doubled again in the 1990s to reach 20 to 22 pages. There are also more human-interest stories in the press. The Lebanese-Saudi *al-Hayat* has regular weekly supplements directed at different reader segments – young people, business, travel – and this type of news is also in the daily paper.

Television broadcasting in the Arab world has also experienced drastic changes, from single terrestrial national television markets to regional and global ones. There are now well over 500 channels available to individual viewers across the region, most managed by private corporations. Of these, it is estimated that 22 news channels broadcast along with many more music and entertainment channels (For an overview of these channels, see ASBU tables, http://www.asbu.net/www/ar/directdoc.asp?docid=117). The largest and most successful of the entertainment channels are the Middle East Broadcasting Corporation (MBC) and Rotana-LBC. MBC was launched in 1991 in London before moving to Dubai Media City in 2001. It is owned by Arab Group International Holding Company, which is owned by Walid al Ibrahim, a relative of the late Saudi King. MBC has nine TV free-to-air channels including MBC1 (a family variety channel), MBC2 (films), MBC 3 for children's programs, MBC 4 for international talk shows such as *Oprah* and *Dr. Phil*, MBC Action, MBC Max, MBC+ Drama, Al Arabiya News, and recently MBC Persia (in Farsi). The group also owns three FM radio stations, MBC FM, Hala FM, and Panorama FM, in addition to one magazine, *Haya MBC*, and two websites (Alarabiya.net and MBC.net).

Rotana-LBC is owned by the Saudi prince Alwaleed Bin Talal Bin Abdul Aziz, who has become known in world media through his business ventures, particularly his buyout of shares in several media corporations including News Corporation, Time Warner, EuroDisney, and various Arabic newspapers (Khan 2005). His presence on the Arab media scene began in 1993, when he bought 30 percent of shares in the Arab Radio and Television network (ART) owned by the Dallah al Baraka group. Later, he bought Rotana Audiovisual Company, which was the largest recording company in the Saudi kingdom. In 2003, he struck a deal with ART owner Sheikh Saleh Kamel to "convert ART Music to a new Arab-language music and entertainment channel," which later developed into the Rotana Music Channel. Shortly after that, Rotana Clip was launched with SMS service for viewers, followed by Rotana Classic (see also Chapter 6, which discusses in more detail the Gulf businessmen's entry into the cinema and film industry).

Expansion of media markets

The explosion of the number of satellite channels, and the fact that Arab populations depend on television for their media consumption, has meant that the pan-Arab satellite television market dominates the advertising market. The revenue in 2008 reached more than 1.5 billion USD for the satellite television market alone (or 88 percent of the market) (Arab Media Outlook 2007, 55). Pan Arab Research Center (PARC) also revealed that pan-regional media, particularly TV, received 40 percent more advertising revenues in the first six months of 2009, compared to the same period the year before. Top advertising markets are the UAE, Saudi Arabia, and Egypt. Advertisers focus on MBC and Fox Movies; retailers or construction companies advertise, but so do government organizations and telecommunications companies. In 2009, the United Arab Emirates advertising amounted to more than 1.4 billion USD, which is 30 percent less than ad spending in 2008, which was 2 billion USD. The TV advertising share amounted to 177 million USD in 2009, compared to 987 million USD for newspaper advertising, 174 million for magazines, and 27 million for radio. The next biggest market was Egypt, where TV advertising revenue reached 348 million USD in 2009, and 509 million for newspaper advertising, 54 on magazines, 64 million on radio, and 228 million USD on outdoor advertising. On the other hand, TV advertising in Jordan was 16 million USD in 2009, compared to 117 million USD on newspaper advertising and 8 million on magazines (PARC 2009). Advertising rates tend to soar during the holy month of Ramadan, when viewer ratings also increase. For instance, a 30-second ad on Dubai TV costs 1,748 USD in the off-season but during Ramadan it jumps to 6,588 USD. Likewise, on Saudi-owned MBC1, an ad spot is 4,450 USD in the off-season but jumps to 12,104 USD during Ramadan (Deane 2009). The expansion of Arab media markets to include regional and global Arab audiences has become a part of the marketing strategy of several outlets aiming to benefit from increased market share.

As the worldwide economic downturn deepens in the region, television broadcasting is likely to be affected, as its advertising-generated revenues continue to diminish. Only television networks with solid and sustainable financial resources will be able to survive, which means the huge range of television outlets available in the early part of the twenty-first century may well shrink in the future (Arab Media Outlook 2007, 55).

As the pan-Arab market is controlled by business tycoons from the GCC countries, particularly Saudi Arabia, it suffered the consequences of the slowdown in the global economy, as capital flows and oil prices declined (Booz & Company 2009).

The MBC, which is the largest free-to-air network, is considered the barometer for the industry. Its COO Sam Barnett claims that the MBC is not greatly affected by the global recession:

> We cannot give advertisers any reason to reduce their budgets for MBC. We are realistic enough to recognize that overall advertising budgets will be

reduced but as the market leader, our larger channels are the least risky option for advertisers looking to recover their investment . . . we have spent more on research this year and the speed with which we are reacting has gone up. If programs are not working, they get changed. If things are working, we expand them. We are also conducting more experiments . . . Gulf comedy . . . seems to be working so we'll do more of it. (Parnell, 2009b)

The growth in the number of satellite channels has outstripped the TV advertising market. TV channels are now forced to differentiate their programming (such as the sitcom *One Man and Six Ladies* broadcast on the Egyptian Satellite Channel) and produce more TV series, which are the major magnet of advertising revenues, hence the need for new productions from the Syrian and Gulf States as well as Arabized Turkish series (Booz & Company 2008). The Syrian series *Bab al-Hara*, or *The Neighborhood Gate* has been run for three seasons; it focuses on a Syrian family feud during the French mandate between the two world wars (Black 2008). When the handsome Turkish actor Kivanc Tatiltug, who starred in the popular soap *Noor*, visited Jordan and Dubai, he was met crowds of screaming young women. The series *Noor* had 3 to 4 million viewers in Saudi Arabia alone, and Arab parents have reportedly been naming their babies after characters in *Noor* (Black 2008).

Satellite channels now offer a variety of program genres addressing the large youth consumer group. Rotana Cinema was host to one of the more daring television presenters in the region, namely, Hala Sarhan, whose program caused significant controversy concerning its on-air discussions of sensitive issues such as prostitution and masturbation. Reality television has also gained a foothold in the Arab media with such shows as *Hawa Sawa*. This featured a group of Arab women living alone, showing their domestic skills as future wives. Young men who watched the show would then call up to meet the girls. A recent study on the impact of this program on youth values found that Egyptian youths accepted this show as a means of finding a life partner. MBC has also produced an Arabized version of the American weight-loss program *The Biggest Loser*, calling it the *The Biggest Winner* in order not to add a negative twist (Wise 2005). Reality TV programs range from *Star Academy*, *The Valley*, *Album*, on which the winner gets an album produced; *Destiny*, modeled after *The Perfect Bride*; *Mission Fashion*; *Super Star*; *Project Fashion*; and *Street Smarts*. *Star Academy* alone had registered 23 million calls from Egypt, 18 million from Lebanon, and 16 million from Syria (Al Sharq Al Awsat, 2007). This development has been accompanied by increasing concerns that the new media outlets may propagate Westernized cultural ideas that threaten Islamic social and cultural values and annihilate national identity. But Arabized programs such as *Star Academy* prove to be a magnet for young consumers. One of the program contestants, the Iraqi Shada Hasson, succeeded in unifying Iraqis across religious divisions to vote for her, thereby achieving what politicians have failed to do[1].

This content is broadcast to the dismay of conservative Arabs such as the Saudi Mufti Sheikh Abdul Aziz Al-Asheikh, who issued a fatwa in 2008 condemning the broadcasting of "immoral TV series." He claimed, "Any TV station that airs them is against God and His Messenger (peace be upon him). These are serials of immorality. They are prepared by people who are specialists in crime and error, people who invite men and women to the devil" (quoted in Black 2008). To compensate for this daring wave of shows, a number of religious channels have been launched. Prince Al Waleed has recently launched an Islamic channel called al-Risala (or Message), to exist side by side with his bouquet of Rotana music channels. Its rival channel, Iqraa (or Read), is part of Arab Radio and Television (ART), owned by the Saudi business tycoon Sheikh Saleh Kamel. In 2008, there were more than 47 Arabic Islamic channels available via satellite to audiences inside and outside the Arab region. Chief among them are Iqraa, al Risala, and Al Majd channels (Galal 2009). Even religious channels such as al Risala seek to compete in the reality television market by offering special shows with "ethical" content. The al Risala Cairo manager explains the interest in reality shows: they "present something nice" to the average Arab family rather than boring religious content (Wise 2005). Iqraa channel has launched Iqraa's Beauty Queen contest; young Muslim women compete for the title using their manners and abidance by Islamic laws rather than their physical beauty (Galal 2009).

Despite the increase in the satellite channels, terrestrial channels still enjoy a large viewership. In Lebanon, more than 90 percent surveyed said they watch terrestrial channels (PARC press release, June 5, 2009). There are still 129 terrestrial TV stations in the region, with the largest number in Egypt. Moreover, liberalization across the region was the reason for the growth in private FM radio stations. Algeria and UAE have the highest number of state-owned stations while Iraq, the Palestinian territories, and Lebanon have the greatest numbers of private ones (see Chapters 4 and 5 on broadcasting industries).

State control or self-censorship?

Arab governments tend to see in the media a double-edged weapon: on the one hand, the media can be used to influence public opinion, and on the other, the media can be a power to menace the ideological foundations of Arab regimes. Arab regimes tend to stress the moral and social responsibility of media professionals not to agitate public opinion, but rather keep the status quo for the sake of national unity (Abdel Nabi 1989). Recent political turmoil that has characterized the region, particularly in the wake of the 9–11 attack, makes this duality evident: this situation has given Arab regimes more reasons to exert more control over media industries in the name of protecting their nations from terrorism, and on the other hand it has forced the same regimes to embrace political reforms, even modestly, to meet the pressures of their Western allies to promote democracy in the region.

Indeed, the fierce state censorship is often out of sync with post-independence constitutions, which usually attach great importance to freedom of speech. Several countries in the Middle East region, therefore, enforce contradictory laws regulating media and free speech. Egypt, for instance, has since 1981 applied an emergency law, following the assassination of President Anwar Sadat, and Jordan allows authorities to prosecute journalists despite Article 15 of the Jordanian Constitution, which affirms the citizens' freedom to express their opinion freely by speech, in writing, or in photographic representation and other forms of expression. Other countries such as Syria enforce emergency laws that tend to supersede constitutional rights of free speech. In 2002 Bahrain enforced a new referendum that supports free speech – while keeping Law No. 47, which gives free rein to the authorities to prosecute journalists, thereby encouraging self-censorship. In Algeria, more than 100 cases of defamation were brought to courts in 2005 alone (IREX 2005).

Increased commercialization has turned the media into a liaison between advertisers and customers rather than between politicians and citizens. In the Arab context it has transformed content: soft news has increased, as well as rival political news presentations, such as party press in Egypt. Despite the differences in ethnic, religious, class, and gender aspects, some regional media outlets, such as the so-called pan-Arab press and satellite news channels, attempt to address as wide an audience base as possible. Hence, pan-Arabism has become a selling point, a marketing strategy that aims to benefit from the increased market share (Kraidy 2005).

The Arab region's media system is unique: media businesses seem to thrive on ever-increasing advertising revenues, despite the region's limits on free speech. Thus, while Arab investments (particularly by the Gulf States) have increased and several states have launched media cities as free zones to encourage more investments, rigid media laws and self-censorship are still the norm across the region. The thriving Arab media scene is often claimed to be the result of the combination of Gulf wealth and the unifying Arabic language (IREX, 2005, x-xi).

The increasing injection of Gulf investment has been met with skepticism from several Arab journalists and commentators such as the Lebanese Hazim Saghiya, who warns that "media investment is a field that is left to the regimes and those close to them who believe that presetting the status quo is a prerequisite for the continuity of their concessions and interests" (Saghiya, 2006, 565). For instance, Abu Dhabi's ruler, Sheikh Khalifa bin Zayed Al Nahyan, is said to have ordered Abu Dhabi TV to stop broadcasting the drama *Saadoun Al Awaji* upon receiving a personal request from the Saudi king, because it was claimed that the episode could stir tribal rivalry. The same happened with MBC's *Finjan al Dam* series, which was cancelled after claims that it stirred public anger in the Arabian Peninsula (Jaafar 2008).

In summary, Arab state governments tend to see media, particularly broadcasting, as their absolute monopolies. There are three main reasons for this: First, broadcasting reaches all citizens, regardless of their education. Second, these media play a major role in sustaining national unity and spreading the feeling of community among citizens. Third, electronic media may serve as a primary tool of the political propaganda machine – and it would be dangerous to let this slip into hostile hands (Amin 2001, 29). Arab media have served the local purposes of educating and informing local citizens, as well as consolidating a sense of pan-Arab identity and solidarity with neighboring Arab countries. The following section elaborates on this particular role of media as a mobilization tool.

Role of media in mobilizing the Arab nation

During the 1950s and 1960s, Arab media were also used as a platform to proliferate Arab unity discourse by calling on all Arab populations to embrace and take pride in their Arab national identity and their membership in one *umma* (or nation). Films, for instance, were used to parade this national identity: *Jamila the Algerian* (1958) followed an Algerian woman who took an active part in the resistance movement against the French presence in the country. Three years later, the film director Youssef Chahine was asked to direct *al-Naser Salah al-Din*, which depicted the Arab view of the Crusades. Not all was harmonious among Arab states, however; the socialist ideologies of Egypt, Iraq, and Algeria were feared in other countries such as Saudi Arabia, which launched the Voice of Islam radio to counter the Egyptian Voice of the Arabs broadcast (Mellor 2008).

The prevalence of Arab nationalist discourse in the Arab media is rooted in combating foreign influence. National governments tended to depend on the media to promote certain policies. The Egyptian government used Sawt Al Arab (Voice of the Arabs) radio to mobilize Arab public opinion in the 1950s and 1960s. The Egyptian state, following the 1952 revolution led by the Free Officers, subsidized the production of patriotic songs expressing themes of Arabism, socialism, and even Syrian-Egyptian unity (1958–1961), using the "new medium of state-owned television" (Massad 2003, 23). The lyrics of one such song, *Watani Habibi* (My Beloved Homeland), expressed the birth of a homeland that is "Arab and free, and not an echo of West or East," although the song "lacked a single Arab or Eastern instrument." While the lyrics expressed patriotic feelings of one united homeland and identity, the music "is appropriated as global culture that has been Arabized" (Massad 2003, 23).

The 1967 defeat put a temporary stop to such songs, however, and they were replaced by songs expressing despair. The 1991 Gulf war, following Iraq's invasion of Kuwait, constituted another blow to the dream of Arab unity (Massad 2003). Other pan-Arab media projects, such as a pan-Arab news agency to counterbalance the dominance of foreign news agencies, could not provide a unified platform for Arabs regionally and globally. These efforts failed due to the disagreement among Arab governments themselves on the form such an agency would take.

Major political conflicts such as the Palestinian intifada or the war in Iraq can still trigger a wave of national and religious songs. Indeed, the recent decade or so witnessed a new wave of Arab unity songs such as *Al Hulm Al Arabi* (The Arab Dream), produced in 1998 by the Saudi Prince Waleed bin Talal. Moreover, the turbulent situation in Lebanon has also given rise to nationalist songs such as those by Julia Butrus. She participated in demonstrations in Beirut against the Israeli attacks and prompted Al Jazeera to launch a special episode on the role of art in promoting Arab political issues[2].

There was also a wave of new films driven by shared political issues such as the Iraq war and the Palestinian issue. For example, *Assifara fil emara* (The Embassy Is in the Building), concerns an apolitical Egyptian man whose apartment is next to the Israeli embassy. The man suffers from the strict security measures surrounding his apartment building, and he decides to sue the embassy. This action turns him into a hero overnight and a symbol of the Arab struggle. The TV producer Ismail Kutkut claims that TV series focusing on pan-Arab issues, using actors from different countries speaking different Arabic dialects, have become tremendously popular (Deane 2009).

This agitation of nationalist feelings is what Rinnawi (2006) dubbed "McArabism." This refers particularly to the increasing intake of the same sociocultural content on satellite channels, such as news bulletins focusing on "shared" political issues. This "McArabism" is also evident in the products targeting children, so for instance pan-Arab children's magazines such as *Majid, Alaa Eldin,* and *Al Arabi Alsaghir* address children's issues across the

Arab region (Peterson 2005). The creators of these magazines "are actively engaged in the process of creating an imagined community of transnational kids by encouraging readers to encounter, and imagine one another, within and through the pages of the magazine" (Peterson 2005, 187). *Al Arabi Alsaghir* includes a news section dedicated to the intifada; also on the rise are new pan-Arab children's channels (some estimate there are around 16),[3] such as Al Jazeera's. Nonetheless, Arab audiences seem to grow more attentive to their distinct local identities. For example, when asked to share their views on possibilities for Arab political unity in a recent debate at the BBC Arabic channel and website, Arab audiences revealed their skepticism of such unity by highlighting the local and national differences in their political situations.[4] But if more and more media outlets are now categorized as pan-Arab and hence target Arab populations across and outside the region, it is because this market expansion serves the commercial interests of media tycoons, rather than the ideological purposes of Nasserist or Baathist regimes.

With a market strongly marked by a large segment of Arab youth, media tycoons like the Saudi businessman Prince Al Waleed have spotted a lucrative submarket, or as Al Waleed put it, "Sixty percent of the population is youth. That's my niche" (Khalaf 2005). In addition, the emergence of free newspapers has prompted the increasing advertising revenues in the region, as these publications depend entirely on advertising. They usually target the young market, which is growing in numbers (as discussed below) in all Arab states. One such free newspaper is *Al Emarat Al Youm* (Emirates Today), which targets youth between 15 and 40 years old. The format of *Al Emarat Al Youm* is designed to appeal to this particular segment, offering easy-to-digest news stories rather than complex analyses (Arab Media Outlook, 2007).

The following section discusses in more detail the characteristics of Arab media consumers, particularly youth and expatriates.

Media consumers inside the region

With the decline of the traditional role of family and the state's authority, young people were influenced by street impulses: "whether in the form of the Islamist movement or alternative cultural expressions" (Meijer 2000, 8). The postcolonial Arab state took over part of the traditional family's responsibilities "in the field of culture, politics and employment through its ambitious educational programs and its massive interference in the economy" (Meijer 2000, 1). Consequently, Arab youths found themselves situated at the borderline between the global and the local; they are usually the center of

Table 5: Percentage of Arab Youth of Total Population

	Youth ages 10–24 2006		Youth ages 10–24 2025	
	Millions	% of total pop.	Millions	% of total pop.
Algeria	10.9	33	10.1	23
Bahrain	0.2	24	0.2	20
Egypt	23.3	31	27.3	27
Iraq	9.6	32	13.3	30
Jordan	1.8	31	2.2	27
Kuwait	0.6	23	0.8	21
Lebanon	1	28	1	22
Libya	1.8	31	2	25
Morocco	9.7	30	10.1	25
Oman	0.8	32	1	26
Palestinian Territory	1.2	32	2.1	32
Qatar	0.2	20	0.2	20
Saudi Arabia	7.6	30	9.9	27
Sudan	11.8	32	15.2	30
Syria	6.6	34	7.9	28
Tunisia	3.1	30	2.4	20
United Arab Emirates	1.1	24	1.3	19
Yemen	7.6	35	12.2	33

Source: http://www.unfpa.org/arabstates/overview.cfm

attention when the evils of "neoliberalism" are debated (Winegar 2006, 180). Recent statistics show that in several Arab states young people constitute the majority of the population, with 34 percent of the region's population below the age of 15. Table 5 shows the percentage of youth in 2006 and the estimate of this percentage in 2025.

The region has experienced high population growth during the past few decades, making it very difficult for Arab governments to create enough jobs for young people. One in five young adults aged 20–24 is unemployed, and unemployment is particularly high in the Maghreb countries (Muñoz 2000, 20). Economic forecasts for the region predict the need to create 100 million jobs by the year 2020 in order to accommodate new entrants to the labor market (Dyer & Yousef 2007, 31).

Youth are also the major consumers of new media. Mobile phones have penetrated Arab markets, particularly in high-income countries in the Gulf. In 2007, the percentage of mobile phone ownership in the whole population in the UAE, Saudi Arabia and Kuwait was 113 percent, 76 percent, and 98 percent respectively (Arab Media Outlook 2007). The use of mobile phones, particularly among the youth, has given rise to satellite channels targeting this segment and offering SMS services such as the Rotana Clip. Moreover, the youth have taken advantage of media and technological advances to reorganize their roles, even if they challenge traditional customs. They use the new technology of SMS "as a means of communication, and even dating, which has paved the way for the rise of tens of music/SMS channels broadcasting music videos while having an SMS scroll bar moving across the screen with messages exchanged between men and women. Some of the messages are overtly sexual, carrying even marriage proposals" (Mellor 2007, 38). Mobile phone communication practices have changed the traditional sociality in Morocco, for instance, with the increasing use of networking through random phone calls and text messages between strangers (Kriem 2009).

Youth, particularly females, also use the Internet as a dating forum, thereby sidestepping the family and social restrictions that regulate meetings between sexes (Galal 2004). The new generation has been dubbed the *"rewish"* generation, referring to their being distracted and confused (Mellor 2008, 362). Surveys show that young people hardly identify with their political institutions and feel more and more marginalized (Muñoz 2000). Studies among a large sample of Tunisian youths, originally conducted in 1988 and repeated in 1994, revealed that Western countries such as France, USA, and Spain, tended to be favored by girls, perhaps because they related these countries to gender equality (Suleiman 1997).

The spread of media, particularly satellite television, and media's increasing advertising, is regarded as an important driver of the spread of consumerism in the Arab world. Arab youth have also been blamed for falling prey to Western consumerism, particularly in the Gulf countries (Assad 2007).

Arab media consumers across the globe

The past few decades have witnessed diverse migrations in the region. The Mashreq countries (Egypt, Iraq, Jordan, Lebanon, Syria, and the Palestinian territories) have been sources of migrant workers for the rich Gulf coast countries (GCC: Saudi Arabia, Kuwait, Oman, the UAE, Bahrain, and Qatar) (International Migration in the Arab Region 2006). The Arab region is home to "the major receiving countries in the world" (2) with immigrant numbers increasing from 13 million to 20 million in the period between 1990 and 2005. The majority of those migrants reside in the rich GCC countries. Saudi Arabia has an estimated 6.4 million migrants, while the UAE has 2.3 million. Increasingly, migrant-driven new "nationalization" policies in the GCC countries favor native Gulf Arabs over migrant workers (except in the media industries). These policies range from restricting the access of foreign workers, for example via taxing or strict visa regulations, to creating more jobs for the natives via the imposition of new regulations prohibiting the employment of foreigners, particularly in the public sector (International Migration in the Arab Region 2006). The increasing immigration rate from the Arab region is dominated by male rather than female migrants, and the Arab region thus has the lowest rate of women migrants.

Arab migrants improve the situation of their families inside the region, and improve the GDP figures due to the huge remittances going back to their countries of origin. For instance, remittances of Egyptians abroad mounted to $4.5 billion USD in 2006, while in Morocco it was $5.2 billion for the same period (World Bank 2007).

The GCC also hosts a large number of Asian workers. This number is steadily increasing, while the number of Arab immigrants has been in decline. Asian migrants (particularly from Bangladesh and Sri Lanka) have increased in other poor Arab countries such as Jordan or Lebanon as well, with the latter receiving around 18,000 workers from Sri Lanka in 2004. There are a number of television and radio stations in English and other languages targeting the expatriate communities in the Gulf. In Kuwait, there are several radio stations airing programs in Arabic, English, Urdu, and Farsi (Al-Menayes 1996).

Generally, Arab migration to Western countries increased remarkably during the twentieth century. This cohort of expatriates and émigrés constitutes a lucrative market for Arab satellite channels. This group of media consumers is offered "at least one channel from almost every Arab country and multiple channels from every genre" (Stanton 2007, 29). For instance, the private corporation TV2moro has launched a subscription service to about 40 Arab TV channels for the 500,000 Arabic speakers in the USA and Canada (Parnell 2009a). The number of Arab immigrants to Europe is about 30 million; France is the major destination for Arab immigrants, particularly those from the Maghreb region. Other countries are also experiencing an increase in their Arab communities, such as the Netherlands, where the number of Arabs is estimated at 1.2 million (Dumont 2006).

The concentration of Arabs from certain countries varies across Organisation for Economic Co-operation and Development (OECD) countries. Egyptian immigrants, for example, are the majority of Arabs living in Austria, Greece, and Japan. The Lebanese are the majority in Australia and Mexico, with Moroccans the majority in Belgium, Italy, the Netherlands, Luxemburg, Portugal, and Spain. Algerians are the majority in France while Iraqis are the majority in Denmark, Finland, Norway, New Zealand, and Sweden. The United States normally attracts the highly skilled Arab immigrants, compared to the number of less skilled immigrants who reside in Europe, particularly France (Dumont 2006). Arab Americans are said to do better compared to average Americans in terms of education and wealth accumulation (Naim 2005). There are also a number of immigrants from GCC countries residing in the OECD, but most of those are students staying short-term (Dumont 2006). The integration of these communities varies from one country to another; for instance, Lebanese diasporic communities are characterized by "different terms of social and political participation" ranging from assimilation to nonassimilation in the host countries (Humphrey 2004, 35).

Integration and assimilation polices in the West have had an impact on the development of the so-called diaspora media, which serves Arab consumers in Western countries. In France, for instance, which is known for its assimilationist ideology, North African immigrants, accounting for about 40 percent of all migrants in France, have had difficulties accessing the media field as producers and journalists. French media output has not covered the needs of this cohort of media consumers (Echchaibi 2001, 301f). Consequently, North Africans have been very active in launching their own local media outlets, whether in Arabic or Berber (Echchaibi 2001, 303). Sweden, which hosts more than 80,000 Iraqis, has supported the publications and setup of periodicals and local radio catering for this group (Camauër 2003, 79).

New media; new challenge

Seen from a cultural perspective, globalization is associated with neo-colonialism, in which Western cultural practices displace Arab ones. This includes dependence on Western media: news agencies, imported sitcoms, program ideas, and consumerist values. But globalization has also brought new opportunities for small states, such as the United Arab Emirates (UAE), which now profile themselves globally as the perfect hybrid link between East and West. Indeed, Arab cities now compete among themselves to illustrate this successful hybridization of East and West. Dubai managed to profile itself as a cosmopolitan city, thanks to the money and attention poured into it by its ruling family. Four decades ago, Dubai resembled a medieval village in which people lived in extreme poverty. Now it ranks as one of the richest and most globalized cities in the world (Abdulla 2006). Nowadays, Dubai is said to be the Arab "trendsetter" city, replacing other traditional cities such as Cairo and Beirut (Abdulla 2006, 63). Dubai also prides itself on its Media City (DMC), which serves 550 media organizations such as CNN, Reuters, Sony, and McGraw Hill Publishing. The vision behind DMC, as articulated by its chief executive, Saeed al-Muntafiq, is "not to be a regional base for broadcasters, but to be one of four or five global bases for broadcasting as we move forward over the next few years" (cited in Mellor 2007, 27).

Likewise, Qatar profiles itself as the host of freedom; this is embodied in the Emir's project, Al Jazeera Satellite Channel, as well as the Doha debates. In fact, part of Al Jazeera's success lies in its stirring debate in Western media, which in turn adds to its market value in terms of audience share. Likewise, the Jordanian government established a free media zone serving the Jordanian Media City Company, while Egypt chose to invest in Media Production City, "envisioned as a 'Hollywood of the East,'" as well as a Media Free Zone (Mellor 2007, 27).

Arab governments also capitalize on the power of the new media in polishing their image internationally. A sample of ten official English-language presidential and government websites in the Middle East showed that the main purpose behind these websites was to communicate with media practitioners within and outside the Middle East (Curtin & Gaither 2004).

Indeed, media outlets across the region are now ready to expand their digital and online offerings, such as the Qatar News Agency, the Lebanese newspapers *Al Balad* and *As-Safir*, the Jordanian newspapers *Al Ghad* and *Ad-Dustour*, as well as the Saudi site *Arab News*. For instance, the Middle East Broadcasting Corporation (MBC) channel has entered into an agreement with the Chinese game developer, CDC Corporation, to develop online games in English and Arabic (Arab Media Outlook 2009, 74, 93). In addition, most Arab broadcasters are now represented on the World Wide Web and some websites include interactive features such as online forums. One example is Beirut Nights Radio (http://beirutnights.com) which features live webcast, chat, forum, and community sites (Zamom 2007).

Other Arabic-speaking transnational media such as BBC Arabic have operated in multimedia platforms. BBC Arabic Online was launched in November 1999, targeting Arab youths; it was chosen as the best news service for the year 2000 by Arabianbusiness.com (Abdel Latif 2001). The distinct feature about the BBC Arabic service in general is its dedication to a tri-media platform, through integrating radio, TV, and web contents. Following the launch of BBCArabic.com, other media outlets followed suit and launched their own web services. Al Jazeera launched Aljazeera.net in 2001 as part of the Al Jazeera group and it provides a huge database of news and archive of Al Jazeera Arabic channel programs. In 2008, Aljazeera.net won the Pan Arab Web Awards Competition, which was launched in Dubai in 2004. The rival channel, Al Arabiya, based in Dubai, also launched the web service Alarabiya. net in 2004, after reviewing competitive sites in order to define the topics that interest young Arabs. For other channels, moving to new media should be cautious, or as the head of MBC, Sam Barnett, put it, "our take on the shift from TV to new media is that it is important to monitor, but it is TV advertising which is the dominant force and it is likely to remain so for a long time" (quoted in Parnell 2009b).

New media have brought about new challenges for state regulation and policies. In Egypt, for instance, radio licenses are authorized by the government and at times the president himself, which has resulted in the refusal of several FM radio applications. However, when the Al Ghad Party, led by the presidential candidate Ayman Nour, was denied an FM license, they launched their online radio station in 2005. Later, two groups of the Al Ghad Party, launched online radio stations, Mahrousa and Bokra, following the arrest of Nour on the charge of bribery. Other political parties followed suit: the Muslim Brotherhood launched their online station in October 2005. These new ventures have thus taken advantage of the laws that do not cover the Internet (IREX 2005, 21).

Chapter 7 discusses in more detail the impact of new media in the Arab world and whether new media have indeed served as a new virtual public sphere.

Conclusion

This chapter argues that media have been a keystone in post-independence Arab states, due to their importance in forming and consolidating a shared Arab identity. Media institutions have helped in forming a new distinct Arab identity that combines Western material progress with Arab traditional heritage.

The economic reforms spreading across the Arab region have resulted in massive privatization programs in several sectors, including media industries. Several Arab states (such as Egypt) that championed socialist policies following their independence have embraced an open-market policy and have competed with other nations in liberalizing and privatizing their markets, as seen for instance in the set-up of several free-zone media cities in Egypt, Dubai, and Jordan. Also, Arab governments encouraged the establishment of super-malls and skyscrapers and the removal of slums (Mellor 2007, 26), which was seen by some scholars and commentators as a mere imitation of Western lifestyle and a cause of deteriorating values, particularly among the increasing youth population.

This economic development coupled with technological advances and the spread of new media by means of the internet have prompted scholars to warn against the lack of distinct Arab identity and hegemony of Anglo-American values (Abdel Rahman 2002). The new pan-Arab satellite channels, for instance, have been accused of depending on imported programs and copying existing American programs rather than producing distinctly Arab content. The next chapters will provide detailed discussions of the proliferation of these new outlets and their role in uniting (or dividing) the Arab populations. Each chapter will deal with one particular industry, although the discussion will show how they overlap, particularly with the advance of technology and the development of multimedia platforms.

Notes

1 See "Idol TV show contestant unites war-weary Iraqis," http://www.cnn.com/2007/WORLD/meast/03/28/iraq.star.academy/index.html
2 See http://www.aljazeera.net/Channel/archive/archive?ArchiveId=428168
3 See figures on ASBU website: http://www.asbu.net/www/ar/directdoc.asp?docid=117
4 See http://newsforums.bbc.co.uk/ws/thread.jspa?forumID=5810

2 Arabic Books
Nabil Dajani

This chapter reviews the development of publishing as an industry in the Arab region, discussing regulations and restrictions surrounding it throughout history. Books and publications have long been regarded as a dangerous tool that only heads of states should control. An account of the development of printing in the Arab world is a prelude to understanding the foundation on which the present Arab media institutions are shaped.

Historical background

While the Arab world knew the art of printing on paper and silk by engravings made on wood (xylography) long before the Gutenberg printing press, it is often incorrectly suggested that the Arab world was quite late to print Arabic script because Islam prohibited the reproduction of images. According to Geoffrey Roper of the Institute for the Study of Muslim Civilizations in London, the Arab Muslims were printing texts, including passages from the Quran, as early as the fifth century. He reports that "nearly 60 examples of . . . Arabic printed pieces survive in European and American libraries and museums, and an unknown number in Egypt itself" (Roper 2008). Richard Bulliet of Columbia University suggests that the Arabs employed block printing through the use of wooden molds in the ninth or tenth century (Bulliet 1987).

Fifty documents printed on parchment, paper, and linen cloth were discovered in Fayyum Oasis in Egypt, most of which are preserved in the national library in Vienna (As-Samara'i 1996, 46). Some of these documents were in two colors and with a wide variety of calligraphic styles: "from an archaic-looking Kufic to an elegant naskhi . . . suggesting that Arabic printing in Egypt was the product of long evolution and must have employed a number of craftsmen. . . . One example is printed on a linen envelope while another contains the first six verses of the 34th Sura of the Koran" (Munro 1981).

Philip Hitti (quoted in Dabbas and Risho 2008, 13) submits that there actually was a primitive Arabic press in Andalusia (Spain) but its process is unknown. The account relates that two early Andalusian sources indicate that Arabs contributed to the development of printing in Andalusia before the fall of Granada in 1492. A 1375 manuscript, *Covering the news of Granada* (*al-ihata fi akhbar gharnata*), by Ibn al-Khatib recounts that Aba Bakr al-Kalusi al-Andalusi presented to the governing minister a volume about the characteristics of producing ink and printing instruments and that this volume is unique in its content. Additionally, a 1424 manuscript by Ibn al-Athir, *The Secret Ensemble* (*al-hillah as-sirriya*), reports that "the vassal of Prince Abdallah used to write down the records in his home then send them to get printed" (Dabbas and Risho 2008, 13).

Bulliet proposes that Arabic block printing "persisted into, but possibly not beyond, the fourteenth century. It had certainly disappeared without a trace by the beginning of the eighteenth century" (Bulliet 1987). Only during the later days of Arab Islamic rule and with the development of variant Muslim schools of thought as well as deterioration in adherence to the Muslim faith did the authorities show concern about the possible distortion or forging of religious texts. Because premodern writing was related to sacred texts (Ayalon 1994), Muslim authorities that faced European modernization waves as well as crusades of Christian missionaries were hesitant to employ the use of movable type to print Arabic books for fear that some may have distorted religious texts and weakened their control.

There are numerous but scattered accounts concerning printing of Arabic script in Europe. The first attempt by Europeans to print Arabic script was in 1486 when Martin Roth, a Dominican priest, printed a book in Latin by Bernard von Brandenburg on his travels to the Holy Land. Europe did not recognize the need to print in Arabic until the repossession of Granada (Spain) from the Arabs when the bishop of Granada upon the direction of King Ferdinand and Queen Isabella convened learned men from the university city of Salamanca and asked them to prepare two books for missionaries who did not know Arabic. The books – *Ways of Teaching and Reading Arabic and Its Knowledge* and *A Dictionary of Arabic* – appeared in 1505 and 1506. Both used illustrated plates (Nehmeh 2008).

Orientalists also contributed to the development of early Arabic printing in their effort to reproduce Arabic manuscripts that preserved Greek philosophy and science (Lunde 1981). In 1538 Guillaume Postel, a French Orientalist, used wooden type to print an Oriental languages grammar book. In 1613 a French diplomat, Francois Savary de Breves, who served as French Ambassador in Constantinople and later in Rome, established an Arabic printing press in Rome. He moved it to Paris in 1616 (Sabat 1966, 23–29).

The situation in Andalusia, however, was different from that in the Arab world, which was then part of the Ottoman Empire. By the time of the spread of the use of movable type in printing, the Ottoman Empire was the dominant Muslim state, but it was an aging state, often referred to as "the sick man of Europe." While Constantinople, the capital of the Ottoman Empire, was ahead of other eastern capitals in printing, its Muslim Sultans were apprehensive about using Arabic script in printing, which was the script used by most ethnic groups in the Ottoman Empire, including the Turks. Their apprehension was triggered by two fears. The first fear was consequent to the resistance of a segment of the Muslim 'uluma (defenders of traditional values), who were suspicious that printing would endanger their uncontested authority and feared that it might result in the sacrilege of God's name. Like their Catholic counterparts during the dark ages in Europe, these 'ulama were concerned about the dangers printing could pose to their standing as spiritual leaders by undermining their monopoly over the written word and permitting lay people easy access to sacred writings. They were afraid that printing would erode the traditional basis of the old order on which their status was established. With the passage of time, however, "many ['ulama] not only tolerated or even welcomed the press but also took part in it themselves (Ayalon 1994,172). Among these were distinguished Arab religious scholars such as Muhammad Abdouh, Jamal ud din al Afghani, and Rashid Rida. By the end of the nineteenth century printing and the press in general were viewed as "a continuation of a legitimate tradition." Another factor that contributed to the tolerance of Arabic printing in the Arab regions of the Ottoman Empire was the rising struggle against foreign hegemony, and the political state of affairs that united the 'ulama and the press and contributed to the weakening of religious resistance to printing.

Many of the printing presses and religious schools established by the Popes during the sixteenth and seventeenth centuries printed or used eastern languages. The first book to be printed in Arabic script in the form of movable type is *Kitab Salat Al-Siwa'i* (also known as *Septem Horae Canonicae* and translated as *The Book of the Prayer of the Hours*). It was intended for distribution among Christians of the Orient and printed by a press subsidized by Pope Julius II. It appeared in 1514 in Fano, a small Italian city south of Venice. According to Krek (1979) at least eight copies of this book are known to exist. One copy is in the collection of the national library in Paris, another can be found in the Treasure Room of Princeton University Library, three other books are in Italy: in the Estense Library at Modena, in the Medici Library in Florence, and in the Ambrosiana in Milan, and copies are in the collection of the British Museum, Dar al-Kutub in Cairo, and Bayerische Staatsbibliothek in Munich.

The Catholic Church in Rome accommodated Christian clergy from the Orient in its religious schools and sought their assistance in the printing of Arabic and Syriac texts, in order to ensure that the printed material was in line with the directions of the Catholic Church. Pope Gregory XIII took the initiative to establish a Maronite institute in Rome in 1584. The Pope assumed this undertaking to meet the need of the Maronite church to educate its clergy and to augment his interest in strengthening the relationship of the Maronite church with the apostolic chair. This institute graduated several clergy who played important roles in the development of Lebanese society. They became pioneers in establishing a network of schools in Mount Lebanon. The Maronite clergy profited from their printing experience in Rome. A Maronite priest, Sarkis al-Razi, brought a printing press from Rome to St. Antonius Qazhiya monastery in Lebanon in 1610. This printing press used Syriac letters. It managed to print only one text before it went into oblivion (Dabbas and Risho 2008, 32) According to Sabat, the press was neglected because Rome flooded the Maronite churches with free religious books that were superior in printing and production and because of the low literacy rate in the region at the time (Sabat 1966, 19, 35–38).

Russia and the Orthodox Christian European states also became interested in Arabic printing as a consequence of their direct contact with Islam and Muslims in the neighboring Ottoman Empire. After acquiring some Turkish territories in the Russo-Turkish War in the eighteenth century, Empress Catherine the Great of Russia founded a "Tartar and Arabic typographic establishment" in St. Petersburg "to print decrees and school books for her Muslim subjects" (Davis 2002).

Printing regulation throughout history

During the latter part of the fifteenth century Ottoman subjects experienced a "dark age" of suppression, when Ottoman officials feared that the mass production of the printed word would endanger their uncontested authority. Thus Sultan Bayazid II issued an order in 1485 banning the use of Arabic script in printing. However, under the pressure of European powers which defended minority groups in the Ottoman Empire, in 1494 he granted permission to the Jews who settled in Turkey after their expulsion from Spain to establish presses using Hebrew script. The Jews in the Ottoman Empire printed religious books as well as literary, historic, medical, and other texts (Sabat 1966, 23–25). The Jewish press lasted for three centuries and used Hebrew letters as well as printed Arabic texts in Hebrew script. Bayazid's son Salim I reiterated his father's order in 1515 (Sabat 1966, 18) but also yielded to European pressure and granted the Armenians printing privileges identical to the Ottoman Jews (in 1567). The Greeks were granted similar privileges (in 1627). The permission for these minorities to print was conditional on not using Arabic script (Dabbas and Risho 2008, 13–15).

During the reign of Sultan Ahmad III (1673–1736) the sociopolitical orientation in the Ottoman Empire moved toward reform and openness to Europe; regulation of printing was relaxed. The Sultan was convinced that through the rapid and wide circulation of scientific and technological knowledge the authorities could arrest the decline facing the Ottoman Empire (Lunde 1981). The 'ulama began to articulate the role of the press "not as a harmful innovation but as a continuation of a legitimate tradition . . . [as] a branch of the study of history" (Ayalon 1994, 171).

The Ottoman Ambassador to France during that period, Mehmed Chelebi Yirmisekiz, played an important role in advancing change. Chelebi and his son Sa'id Afandi were fascinated by the advancement of printing in France and were determined to end the ban on printing in their country. Upon their return to Istanbul they cooperated with an Ottoman diplomat of Hungarian origin, Ibrahim Muteferrika, to establish an Arabic printing press in Istanbul. Muteferrika had printing experience and had contacts with the Grand Minister, Ibrahim Pasha. Accordingly, Ibrahim Muteferrika submitted a petition to the Ottoman authorities in the form of a long essay entitled "The Utility of Printing." The essay explained the benefits of introducing printing and concluded by pledging not to print religious books that dealt with interpretation of religious texts. The Sultan presented the essay to Shaikh al-Islam Abdallah Afandi, the leading authority of Islamic law, with the following question: "A certain man has cast metal letters in order to print the classical works of literature and science, such as dictionaries, works on logic, philosophy, astronomy, and so on, and has offered to undertake to print them. Can he, in accordance with the rules of justice, execute his design?" (Lunde 1981).

Shaikh al-Islam responded by issuing a fatwa (religious decree) in 1727 sanctioning Arabic printing provided it did not include printing religious texts (Sabat 1966, 54). The fatwa declares:

> If a person with an ability to impress letters and words for a book that is properly corrected on a mold, and brought to us without effort many copies through the process of pressing paper on the mold, so indeed the abundance of books would lessen their cost and increase their acquisition. Since there is great advantage in this, so indeed this matter is worthy of wide praise, and therefore, permission should be granted to this person, but it is necessary to appoint scholars to correct the book whose letters will be engraved (translated by the author).

Supported by the fatwa of Shaikh al-Islam, Sultan Ahmad issued a decree (Khat Hamayuni) authorizing Muteferrika and his partner to establish a printing press using Arabic script. The press began printing texts in 1728 (Dabbas and Risho 2008, 109–12). This decision was a landmark in changing printing regulation in the Ottoman Empire and marked the granting of a legal status to printing in the modern Arab world.

Printing in Arabic by missionaries and Orientalists flourished in Romania, Italy, France, Holland, Germany and England in the seventeenth century. Most of these printing presses were linked to religious authorities or educational institutions and universities. The majority of the Arabic books published during this period also included Latin script, and some included print in Hebrew and Syriac (Dabbas and Risho 16–33). Regulation of missionary printing was mainly by the higher religious authorities and was largely supportive of missionary work in the Arab regions. Thus missionary printing presses produced religious texts, and later school textbooks for the use of the missionary schools.

While early Ottoman rulers opposed the use of movable Arabic type, foreign parties in force in the Arab region were not troubled with this, and encouraged their missionaries to set up printing presses to advance their purpose. Thus the Roman Catholic Church (later the Orthodox Church, then the Protestants) employed printing in their missionary work in the Arab world. Early missionary printers did not only have regulatory limitations; they also faced technical problems. Unlike Latin script, Arabic is written in a flowing style with the letters joined together; they do not locate in isolation. To add to the difficulty of printing Arabic script, each letter has up to four different forms or shapes. Different attempts were made by Arabic printers to overcome this problem, but not until the introduction of the computer in printing was a definitive solution reached.

The use of printing presses gained ground in the Arab Orient, particularly in the areas populated by Christians, as a result of the competition between the different Christian missionaries to attract adherents. After the death of Patriarch Dabbas, Zakher moved to Mount Lebanon, where he established in 1733 a printing press in the St. John (Mar Yuhanna) Catholic Monastery near Shweir. Competition between the different missionaries in producing printed matter moved from Aleppo to Mount Lebanon.

The Greek Orthodox priests reacted to the challenges of the Zakher press by establishing the first Arabic printing press in the city of Beirut, in 1751. The Maronites followed by establishing an Arabic printing press at the St. Isaiah monastery in 1808. In 1834 the American Protestant missionaries moved their Arabic printing press from Malta to Beirut. The Catholic Jesuit missionaries also entered the race by setting up the third Arabic printing press in Beirut in 1848. Both the Catholic press and the American Protestant Press played an important role in the advancement of printing in Lebanon and the region. They continued to be the leading printing presses in the region until the 1950s.

Popular printing not connected to religious orders appeared in 1857 with the establishment of the Syrian Press, the fourth Arabic printing press in Beirut, by Khalil el-Khuri, a former director of publications in the Ottoman administration. El-Khuri published the first popular Arabic newspaper in Lebanon, *Hadikat al-Akhbar*.

While Syria and Mount Lebanon were ahead of other Arab areas in printing through the use of movable type, this method was mainly used to produce religious texts, dictionaries, or perhaps a few literary publications. It was also used to reproduce old Arabic manuscripts.

Printing in Egypt was launched for different purposes. Egypt did not know printing using movable letters until the French expedition in 1798. Lunde (1981) reports that the Copts in Egypt were in receipt of printed religious material in Arabic that was made available by the Catholic Church. A 1996 text by the Center for Judaic Studies at the University of Pennsylvania, *From Written to Printed Text: The Transmission of Jewish Tradition*, states that the grandson of Greshom ben Moses Soncinos, who introduced printing of Hebrew script in the Ottoman Empire, introduced Hebrew script printing in Cairo in 1557. Steinberg (1996, 52) supports this report but mentions that the printing of Hebrew books took place between 1562 and 1566. No other sources support this account.

Napoleon brought with him three printing presses equipped with Arabic, Latin, and French typefaces to communicate his messages to the Egyptians and to his troops. With the end of the French expedition in 1801, however, these presses were returned to France. Later, when Mohammad Ali Pasha emerged as the strong man of Egypt, he introduced movable-type printing to support his plan to put together a system of schools in an effort to modernize the country.

Among the major obstacles for the development of a publishing industry in the Arab region is censorship. Censorship in the Arab world is today a major barrier to the development of publishing. Criteria of censorship differ from time to time and from one Arab state to another. It varies from careful watch over religious texts, as in Tunis and Algeria, to the banning of texts by Muslim reformers and secular authors, as in the Arab Gulf States (Mermier 2006, 97).

Modern Arabic printing

The coming to power of Mohammed Ali Pasha in Egypt ushered in a new era in the Arab world: it began to move out of the dark ages. Mohammed Ali established in 1821 a printing press in Cairo on the grounds of the earlier

French press. It was moved later to Bulaq and became known as the Bulaq Press, gaining great fame as the leading press in the region. Today it is the official government press in Egypt. This press brought about an information revolution in the region and managed to print more than half a million publications in its first six years of operation.

Printing in Egypt during the rule of Mohammad Ali was a government monopoly designed to aid in the modernizing of the state. It focused on the production of administrative directives, as well as publications that dealt with medicine, science, music, the arts, and education. These publications, however, did not bring about the change desired. Most ended in warehouses, as few Egyptians were literate, and among the literate few were ready to accept reform messages, or were interested in reading what was chosen to be published (Sabat 1966, 170). The collapse of the rule of Mohammed Ali was followed by weak leaderships that could not carry on the educational reforms.

Like Syria and Mount Lebanon, printing in Palestine – the home of the three major "religions of the Book" – was introduced through the efforts of religious groups. Printing began in 1830, when a press was established to print Hebrew script. In 1846 an Arabic press was set up in Jerusalem by the Franciscan monks, to be followed in 1848 by two printing presses, one established by a group of English preachers, and the other by Armenian preachers. Before the First World War the area of present-day Jordan was distributed between Syria, Palestine, and Hijaz; printing there dates after this period. The first press in Jordan was started by Khalil Nasr, who moved his press from Haifa to Amman in 1922. A government press was instituted there in 1925.

The introduction of printing in the rest of the Arab states was slow and mostly came about as a result of the interest of local and Ottoman authorities in circulating their views as well as their administrative decisions. There is scattered information about the development of printing in these states. Some of the reports vary. One source suggests, for example, that printing in Iraq was introduced by Dominican monks in 1856 in the city of Mosul. Another source states that printing in Iraq was introduced by an Iranian of Turkish origin in 1821 or 1830 (Sabat 1966, 19, 295).

Yemen had its first printing press upon the order of Sultan Abdul Hamid II to serve the purposes of the Ottoman authorities. The press was known as Al-Wilayat Press or the Press of Wilayat al-Yaman. There are different reports as to the date of the establishment of this press. The accounts range between 1872 and 1879, but all agree that it was primitive and printed only Turkish texts (Sabat 1966, 327).

In 1882 the Ottoman Empire established the first printing press in Hijaz, which later became part of the present Kingdom of Saudi Arabia (Sabat, 1966, 19). This press, Al Matba'ah al-Miriyeh or the Press of Wilayat al-

Hijaz, was founded by the Turkish ruler of Hijaz, Minister Othman Nuri Pasha in the city of Mecca. The press was manual and could not compete with the advanced printing presses in Egypt. Thus Hijazi scholars and officials preferred to print their work in Egypt. Printing presses spread during the Saudi rule and special attention was given to training printers in Egypt.

The other Arab Gulf states were late in introducing printing presses. These presses were first introduced through individual efforts, and then with government support. Bahrain had its first printing press in 1938; Kuwait introduced its first press in 1947 and Qatar in 1956. In the Arab Maghreb states printing did not spread as fast as in the Arab Orient. It took a longer time to play an important role in introducing change in the Maghreb states, where printing was mainly introduced either by private enterprise or upon the initiative and with the support of military occupiers.

The first printing press in Algeria was introduced in 1830 by French troops. In Tunis the first press goes back to 1849, when a French priest printed a religious book in French. A number of new printing presses followed, mainly through the initiative of private individuals (Mermier 2006, 18). Printing in Morocco dates back to 1865, initiated by a state official in Meknes. It was subsequently moved to Fas. The first press in Libya was introduced by the governor of the province of Tripoli in 1866.

The situation of publishing Arabic texts in the Arab region today is in direct contrast with the status of publishing in the Arab region during the early days of Islam. Almost one thousand years before books appeared in the same quantity and quality in the West, around the middle of the eighth century, the Muslim civilization had a remarkable publications industry. "The vast [publishing] industry was . . . in existence when Europe began to occupy Muslim lands, and [it] was systematically killed off by the colonial powers, along with the Muslim systems of education and medicine and other cultural institutions" (Sardar and Davies, n.d.).

Challenges facing Arabic printing

The rapid development of typesetting technology during the past half century posed a serious challenge to Arabic printing, since the new technology addressed the problems of printing Western European languages that use the Latin alphabet, consisting of some 60 letter forms. Arabic printing can entail more than seven times as many, up to 450 forms (Munro 1981).

The primary modern challenge to Arabic printing was the one posed by the replacement of the old hand-setting of type by linotype and monotype machines that resembled typewriters but with keyboards that could accommodate large numbers of typefaces. With a good deal of creativity, Salloum Mkarzel of *Al-Huda* daily newspaper in the US was able to reduce the Arabic letter forms needed for printing and to lodge 122 Arabic letter forms in a linotype machine. Kamel Mrowa of Beirut's *Al-Hayat* newspaper managed to reduce the Arabic characters on his machine to 88 (Munro 1981).

Changes in printing technology during the twentieth century were massive, and provided, particularly through the introduction of computerized typesetting, an opportunity for Arab printing to free itself from being a mere adaptation of Western technology. Arabic printing today has better prospects to accommodate far more letter forms and typefaces and to seek new solutions to the problems of Arabic type design. Arabic texts can now be typeset more rapidly and more correctly than ever before.

Resolving the technical difficulties of printing Arabic script was an advance, but such hurdles are only part of the difficulty of printing in Arabic. The nature of the classical Arabic language and its style of writing posed several other problems for journalistic and scientific writing. Arab writers adopted a pan-Arab vernacular or a written variety of Arabic, rather than one dialect. This pan-Arab vernacular does not go well with journalistic or scientific writing, as it is characterized by a classical literary prose that strove for "formal and verbal perfection at the expense of clarity" (Ayalon 1994, 173). The traditional classical literary form places high value on form, rhyme, imagery, and ornamentation. Accordingly, clarity of meaning is often lost (Hamza 1963).

Another problem that beleaguered Arabic scientific and journalistic writing was adapting the Arabic vocabulary to meet the challenges of accommodating foreign terms and concepts. Arab writers, particularly journalists and scientists, had to adapt Arabic to the new foreign usages. Some attempted to introduce equivalent Arabic words, but this often resulted in confusion, as different Arabic words were sometimes adopted for the same foreign term by different writers. Other writers borrowed or "Arabized" foreign terms, but this could contribute to literary poverty. Sometimes proper Arabic words are replaced with foreign words that are not appropriate, or which even have crude connotations.[1] This latter approach has been on the increase since the advent of a generation of Arab television personnel whose command of classical Arabic vernacular is shabby and who often "throw in" foreign terms when the Arabic terms fail them.

In addition to the technical and literary difficulties faced by those involved with Arabic printing, the Arab world today faces a number of other challenges that need addressing. Among these challenges are the problems of the inadequate level of readership of printed matter and that of censorship.

According to the chairman of the Arab Publishers' Association, Ibrahim al-Moallem, "no exact statistics are available, but the quantity of books published in the Arab world is small, especially relative to the region's population" (Del Castillo 2002). In addition, Arab publishing suffers from the lack of proper distribution of the published books, according to Nasser Jarrous, head of the Lebanese publishers' association.

Accurate information about the data relating to printing and publishing in the Arab region is hard to obtain and even harder to validate. This author had first hand experience about problems of securing reliable official data when he edited the Arab region section in the 1989 UNESCO World Communication Report. Whatever outlook one adopts on the present state of affairs of Arab publishing, one can safely attribute the present situation of consumption of the print media to the low literacy rate in the Arab world, to weak purchasing power, to an undeveloped Arab publishing sector, and to censorship that suppresses the development of the medium as well as the publishing industry in the Arab world.

The Arab League Educational, Cultural and Science Organization (Alecso) reported that the number of illiterates in the Arab region has increased from 50 million in 1970 to 70 million in 2007. The report states that the level of illiterate Arabs who are older than 15 years old is 35 percent, which is above the level of illiteracy in undeveloped regions of the world: 23.4 percent (*Islamic News*, 2007).

Efforts to implement compulsory and free education for Arab children are underway. The Arab Maghreb states have made good strides in this direction, with the level of elementary school children reaching 90 percent and with the women students comprising half the school population in both Algeria and Tunisia. The Alecso figures indicate that the level of Arab illiterates who are above the age of 15 is 29.7 percent (46.5 percent among women) (National Commission for Childhood, 2008).

Alecso, however, warned that the present efforts to fight illiteracy mainly focus on teaching basic reading and writing as well as elementary mathematics. This gives little or no attention to attending to cultural and functional illiteracy or to improving the professional skills of the citizens (Watani 2007).

More optimistic data on Arab education is reported by *Al-Watan,* a Saudi newspaper, which suggests that more Saudi children below the age of 15 are literate. A Saudi government report suggests that illiteracy among Saudi children between the ages of 10 and 14 is only 1.4 percent, while it reaches 73.9 percent for Saudis above the age of 65 (*Al-Watan* 2008).

In most Arab states there are several authorities that are involved with the censoring of printed matter. In Egypt, for example, there are censoring authorities in the Ministry of Information as well as in the Ministries of

Defense and the Interior. The Islamic research center of Al Azhar University also practices censoring power over printed matter (Mermier 2006, 100). According to the Arab Human Development Report 2003, most Arab states "place the media under the dominant political authorities and institutions, and employ media channels for political propaganda and entertainment, at the expense of other functions and services." The Report also suggests that Arab media "operate in an environment that sharply restricts freedom of the press and freedom of expression and opinion . . . censorship is rife" (UNDP, *Arab Human Development Report 2003*).

Censorship of the press usually takes the form of letting the editors know what is expected of them. A senior editor of the leading Saudi paper *Al-Hayat* reports: "I have never been told to publish anything. But I have been asked not to publish something more times than I can remember." He maintains that "the most prevalent form of censorship is self-censorship . . . it is a matter of economics, even of survival. . . . It is the case that some kind of subsidies, whether by state or by individuals, will continue to be necessary to the survival of much of the Arab media" (Khazen 1999).

Not only is censorship practiced on printing presses and on the media but it also covers national and international book exhibitions. In general publishers in most Arab states are required to secure permission to exhibit books by submitting a list of books that are intended for exhibition. In 2000 the Kuwaiti officials did not allow some 300 books to be exhibited in a book fair. The Saudi officials submitted a 200-page list of corrections that they required the publisher of a well-known Arab dictionary, *Al-Munjid*, to make before allowing its sale in the kingdom (Mermier 2006, 98).

Book market

By the late nineteenth century both Egypt and Lebanon emerged as important places for printing and publishing. Cairo became the Arab world's most important intellectual center in the first part of the twentieth century. Due to geopolitical changes in the Arab region, however, and with the Egyptian change of political system in the 1950s, Egypt's predominance in Arab publishing was lost to Lebanon (Mermier 2006, 25).

Modern Arabic publishing in Egypt and Lebanon developed mainly through private ventures and individuals. Publishing in these two countries became the main force in introducing modern thought and instigating reform movements in the Arab world. These two countries dominated Arabic printing and publishing during the past century. Iraq was not as advanced as both countries in the areas of printing and publishing, but it had the highest relative consumption of Arabic printed media until the early 1990s. Thus it was commonly stated that "Cairo writes, Beirut publishes, and Iraq reads" (Mermier 2006, 23). The Gulf States to date are the major consumers of Arabic printed matter.

Arab publishers usually operate on very small budgets and face difficulties in distributing their books across the Arab world. Publishing establishments in the Arab region are often extensions of family-run bookstores. Recently, however, a number of small-scale and independent publishers came into the publishing scene, particularly in Beirut, Cairo, and the Gulf. "All the ingredients for a take-off in Arab publishing are in place" (Tresilian 2006).

The UNDP's *Arab Human Development Report 2003* suggests that the Arab states suffer from a lack of consumption of print matter (UNDP, *Arab Human Development Report 2003*, 51–67). "With a combined population of 284 million, a 'best seller' may have a print run of just 5,000 copies. Translations of foreign works into Arabic lag far behind figures in the rest of the world. Just 53 newspapers per 1,000 citizens are published daily in the region, compared to 285 papers per 1,000 people in the developed nations" (Shamounki & Orme 2003).

According to the First Arab Report on Cultural Development (Arab Thought Institute 2008) the total number of books (excluding textbooks) published in 2007 in 17 Arab countries was 27,809. These are broken down into the following categories: literature, 7,060; social sciences, 6,351; religion, 5,157; history and geography, 2,769; applied sciences, 2,208; pure science, 1,129; general knowledge, 960; languages, 909; philosophy and psychology, 714; and arts, 552. First printings of Arabic books usually range between 1,000 and 3,000 (some print only 500). There are exceptions: the series of Reading for All in Egypt and the series of books of the Kuwaiti National Council for Culture, Arts, and Literature print 50,000 copies.

A noted problem concerning Arabic publications is the paucity of Arabic books translated into foreign languages. Similarly, few books are translated into Arabic from foreign languages. Mermier (2006, 143–44) notes that *The 2002 UN Report on Arab Human Development* gives the annual number of books translated as 230 while Jalal (1999) reports that the figure is 450.

Most of the translated books are from English, French, Russian, Spanish, and German, and some of these are done from secondary texts that are translations of texts from a language other than the five listed languages (Arab Thought Institute 2008, 413–14).

A serious flaw in Arabic publishing is the scarcity of the publication and circulation of research and academic work. Academic publishing in the Arab world is kept minimal by the insufficiency of funds allocated by academic institutions to research and to publishing, as well as by undue restriction of academic freedom by many of the ruling regimes. Arab academic journals are insufficient and many are short-lived. As a result many Arabic scholarly works are not widely circulated, and accessing the texts of masters' and doctoral theses in Arab universities usually requires hard labor (Nasser and Abouchedid 2001).

A recent study on the economic performance of four key copyright industries, including book publishing, in Morocco, Tunisia, Egypt, Jordan, and Lebanon argues that there is a recorded good economic performance of book publishing in Lebanon and Jordan due to positive production factors such as available labor in Jordan and capital in Lebanon, positive demand conditions (domestic in Jordan and foreign in Lebanon), and favorable interaction with the upstream and downstream industries (Harabi 2004). On the other hand, Morocco and Tunisia do not have favorable industry conditions, perhaps due to poor production factors (mainly lack of capital), weak support from peripheral industries, and insufficient government support. The Egyptian book publishing industry enjoys positive production factors and demand conditions as well as healthy domestic competition, but still encounters serious obstacles due to the lack of support from upstream industries, such as paper manufacturing or book and publishing equipment. Overall, Arab governments still need to enforce immaterial property rights (IPR) and antitrust laws to regulate the competition and to encourage investment in this sector.

While the internet is still in its early infancy in the Arab world, mainly due to the high illiteracy rate, the limited distribution of computers, and the high cost of getting an internet connection, this medium is nevertheless quite effective among urban, educated, and rich Arabs. The internet can be employed among the Arab elite to develop the Arab public sphere to cover what are usually taboo subjects, such as the promotion of democratic structures and good governance. Censored books and articles can now be available on line.

A successful attempt in this line is the Egypt-based e-book series Kotobarabia, which is devoted exclusively to Arabic-language titles. The venture www.kotobarabia.com "now offers over 8,500 books in 31 subject categories, ranging from 'Literature' to 'Business Management,' 'Banned Books,' and the provocatively titled 'Hot Topics.'"(Rossetti 2009). To avoid censorship, Kotobarabia's servers for the site are in the United States, rather than in the Arab world. A study of 150 Arabic titles by the founder of Kotobarabia found that "the top 10 percent of the books were available along any conventional distribution route, and could be found at most bookstores. The bottom 10 percent was not available anywhere: Basically, you could only get them at the publisher's office or at the author's home. The middle 80 percent was only available within a five kilometer radius of the publishing house" (Rossetti 2009).

Such an individual initiative is not enough. What is needed are joint and cooperative Arab ventures that will succeed in encouraging Arab scholars and activists to accept the use of the internet in their public exchanges. Another serious challenge to printing and publishing is the mushrooming of television channels that mainly distract the viewers from published work and have addicted Arab viewers to kitsch and low cultural products. Improving the quality of television programs can perhaps stretch the viewers' interest to seek more information in published works.

Conclusion

Like most areas of communication in the Arab region today, Arab printing and publishing have witnessed immense technological developments. This development, however, focuses more on the physical element at the expense of the human. It lacks serious and genuine attempts to develop the human component involved in this endeavor – a commitment to participatory development that stresses human involvement and is not merely based on copied technology and parachuted programs. Participatory human involvement would yield solutions to the problems of printing and publishing through focusing on understanding the cultural norms and values of the Arab world, rather than merely studying Western developments in these fields. What is needed is more than simple copying. The need is for solutions that emerge from within. The Arab world today is in urgent need of planning to get rid of cultural illiteracy. Most important is the need for a commitment to democratic structures and systems of governance. Developments in Arabic printing and publishing need to center the attention on this goal.

A starting point would be to pool the different Arab efforts in the area of printing and publishing. What is needed is the cooperation of Arab printers and publishers in addressing their problems, and not dependence on outside help or copying of successful distant solutions to alien printing and publishing problems. Arab cooperative ventures are needed. Arab intellectuals and experts need to join their efforts and come up with effective Arab solutions to Arab problems. An example of a simple but successful venture is the cooperative monthly publication of a popular series of influential books from the past that are distributed at no cost with a select leading Arab newspaper in Egypt (*Al-Kahirah*), Iraq (*Al-Mada* and *Al-Itihad*), Arab Emirates (*Al-Bayan*), Kuwait (*Al-Qabas*), and Lebanon (*As-Safir*).

Note

1 For example, while the Arabic language has a suitable Arabic word (*mazhar*) for the English term "look," the Arabic television term regularly used is *luk*. A term that has recently gained usage for charging a cell phone is *tashreej* (from the English word "charge") while there is a perfectly appropriate Arabic word for it: *ta'bi'ah*. The irony is that in Arabic the word *tashreej* originates from the word *sharj* which in Arabic means "anus."

3   Arab Press
Nabil Dajani

To understand the development of Arab print media it is necessary to understand the emergence of popular demand for news sheets. Popular papers in the Arab world could not develop until necessary and sufficient factors for their need by the population materialized. These factors are printing, literacy, and, most important, conflict. While printing and literacy are necessary ingredients, they are not sufficient for the emergence of a popular press. Popular need for information develops during times of conflict or discord. Conflicts prompt the population to seek information that will help them understand events and reduce public dissonance.

The development of the popular Arab press was influenced by major social and political events that produced discord among the general public. Most important among these events were the intensified conflicts among minority sects and the spread of the call for Arab nationalism, which advocated independence from Ottoman, French, and British domination and "the creation of the state of Israel and its ensuing wars, military coups d'états, civil conflicts and the Gulf War, as well as the development of a politicized Islam . . . [and] the oil boom" (Essoulami 2009).

This chapter reviews these factors in each region of the Arab world, and discusses the changing roles of the print press from the nineteenth to the twenty-first centuries.

Historical background

In their attempt to understand the early development of print media, scholars of Arab media often focus on this medium as operating within separate state entities and recount when and where the early Arabic papers appeared. Because of scarcity of documented records on the subject, conflicting assessments are circulated. For example, the respected historian of the Arab press Philip de Tarrazi reported that the earliest Arab paper was *At-Tanbih* (L'Avertissement) and that it appeared in Egypt in 1800 upon the orders of Napoleon during his Egyptian expedition. It was reported that French General Menou issued a decree in November 1800 to establish *At-Tanbih* newspaper. He appointed Ismael el Khashab as its editor, to be supervised by scholars of the French mission in Egypt. The paper was to deal with the affairs of the French government as well (Tarrazi 1919; Abdo 1942, 5–6).

Later research proved that this paper never saw the light, although Napoleon made plans to produce it. Political developments and the deterioration of security did not allow for the implementation of this project (Abdo 1951, 29). The publisher of the Iraqi *Al-Mu'arikh* magazine, Razzouk Issa, asserted in a 1934 article that the first Arabic paper was *Journal al-Iraq*, which appeared in Baghdad in 1816, and that it was published by the Ottoman Wali Dauod Pasha al-Karkhi (Al-Wandi 2008). However, Raphael Batti, historian of the Iraqi media, argued that this information "lacks a great deal of proof and documentation as its bearer did not provide any source for this information" (Batti 1955, 10). In the Arab Maghreb some media scholars designate *Al Mubashir,* which was published in Algeria in 1847, as the first Arabic paper (Azzi 1998). There is general agreement, however, that the first Arabic paper regularly published was *Al Waqa'e al Misriyyah,* published by Mohammad Ali Pasha in Egypt in 1828.

This concern and confusion over the date of the appearance of early Arabic newspapers has diverted attention from investigating the causes or factors that contributed to the emergence of newspapers in the first place. No matter where and when early Arabic papers appeared, they were clearly founded in an effort by authorities to address and direct their subjects. They did not represent a popular need for information, but rather were published by ruling powers whose purpose was to convey directives to their subjects. Their impact, therefore, was limited to few targeted elite. Hamza (1963, 29), Abdo (1951, 9–12) and Aziz (1968, 12) report that Mohammad Ali published his paper to be read by his senior administrators and staff.

The beginnings of a popular Arab press were realized by Arab men of letters and social reformers. The first Arabic popular paper is perhaps *Miraat al Ahwal* (Mirror of Events), published in Istanbul in 1855 by Rizkallah Hassoun el-Halabi. This paper, however, was soon suspended by the Ottoman authorities. A series of popular papers followed soon after in Lebanon, beginning with *Hadikat al-Akhbar* (The Garden of News) by Khalil el-Khuri, in 1858.

The strict Ottoman control of the press "drove Syrian-Lebanese journalists to Egypt where press regulation was [more relaxed]. It was these Syrian-Lebanese journalists, bent on resuscitating Arab literature in the name of past Arab glory, who were in the avant-garde of modern Arab journalism and launched [elite] newspapers which . . . became models for the Arab press" (Essoulami 2006).

By the time the popular press was mushrooming in Lebanon, Egypt, which already was introduced to printing and had a relatively modern and developed system of education, was experiencing struggle among members of its ruling elite and was facing political unrest. The army was impatient about the increasing British influence in Egyptian affairs during the reign of Ismail Pasha, who was attempting to introduce a Western style of modernization. This agitation culminated in an army revolt. With printing, education, and public unrest, Egypt was ready for a popular press, and the first popular paper in Egypt, *Wadi el Nil*, appeared in 1867.

It can be assumed that the popular print media emerged in Arab areas that were witnessing internal conflicts and that possessed printing presses as well as a developed educational system. These areas were Lebanon and Egypt. Lebanon was going through sectarian strife and Egypt was going through political unrest, as well as undergoing the pains of modernization and foreign intrusion. The early popular papers in Lebanon were thus more literary and social in their initial stages. With increased Ottoman oppression during the reign of Sultan Adbul Hamid II, however, the Lebanese press began taking political positions and the call for Arab nationalism gained ground. In Egypt, the popular press was political from its start.

The modern Arab press, which has roots in its response to popular needs, can be understood better by viewing media regulations within the sociopolitical and geopolitical developments affecting Arab political, economic, and social forces. While the Arab world was part of the Ottoman Empire, its regions included people of different religious and ethnic backgrounds. These regions, and the social and ethnic groups within them, were not evenly controlled by the central Ottoman authorities. The freedom exercised by Arab editors in the different Ottoman regions, therefore, was varied.

Regulation of the Arab press

Once a popular press emerges, its regulation is influenced by a variety of factors. In his classification of Arab media William Rugh (1979), following the approach of Schramm et al. (1963), argues that the state is the primary factor in determining regulation of the press in the different parts of the Arab world. On the other hand, Awatef Abdelrahman (1996) stressed the differing colonial and imperial influences on Arab media regulation systems.

An examination of the development of the Arab press suggests that, beyond the role of the state, its regulation is influenced by sociopolitical and geopolitical factors contributing to the materialization of the modern Arab states. For example, while Lebanon and Syria were within the same "political territory" the sociopolitical facts (sectarian strife in Mount Lebanon and social stability due to homogenous religious constellations in Syria) prompted the development of a popular press in Lebanon before Syria. And geopolitical factors contributed to the migration of the press from Lebanon and Syria to Egypt during the strict rule of Abdul Hamid II (ruling from 1876–1918). It was this period, when the Arab press experienced the harshest press controls, that contributed to the emergence of a politically oriented popular press that championed Arab nationalism – even though some journalists had to emigrate. On the other hand, a reverse migration took place following the political coup d'état of the free army officers in Egypt in 1952. Similarly, Lebanese press migration to Arab Gulf states as well as to Europe occurred during the 1975–1990 Lebanese civil war.

While the desire of Lebanese intellectuals to address the religious conflicts in their country played a role in the emergence of the popular press in Lebanon,

> the growth of the popular press in Syria came about as part of a general trend in the Ottoman Empire by intellectuals to reform the administration. The Lebanese and Syrian press developed into a political press with an Arab nationalist Orientation early in the twentieth century, with the coming to power of the Young Turks whose rule became clearly in favor of the Turkish subjects of the empire. (Dajani and Najjar 2003, 75–88)

The French mandate imposed strict press censorship and administrative suspension of opposition papers. The French authorities tended to "manage" the press through resorting to rewards or punishments (el-Ghrayyeb 1971; Rayashi 1953, 1957). After independence the press regulation systems in Lebanon and Syria took different paths. Lebanon adopted a liberal system of governance and, because of the strife among its different religious sects, developed into a state with a weak central government and strong sectarian bosses. Consequently, the Lebanese press enjoyed relative freedom to oppose the state authority but could not act as a "watchdog" to safeguard the public interest, as it experienced strict control from the sectarian bosses that it represented. On the other hand, Syria adopted a socialist system of governance with strict control of the media.

Lebanon

The Lebanese press passed through four phases of regulation from independence to the present. Newspapers in Lebanon are privately owned, and media management is regulated by press laws. In the first phase, the government of independence continued to make use of the French press law and to apply the same tactics of regulating the press, as was the case with Syria. During this period (1946–1962), the Lebanese press was influenced by the geopolitical changes in the region. Lebanon's policy of free economy and its relative political stability, following the 1948 Arab-Israeli war and the consequent military coups in the Arab world, enhanced its economic and political roles in the region. Lebanon became the diplomatic center of the Arab world and a prominent center for Arab business and finance. Consequently the Lebanese press institutions improved their material facilities and eventually developed into a pan-Arab press, which was a role previously occupied by the Egyptian press.

The second phase (1962–1975) is perhaps the most important and richest period for the Lebanese press. It began with the introduction of a liberal press law, in 1962, that organized the profession and protected it from administrative abuse. Local and foreign interest groups sought the support of the Lebanese press to reach the Lebanese and Arab masses. Lebanese press institutions became occupied with Arab political disputes. Consequently many Arab governments exerted pressure on Lebanon to control the "harmful" coverage of their countries' news by the Lebanese press. Local complaints were also increasing that the press was losing its "Lebanese character."

The outbreak of the civil war in 1975 ushered in a third phase. This period is characterized by the decline in the financial resources of the press as well as in its influence and prestige. The period witnessed the introduction of legislative decrees that imposed strict penalties for press offenses.

The pressure on the Lebanese press to regulate itself was accompanied by loss of revenue due to the drop in distribution and loss of advertising. The Lebanese press lost its pan-Arab character and a number of papers were discontinued. Several of the leading journalists moved with their publications outside Lebanon to countries in the Arab Gulf or to Europe where many achieved recognition.

With the end of the Lebanese civil war and the beginning of the 1990s, the Lebanese press entered its fourth phase, which continues to the present. The press began to rebuild what it lost professionally and materially during the long war.

Syria

The first three years of independence (1946 to 1949) did not witness much change in the affairs of the press in Syria. The ruling elite was overwhelmed with political and administrative problems, thus they did not pay much attention to the press. Granting publication licenses became the prerogative of the Minister of the Interior, who decreed that a city may not have more than one political paper for every 50,000 inhabitants (Abbas 2001, 8). Following the 1948 Arab-Israeli war, Syria was plagued by a series of military coups and political struggles among conflicting political groups. This period stretched from 1948 and 1963; Syria witnessed different political regimes, including a union with Egypt that lasted three years. Consequently varying forms of press legislation prevailed and party ownership of the press became common.

In March 1963, the Baath Party took over power and ushered in a long period of political stability – which Syria is still experiencing. In May 1963, the new Syrian regime established a special body that was to oversee the affairs of the press (Othman 1997, 416–17). The Syrian national council approved in 1965 a law organizing the press, which now became semi-official and was expected to operate within a socialist national orientation.

In November 2000 Syria permitted public entities other than those of the ruling political party to publish newspapers without the need for government licensing. A new 2001 press law allowed more press freedom and contained articles organizing the profession. Licensing of papers, according to this new law, is issued by the council of ministers, which has the right to deny granting a license for reasons of public welfare. However, public entities, political parties, unions, and professional syndicates are simply required to notify the Minister of Information of their intention to put out a paper and do not need the approval of the Council of Ministers.

Palestine and Jordan

In Palestine the Arabic popular press entities were mainly owned by individuals, who were repressed by the Ottomans. After the occupation of Palestine by England, the fear of a British and Zionist conspiracy to establish a Jewish state provoked the development of a popular press in 1919. This press gained momentum following the 1929 "Wailing Wall revolt" (*thawrat al-barrak*). The British seldom managed to control this press by direct regulation, but resorted to playing the Jews and Palestinians against one another. Palestinian newspapers and magazines became an important instrument in the call for independence. They focused on political articles, poetry, and intellectual and literary topics that dealt with the call for reform and change (Suleiman 2009).

After the establishment of the state of Israel in 1948 Palestinian refugees streamed into the East Bank of Jordan from former Palestine, and the West Bank was officially annexed to Jordan in 1950. Jordan until that time did not have popular press. Prior to its acquiring independence in 1946 Jordan had a weekly newspaper – *Al Sharq Al Arabi* (Arab East) – that appeared in

1923 and published official announcements, government legislation, and regulations. It did not have a popular press and its inhabitants relied on publications imported from Palestine, Syria, Lebanon, and Egypt. Palestinian newspapers set the agenda of political discussion in the kingdom, which prompted the Jordanian government in 1967 to force the merger of West Bank papers and to legalize its partial ownership of the merged papers in a move to control their content.

The clash between the government and the PLO in 1970 resulted in the introduction of a strict 1973 press law that increased penalties and imposed prior censorship until July 1974. Press restrictions impelled a number of journalists to leave, some of whom later published on the internet. A new openness to democratic rights and freedoms in 1992 encouraged the publication of new papers. Government partnership in the ownership of these papers was maintained. Although the government periodically announces its intention to liberalize the press law, this has not taken place.

Iraq

Like Jordan, Iraq was late to develop printing and modern schools, and consequently, late to acquire a popular press. Iraq knew only one official paper, *Az Zawraa'*, from 1869 until 1908 when the Ottomans issued a new constitution and established more official papers in the different Iraqi districts. Not until the British occupation of Iraq and its declaration as a Hashemite kingdom did a privately owned popular Iraqi press develop. This popular press, however, was ineffective and was manipulated by the authorities, which continued to apply the Ottoman press controls until 1931 (Al-Wandi 2008).

The Iraqi popular press experienced varying degrees of freedom during the different Hashemite governments. The July 14, 1958, revolution that brought about a republican regime introduced an atmosphere of relative press freedom and initiated many incentives for journalists. The political instability that followed, however, and the consequent coups by military officials were not conducive to the professional development of journalism. After Saddam Hussein took power only a handful of papers were permitted to publish and these were subjected to suppression (Al-Wandi 2008). The fall of Saddam Hussein generated a state of media chaos in Iraq. More than 200 newspapers and magazines mushroomed across the country with US funds channeled into the Iraqi media (Finer 2005; Rugh 2004). The new papers produced pluralistic voices but lacked proper understanding of their responsibility in an era of political, social, and cultural change. The new press system contributed to the spread of sectarian grudges as well as disunity. These newspapers are mostly funded by political or religious parties and "many have a credibility problem among Iraqi readers as they often contain unverified, false or heavily-biased reports, undermining any notion of independent journalism" (BBC News, 2007).

Egypt

The freedom enjoyed by the popular press in Egypt in the late nineteenth century and the progressive governance it enjoyed attracted journalists from Bilad ash-Sham (Lebanon and Syria) who fled Ottoman suppression and were instrumental in introducing newspapers that became foremost Arab papers. Shaheen (1957, 62–63) reports that in 1944 two prominent Egyptian journalists stated, "We Egyptians are not used to being publishers and editors of newspapers. We are only tailored to the role of reporters. Publishing is the concern of the people of Bilad ash-Sham and not ours." Consequently the popular press in Egypt led Arab journalism and developed into a pan-Arab press. The British authorities were relaxed in dealing with the press. Their interference was indirect; it took the form of having postal officials delay the distribution of opposition papers, or of favoring friendly papers with inside information.

This lasted until the 1950s, when the revolution of the "free officers" brought about a regime that instituted stern government regulation. (Iraq and Syria went through similar changes of regimes and the political unrest in the region brought about major changes in the Arab press system.) The new revolutionary regime introduced nationalization of the press and created institutional frameworks that subjected the press to the rule of one party. In 1960 Egyptian authorities issued a decree transferring the ownership of leading papers to the "National Union" which was empowered with the exclusive right to license newspapers and appoint their editors. As a consequence, the presidencies of Abdul Nasser and Sadat experienced a relatively obedient press.

With the declared intention of the Mubarak government to move toward a "pluralistic democracy," and its introduction of a relatively more relaxed press law in 2006, press aspirations were higher than what the government delivered. The 2006 press law allowed forms of censorship and continued to appoint editors for the national press. It also maintained provisions for custodial sentences for "endangering national interests," "displaying bad publicity," or for "insulting the head of state." Accordingly the relationship between the press and the state deteriorated, and press and state clashed in the autumn of 2007 (Black 2008).

As publishing a paper in Egypt requires securing a license or starting a political party, both of which require lengthy and costly procedures, some

Egyptian journalists resort to publishing what is commonly known as the "Cyprus press." The label goes back to early journalists who published Egyptian papers under Cypriot licenses and shipped them to Egypt. At present such papers can be licensed anywhere outside Egypt and then printed outside, mainly in Lebanon, or in Egypt's Free Zone in Cairo. The "Cypriot papers" need clearance by the censorship office like all other foreign publications.

The present press in Egypt may be described as one that operates "in a culture where the political and the moral spheres are subject to rigid controls . . . it is a model of how to maintain state control and allow freedom within certain strictly patrolled boundaries" (Hammond 2007, 85).

The Arab Gulf Region

This region includes Saudi Arabia, Yemen, Oman, Qatar, Bahrain, the Arab Emirates, and Kuwait. The discovery of oil enhanced the importance of this region and its new wealth attracted skilled personnel in many areas, including the press. Arab journalists took up leading positions in newly formed privately owned newspapers. "Unfortunately, these journalists were hemmed in by the traditionalist system governing the countries concerned. The downside of the high salaries they earned was the rigid censorship they had to work under" (Essoulami 2006).

The Arab Gulf states share many demographic and ecological characteristics that delayed the development of a popular press system in all of them. The print media was late to emerge in this region, mainly due to the absence of printing presses as well as the high illiteracy rate. Popular press did not appear in these states until quite late in the second half of the twentieth century. The oil boom, the heavy movement of professionals to the Gulf states, and the political volatility in the other Arab Mashriq regions contributed to the migration of Arab journalists to this area and consequently to the development of an advanced media structure. The governments of the Gulf States, however, "are mindful of two risks as far as the media are concerned. They feel that foreign, especially Western, values could undermine their traditions and roots. Second, they would like to maintain their citizens' respectful attitude to their leaders, governed by tribal and religious guidelines. Support for freedom of the media is therefore circumscribed . . . Gulf reservations were perhaps best expressed by Oman's Information Minister, Abdulaziz bin Mohammed al Rowas. He said: 'We have a duty to immunize ourselves the way you immunize yourself against diseases...We monitor the foreign media and react to it according to our needs'" (Singh 2000).

The affluence of the Gulf states has allowed them to attract leading journalists from the entire Arab world, but most Gulf rulers were cautious in providing space for free media operation. These rulers realize "the need to maintain their heritage and traditions in a fast-changing world, with their oil wealth having given them the comforts and benefits of modern living and conveniences . . . [they] realize that their societies will change, but they do not wish the changes to be disruptive" (Singh 2000). Because Kuwait and Saudi Arabia were early to benefit from the oil wealth, they took earlier and bigger leaps into developing their media systems. Other Gulf countries balance the restrictions by supporting local media but imposing guidelines on coverage or by promoting satellite television, as Qatar did by establishing Al-Jazeera. Yemen experimented with moderate press freedom in 1990, following the unification of its northern and southern parts. However, subsequent to the 1994 civil war, press freedom was curbed drastically (Rugh 2004, 105).

In Saudi Arabia, where the government faces strong conservative religious pressure groups, several members of the Saudi royal family publish papers in European capitals. This absolves the Saudi government from the need to control the content of these papers, while it provides the papers with an agreeable space of freedom.

All Saudi newspapers are privately owned and most are openly or indirectly controlled by a member of the ruling family, or by people close to them. They require a royal decree to publish and they operate under strict censorship. No criticism of the government, the Saudi royal family, or Islam is tolerated (BBC News 2006).

Arab journalists in the Gulf were instrumental in introducing a media transformation in this region. Today the Arab press in the Gulf is among the most advanced of its Arab counterparts. However, press freedom continues to suffer in the Gulf. This is often freely acknowledged by Gulf leaders. The Information Minister of UAE, Shaikh Abdallah Bin Zayed Al Nahyan, once proclaimed: "It is difficult to speak about local Press freedom while the media machine is not run by local journalists" (Singh 2000).

The Kuwaiti local press is relatively the most free among the Gulf's local press. Kuwaiti newspapers are professionally advanced and are characterized by independence and openness, but are not permitted to criticize the amir (ruler) or discuss Islam and religion (Press Reference: Kuwait).

The Maghreb

The print media in Arab North Africa "is the product of at least two historical components: colonialism and post-independence conditions" (Azzi

1998). The early press in this region was introduced and owned by foreigners and the popular press was late to develop. As Libya experienced a different colonial influence (Italian and British) from the remaining Maghreb states, which were influenced by French colonization, two distinct press systems characterized the early popular press in this region.

Italy colonized Libya in 1911 and continued to rule it until 1943, at which time British forces occupied it until 1951 when it achieved independence. Libya did not experience a popular press until the beginning of the twentieth century. The Italian colonizers confiscated the printing presses in Libya and closed down Arabic papers. The Libyans resorted to publishing underground resistance papers in regions that the Italians could not control. When England took over the authority in Libya following its expulsion of the Italian forces during the Second World War it did not contest the development of political parties and a popular Libyan press. After independence in 1951 the government of King Idriss Senusi abolished political parties but retained qualified freedom of operation for the press.

The 1969 September Revolution of Muamar Qadhafi appropriated the existing Libyan papers and declared the necessity for a new "revolutionary" press. Not only did the new authorities work to introduce this revolutionary press at home, they also "invested in the expatriate press in order to rally support for their power and ally themselves to the most eminent and credible pens in the Arab world . . . [Arab] Journalists fell over themselves to offer their services to the rich and draw on the benefits due to them. . . . A critical press was confined to the limits of the Arab community abroad. Other more powerful dailies and reviews had a regional audience that was much more significant " (Essoulami 2006). On the home front a 1972 law forbids "any person who does not believe in the revolution and its goals" from publishing a paper. In the same year another law ended the era of private and independent papers by setting up a special body, the Public Press Institute, which was given the exclusive right to publish the printed media "in a way that serves the revolution" (Human Rights Solidarity 2006).

The Libyan authorities attempted several measures to liberate the press and media in Libya. On January 2006 a son of President Qaddafi announced that the government would allow private radio and television stations and printed news media. This did not materialize for the print media and the Libyan press remains tightly controlled.

The area of the Maghreb that includes the present states of Algeria, Morocco, and Tunis shared, until their independence, a similar media background. From the first half of the nineteenth century until the beginning of the twentieth century the area was under strict rule by France. The colonial authorities imposed a course of confusion, merging of land, and harassment.

This period knew colonial papers that were published mainly by the French authorities, or by European settlers. A 1881 press law "considered Arabic language as a foreign language and printing in Arabic or the importation of Arabic papers and documents were considered serious violations of the law . . . [it] postulated that only those enjoying civil rights were permitted to issue publications . . . [Arabs] were apparently required to seek French nationality and adopt French language and culture to possibly acquire such rights" (Azzi 1998). There were some papers that included a few pages in Arabic but "these were founded essentially to communicate with the local population on colonial administration's restrictive and oppressive laws and policies" (Azzi 1998)

Following this period, between the 1910s and 1930s, the French tolerated the emergence of papers by Arabs under the strict control of the colonial administration. By the late 1930s and until independence the area saw the emergence of a nationalist press that advocated reform and self-government. Many of these papers were underground. After acquiring independence, each of the three Maghreb states worked to advance the state's goals, which usually involved social and economic growth.

> In Algeria the National Liberation Front established the system of one-party rule and journalists became civil servants answerable to the socialist revolution. In Tunisia, the Bourguiba regime tolerated an opposition press, but this press was dependent on the government's goodwill, as was the case in Morocco. Journalists often came up against censorship and a legislation which repressed independent criticism in the name of the protection of public order. (Essoulami 2006)

The press in Algeria, Morocco, and Tunis during this period was an "instrument for political legitimatization and indoctrination." Eventually this press became an advocate for the position of the ruling national elite at the expense of the general public. Additionally the influence of France continues in the three Maghreb states. Many of their leading papers are published in French (Azzi 1998).

Following independence in 1962, intellectuals of the Algerian National Liberation Front operated the print media in Algeria and thus the press enjoyed a high degree of freedom. Within a few years, however, passive civil servants took over the operation of the Algerian media, which became a mere instrument of the state. By the late 1980s popular pressure resulted in political liberalization, and greater freedom was granted to the press and several new papers emerged. An army takeover in 1992 brought about press restrictions that lasted until 2000, when the press regained part of its freedom. The media in Algeria, however, are still under firm government control. The state subsidizes marginal publications, but it imposes a sort of prior censorship on the content of the media and foreign publications require prior license. Algeria, which is a society torn by civil strife, has failed to promote dialogue among the diverse socioeconomic groups (Press Reference: Algeria 2008).

The Tunisian press follows the traditional French press form in which newspapers are highly editorialized. The media in Tunisia are published in the capital, Tunis, and are mostly privately owned. They are mainly directed to the cultural elite. Most of the Arabic-language dailies published in Tunis are the translated versions of French-language newspapers and are owned by them (Press Reference: Tunisia 2008). The press in Tunis usually represents the government position, and criticism of officials is discouraged. With the end of the Bourguiba regime Tunis moved toward more relaxed press controls. "However, the political environment is generally restricted, a fact which is reflected by relative homogeneity of media content in Tunisia today" (Azzi 1998).

While outright censorship of the press is rare, views of minorities are regularly prohibited and journalists are often harassed. Thus most journalists choose to operate within the guidelines established by the Tunisian government. The Tunisian government subsidizes pro-government papers as well as newspapers published by opposition parties.

After it won independence in 1956, Morocco experienced the mushrooming of newspapers that reflected different party links. The impact of the long French cultural influence on the Moroccan press is obvious in editorialized news that it carries and in its reflection of political viewpoints and social agendas. Until recently French-language newspapers had the largest circulation in Morocco.

While the newspapers in Morocco usually represent the different political parties and are mostly independent and liberal, they also realize the necessities of adjusting to the monarchy system that provides them with annual subsidies. Similarly,

> the Moroccan government accepts mild forms of political criticism. The government, however, tolerates no attack on the monarchy or Islam. If newspapers in Morocco expect to remain in business, they must agree to exercise some form of restraint and to practice self-censorship. To guarantee that criticism of official policies remains within appropriate boundaries, the government grants a subsidy . . . to the press each year. (Press Reference: Morocco 2008)

The Moroccan press code of 2002 imposes prison sentences for defaming the king or the royal family and grants the government the right to shut down any publication "prejudicial to Islam, the monarchy, territorial integrity, or public order."

Arab émigré and transnational press

The suppression of press freedom in the Arab world by colonial powers and national authorities has also contributed to the development of a distinct type of Arab press: "press in exile" or an émigré press. The Arab press in exile consists of (usually) magazines that are published by journalists who fled the Arab world because they could not practice an acceptable level of freedom of expression in their home countries. In most cases these publications are sustained by sources that support their position.

An émigré press, on the other hand, is usually published by persons of literary background or out of concern for the emigrant community in the country they have settled. These publications are as

> diverse as the groups which they represent, including literary, political, social, economic, religious and popular weeklies, monthlies and quarterlies as well as bulletins published by compatriotic unions . . . [most prominent among the early émigré papers are] *Abu Saffarah, Abu Naddarah* and *Abu Naddarah Zarqa* edited by Egyptian nationalist Yaqub ibn Sannu . . . and *alUrwa al-Wuthqa*, edited by Muhammad Abduh and Jamal al-Din al-Afghani. (Hirsch, 2005)

The transnational Arabic press is not new in the Arab world. An examination of the history of the Arab press world would confirm that the Egyptian press was distributed all over the Arab world in the forties and early fifties. In the fifties and sixties elite Lebanese newspapers like *Al-Hayat* and *Al Anwar* were pan-Arab papers par excellence. The pan-Arab Arabic press in past decades, however, differs considerably from today's transnational press of the Gulf. Not only were the early pan-Arab Egyptian and Lebanese papers published from their home countries, the content and style of both differed. Even the impact on the Arab audiences differed. The early Egyptian pan-Arab press penetrated the Arab states because of its mature professional style and because it represented the Arab country that was at that time the most politically and culturally influential. On the other hand, the early Lebanese pan-Arab press flourished at a time when most Arab regimes imposed heavy restrictions on their local press, and the Arab masses were hungry for a native press that was both free and professional. The pan-Arab Egyptian and Lebanese papers were, therefore, relatively liberal and were advocates of change, while their modern Gulf counterparts are more conservative, and are supportive of the conservative Arab regimes.

Additionally, pan-Arab Arabic newspapers in the past had to rely on traditional means of transportation, so their extranational readers would receive these papers in the afternoon or the next day. Content of these newspapers was generally pointed at local readers.

Two main reasons may explain the success of Lebanese and Egyptian newspapers in penetrating other Arab borders. The first is the lack of an established journalistic profession in other Arab regions; and the second is the cultural and political importance of Egypt and Lebanon in addition to the relative press freedom they enjoyed.

While most Arab states have by this time developed a relatively capable local corps of journalists, they usually address local readers. The emphasis in these regional presses, therefore, is on local news. Additionally, this press usually presents their readers with a Western image of developments in other Arab regions, as their main sources of regional and international news are the big western news agencies (Dajani 2000). This may explain the rise of regional fervor among the Arab masses, which bolsters regional identities and often leads to regional disputes.

The present-day transnational Arabic newspapers differ from the pan-Arab papers in that they cover the whole Arab world and do not focus merely on one Arab region or state. This allows them to increase their circulation, and consequently their income from advertising. Moreover, Arab journalists find it easier to criticize from outside their own country. The fact that they publish outside the Arab countries frees them from Arab local political influence as well as from the fear of losing their licenses. All Arab countries require print publishers to obtain a license from the authorities.

The 1970s and 1980s witnessed a surge in the publication of pan-Arab publications in Europe. This period was characterized by intensified tensions in the Arab world when regional and international powers were struggling to win the Arab masses to their political perspectives. Lebanon was the main arena of these tensions, and many Lebanese and Palestinian journalists and publishers relocated in Europe, mainly to Paris and London. Because of the lack of sufficient advertising budgets, these publications had to seek political subsidies.

> All these enterprises had the same shortcoming: they were non-profit making . . . the newspapers were largely a showcase for various Arab regimes . . . Most of the journalists who worked for these newspapers were unaware of their circulation figures or how they were financed. They all received advertisement revenue from Gulf states, Libya and Algeria, but this money was not the main source of income . . . apparently [some] got most of [their] money from [propaganda] deals. (*The Middle East Magazine*, 1997)

Changing Roles of the Arab press

In its early stages the Arab print media took different forms, influenced by the sociopolitical and geopolitical circumstances of its region. The local strife in Lebanon in the nineteenth century, for example, gave rise to a social-pamphleteering press, addressing sectarian conflicts; it later became a politically oriented press when the Ottoman oppression became provocative. In Egypt and the Maghreb, where conflicts resulted from colonial practices, the early press took the form of political pamphleteering.

The restrictions imposed later by colonial rule intensified the political nature of the Arab press and political events were its main diet. The focus on politics, at the expense of covering social and other events that concern the average citizen, has become common practice in the present-day Arab media.

After the withdrawal of colonial forces and colonial administration from the Arab countries, the new independent regimes could not free themselves from colonial cultural and political influence. News events that concern the old colonial powers are still given wide coverage, and forms of the old colonial restrictions on the press continue to be practiced by post-independence regimes. In many cases press restrictions were intensified.

The print media in the Arab Gulf differs. The harsh physical conditions of this region as well as the high illiteracy rate delayed the emergence of a popular press. However, the oil explosion and the abundance of funds available in the 1970s, and the desire of the rulers of the Gulf to "modernize," brought about a deluge of expatriate Arab journalists who helped build Gulf media institutions. Fear by Gulf leaders of the consequences of granting a degree of press freedom led to the formation of a transnational Arab press published in European capitals. Hence the local Gulf press publishes under strict governmental control while the transnational press, catering to elite Arab audiences, is subject to the press laws of the European countries that house them. With the development of communication technology these Arab transnational publications print from different locations (Arab and foreign) simultaneously, which allows them speedy distribution to readers all over the world.

Although private ownership of newspapers is allowed in several Arab countries, Arab governments have reserved the right to grant publishing licenses. License issuing laws differ from one country to another. In Kuwait, the Ministry of Information issues licenses, and in Saudi Arabia and Bahrain licenses are granted at the discretion of the Minister of Information. In the United Arab Emirates, this right is granted by a decree from the Ministers Council, and in Lebanon, although it is the Minister of Information who holds the final responsibility, the license is subject to prior acceptance by the National Press Council. This situation is widely perceived as a violation of freedom of opinion and communication in the Arab world (Al Jammal 2001, 130).

As if this were not enough, access to the journalism profession itself is subject to individual countries' policies, despite the fact that the majority of Arab constitutions have not addressed such rules. The authorities justify this interference by the need to maintain political and social stability. The rules address broadcast and print journalists directly, whereas the advertising industry, for example, is not directly affected. While Egypt, Sudan, Saudi Arabia, Lebanon, Tunisia, and Morocco do not limit access to the field, Kuwait, Bahrain, Qatar, Oman, Syria, Yemen, Libya, and Algeria require that journalists obtain a license (Al Jammal 2001, 59ff).

The rapid development of communication technologies and the integration of cable with computer and satellite systems paved the way for the emergence of new communication channels that changed the media scene in the Arab world. Because of the predominantly illiterate composition of the Arab masses television became the most popular information and entertainment medium. In early Arab television citizens had access to few local channels, and these were typically government-owned and controlled by local authorities and media subsidizers. During this early phase television's competition with print media was mostly ineffective, though it spurred some publishers to conduct minor changes to their papers.

The advent of satellite television, however, brought about major changes that greatly affected the Arab print media picture. On the positive side, satellite television fractured the tight regulatory control on media content. Censorship became more difficult, and print media were emboldened to delve into otherwise prohibited subjects, and thus improve their local coverage. Some publishers benefited from the satellite television experience by exploring the possibilities of a transnational Arab press. A number of Arab newspapers are registered and published in European countries to avoid local Arab government controls, and are simultaneously printed and distributed in several Arab capitals. Among the successful ventures in this area are *al-Hayat*, *Al Sharq Al Awsat*, and *Al Quds Al Arabi*, all of which are published from London.

As a reaction to the great success of satellite television, Arab print media began experimenting with their formats. New specialized sections were introduced or enriched. More in-depth and lengthy news analyses, which television cannot provide, are on the increase in the Arab print media. Lately, some print media outlets have been running investigative journalism. A number of nongovernmental organizations were set up with the sole purpose of encouraging Arab investigative journalism. One such NGO is Arab Reporters for Investigative Journalism (ARIJ) which was started by a group of Arab media practitioners and educators with initial funds from the European Union. ARIJ started in 2002 by holding investigative journalism workshops and financing local journalists' investigative projects in Lebanon, Jordan, and Syria. Its activities now cover the entire Arab world.

On the negative side, print media resorted to self-censorship in an effort to curb censorship of their content by the local authorities. To be able to survive the competition, the print media had to rely heavily on subsidies and thus the number of partisan papers is increasing.

The Arab press has not built a true climate of dialogue between citizens and the authorities, nor have they advanced dialogue among the different factions of the population. Structural changes have taken priority over professional competence and ethics; this contributed to the spread of a culture dominated by the market mentality and lacking in social responsibility. As a consequence there is confusion among Arab journalists between the freedom of the press to inform the citizen and its freedom to seek out material profit or acceptance by the government.

If forming political consciousness was a primary function of institutions in societies that were laboring under foreign occupation, then the formation of social consciousness should be the primary function of post-independence institutions. The excessive involvement by the Arab press in its political role came at the expense of its social role. The Arab press failed to give due importance to investigative work for public enlightenment, developing the Arab public sphere, and serving the citizens. Faced with the threat of satellite television, the print media resorted to copying this new medium by focusing on sensationalism in politics and events. As a consequence, the public sphere was trivialized and important public issues are treated in a way that makes them appear less serious, important, or valuable than they really are.

The inability of the local Arab press to carry out its role as a responsible watchdog over political institutions and public organizations, particularly its failure to defend the rights of citizens, is contributing to its decline in both readership and credibility. The Arab press failed to serve as a forum encouraging the development of an enlightened civil society, a just system of governance, and good citizens.

Journalists play an active role in selecting and shaping the content of their messages. They set the agenda: they are instrumental in determining what issues enter public debate. To guard their freedom of expression, Arab journalists need to submit an account to the people and not merely to the ruling authorities. Their moral right of freedom of expression is related to accepting accountability, and their legal right of freedom of expression stands a better chance as long as they continue to undertake their moral obligations toward their society.

The print market: online and offline

Recent figures of newspaper circulation in the Arab region suggest a steady increase from 144 titles in 2003 to 167 titles in 2006 and 189 titles in 2009, with the highest density in the Gulf markets of Bahrain, Qatar, and Kuwait. It is estimated that only 60 percent of newspaper revenues stem from advertising (Arab Media Outlook 2010, 29–31). One way to increase the growth in this sector is through increasing the level of auditing on circulation figures, as only 27 titles of the total 189 dailies available in the Arab region are audited using an official body audit. Morocco, Saudi Arabia, Oman, and Emirates are among the countries that practice auditing, albeit still at a limited scale (40).

New developments in electronic media provoked the emergence of new print media outlets, but at the same time the enthusiasm for electronics cut into the circulation of newspapers that could not maintain their appeal to their readers. Thus, "although total circulation numbers may appear to be increasing at the country level, this does not always translate into increasing circulation numbers for all newspapers in that market" (Arab Media Outlook 2007–2011). Arab Media Outlook continues, "the picture in the Arab region is very different [from that in the West]. Newspaper circulation is growing strongly in the region's less mature media markets and this growth is projected to continue . . . [This] growth is driven both by a range of economic and social factors including: strong GDP growth, increasing literacy levels and improving quality of the press . . . A portion of the projected increase in the total circulation . . . is driven by the anticipated increase in the total number of newspapers because of the entry of new players."

A 2006 article in *The Middle East Journal* reports that "there is a growing readership and viewer base [in the Arab region]. The consumer demand for information in Kuwait and Saudi Arabia rivals that of Western Europe. In Kuwait, for example, there are 374 newspapers per 1,000 citizens, in Saudi Arabia, the number is 318."[1] The article further reports that a specialized publication, *The 2006 Middle East Media Guide*, "lists more than 170 newspapers, as well as 700 magazines, 140 television stations and 145 radio stations across 14 [Arab] countries" (Martin 2006).

Arab magazines were quick to recognize the need for change. Realizing the diminishing interest of Arab audiences in political news and faced by the decrease in political subsidies, as such subsidies were being diverted to the new media, Arab magazines moved into consumerist content. A wave of such specialized magazines is flooding the Arab world and is capturing a good slice of the advertising budgets.

Arab newspapers were not as fast in responding, perhaps because they were unable to free themselves from political subsidies, or because they had trouble developing a new journalistic niche. Instead of decreasing their political news and giving more space to events of interest to the common person, Arab newspapers experimented with changing printing formats. Some newspapers took a tabloid format; others changed fonts. Specialized pages, such as sports and books, were instituted and weekly supplements were introduced. Lack of investigative reporting is still a major deficiency in Arab newspapers. The Arab newspaper readers are still hungry for information about events that concern them. Additionally, Arab newspapers invest heavily in new technologies but very little in the human element that does the work of their institutions.

Almost every major national Arab newspaper has launched a website, although these sites have not recorded any profits. The main reason behind this virtual presence is to compete with other publications with websites. Debatably, the first Arabic newspaper online was *Al Sharq Al Awsat,* launched in December 1995, with its searchable archives free of charge. In the beginning, the newspaper tried to offer the printed content for subscribers only while offering an interactive version for free (Fayez 2000). Other newspapers such as *Al Quds Al Arabi* (London-based) offer their printed content as PDF free of charge. The Egyptian daily *Al-Ahram* provides rich content and a good archiving engine for its subscribers, along with updated information on the weather, prayer times, and links to other media sites (Fayez 2000).

The e-newspapers can be roughly divided into three categories:

1. Websites of established printed publications which provide the exact content of the printed papers with few interactivity features,
2. Websites of printed publications with advanced interactivity features, and
3. Websites of e-newspapers that only exist on the internet (Fayez 2000)

The year 2000 saw the launch of the first Arabic online-only newspapers: *Al Jareeda* (Emirates) and (in 2001) the Saudi-owned *Elaph*, with its network of correspondents across the region (Ali 2007, 43). *Elaph* is edited by the Saudi journalist Othman Al Omair. It draws on news from the wires and other printed publications such as *Al Sharq Al Awsat*. Its editor said that the aim of *Elaph* is to provide a mix of print, audio, and visual material (Al Faisal 2005, 217).

Some publications are also moving to online editions, such as the Saudi *Al Majalla,* which transferred to e-format in 2009 to include interactive features and social networking sites. Several corporations also apply a consolidation strategy to expand their portfolio, such as Dubai Media Inc. which has added Dubai Radio & TV as well as Masar Printing & Publishing to its portfolio in 2009 (Arab Media Outlook 2009–2013, 28).

Arab journalists in the Gulf region were asked about their prediction for the future of e-newspapers. Some, such as Ahmed Abdul Hadi, predicted the death of printed newspapers within a few years, while others such as Hedaya Darwich said that the printed publications still attract readers (quoted in Ali 2006, 44–45).

Overall, Ali (2007, 46–58) summarises the obstacles for developing e-newspapers as follows:

1. Lack of training
2. Shortage of adequate Arabic-language software
3. Limited spread of the internet in the region while the prices of accessing the internet in some countries make it a commodity for the well-off. For instance, in Iraq, citizens had to pay 2,000 Iraqi dinar (or $1) in 2002 for an hour's internet use, while in Algeria it cost a dollar and a half in 2005 for the same service.
4. Lack of laws that regulate the internet (Ali 2007, 46–58).

A move toward Arab electronic publishing and blogging is on, and blogs that allow citizens to inform themselves and engage in debates, dialogues, and interactions are mushrooming all over the Arab world. It is too early, however, to give much weight to the Arab electronic media simply because of the limited spread of such media. The Arab world suffers from a high illiteracy rate, and computers are expensive and have limited distribution, even in urban areas. Consequently, the internet is available mainly among the rich, urban, and university-educated population. The poor and rural population will probably wait a long time for such electronic media.

Conclusion

All over the Arab world the press is oriented to the political and financial elites and does not appeal to the general public, especially the rural, the poor, and minorities. While the Arab print media have achieved a high level of professional maturity, it is still a subservient press that has failed to play its "watchdog" role (Dajani, 1989). These media paid a heavy price and endured suppression and legal pursuit by the colonial and national authorities after independence. However, they continue to give priority to technological developments over the development of the human element: reporters, photographers, and editors. This failure is demonstrated by losses in readership for most Arab newspapers, as well as in the decrease of credibility of the print media. The huge number of publications, combined with low advertising revenues and difficult economic situations in several Arab countries, necessitates dependence on subsidies for survival, and pushes journalists to serve the aims of their benefactors in their domestic as well as regional and international coverage (Dajani 1992).

The challenge facing the Arab print media lies in its innaccurate visualization of the meaning of freedom. It does not lie in the problem of censorship or lack of a free media environment. This distorted visualization of freedom leads to private interests that both override and overwhelm social responsibility. To discuss censorship is no longer to discuss the subject of freedom of expression. The proper perspective for freedom of expression is the subject of human rights, particularly the right of the individual to communicate in an effort to practice true democracy, which requires the active participation of citizens in public debate as well as involvement in decisions that concern public affairs (Dajani 1992).

The revival of the local Arab press can be achieved if it reassesses its role in society, rejects the hegemony of ruling authorities and the business sector, and gives up political agitation. The success of the press can only be achieved by truly serving the public and the society, and not merely the politicians.

Note

1 These figures do not match with the 2003 UNDP Arab Human Development Report which indicates that the Arab region has 53 newspapers per 1,000 citizens. Several Arab scholars, however, criticize this report for presenting a pessimistic and disheartening picture of the Arab world. See, for example, As'ad Abu Khalil, "The psychological war: Zionism in our bedding (and minds)" One could also argue that the other reported figures are inflated.

4   Radio Broadcasting in the Arab World

Muhammad Ayish

The Arab world experienced radio broadcasting as early as the 1920s, when radio amateurs were operating wireless transmitters in some of the region's former European colonies (Boyd 1999). But regardless of the genesis of radio in the region, it is clear that the defining feature of broadcasting in Arab countries has been its heavy state domination and broad audience exposure, especially in communities with long oral communication traditions. The development of radio broadcasting in the Arab world has been a function of numerous variables, most political and cultural, pertaining mostly to the role of the medium as a tool of national expression, political mobilization, and cultural development (Rugh 1979). By the early 1990s, state domination of radio services began to weaken, as new nonstate broadcasters with new political and commercial agendas were appearing on the airwaves with mostly local transmissions featuring light social and entertainment content that contrasts with the highly formal and protocol-oriented government radio offerings. As one international report notes, at the turn of the twenty-first century, Arab radio broadcasting was coming under the aegis of three major trends: the emergence of independent FM stations, the advent of the American station Sawa ("Together" in Arabic), launched in March 2002, and changes in legislation governing radio and television systems (PANOS Institute 2006, 17).

This chapter surveys the radio broadcasting landscape in the Arab world as it began to unfold in the early 1990s. It throws light on the dynamics of radio broadcasting in a region long defined by oral and patriarchal communication traditions. It also identifies the changing role of radio from a tool of classical national development, to political mobilization, to community-based democratization. The chapter also highlights the functions of radio in the age of media convergence, which offers both opportunities and threats to radio broadcasters in an emerging multimedia-defined environment. The main point here is that radio broadcasting in the Arab world is here to stay, with more opportunities for its development as state radio monopolies break up, private commercially funded operations launch, more community-oriented programming is supported, and more open content is catered for as more diverse social groups arise, and radio services integrate with emerging new media through web-casting and satellite broadcasting systems. Despite the potential effects of those trends on radio broadcasting, the medium has a long way to go in the emerging Arab public sphere in order to contribute to substantive debates on issues pertaining to democratic reform and political development. This promised role is a function of the depth and breadth of Arab world societal and political transformations that bear on the whole media terrain, including radio broadcasting (Cairo Center 2006).

The huge expanse and the diverse political, social, and economic nature of the region do preclude a comprehensive account of its radio. Instead, the writer addresses common features and trends shared by national radio broadcast systems without compromising the analysis of outstanding peculiarities of some radio operations in different parts of the region. Paucity of empirical research on radio broadcasting has been a major obstacle in preparing this account of radio. Although the focal point of this chapter is the development of radio broadcasting in the Arab world in the 1990s and beyond, an overview of the region's radio history would be quite illuminating. This is primarily because many of the current radio system features are inherited from six-decade-long radio traditions.

Historical overview

Although it is difficult to pinpoint the genesis of radio in the Arab world, most researchers trace it back to the 1920s when radio amateurs were apparently experimenting with wireless transmissions in Egypt, Algeria, and Tunisia (Boyd 1999). British, French, and Italian colonial powers were credited with the introduction of radio services to Arab countries in North Africa and the Middle East in order to promote their interests in those regions and to keep their fellow colonists abreast of new developments in their home countries. Although radio transmissions were largely controlled by colonial authorities, local populations seemed to have benefited from their exposure to broadcasting in their capacity as both information transmitters and receivers.

Boyd (1999, 20) notes that radio broadcasting in Egypt began haphazardly in the 1920s, with over 100 amateur wireless stations operating, mostly in the Cairo area. In Lebanon, the first radio station was constructed in 1937 by the French government, partly to counter Italian and German Arabic-language radio propaganda. In Syria, radio broadcasting appeared in 1946 with the establishment of the Syrian Broadcasting Organization while Jordanian radio operations are traced back to the Palestinian Broadcasting Service launched on March 30, 1936, by the British mandate authority in Palestine and Trans-Jordan (Stanton 2007). Radio broadcasting started in Algeria in 1937 to serve the one-million-strong French community and was referred to as "French Cinq." Most of the Algiers programs were relayed from Paris,

Table 6: Selected Arab Radio Services

Country	Radio Station	Affiliation
United Arab Emirates	Al Arabiya 98.9 FM	Commercial
	Al Khaleejiya 100.9 FM	Commercial
	City 101.6 FM	Commercial
	HIT 96.7 FM	Commercial
Lebanon	Radio NBN (National Broadcasting Network),	Amal Party organ
	Radio Orient	Hariri Family
	Sawt Al-Shaab	Lebanese Communist Party
	Sawt Lubnan	Lebanese Army
	Lubnan Al-Hur	Phalangists
	Radio Lebanon	Government
	Radio Al Nour	Hizbullah Party
	Radio Mont Lebanon	Junbalat Party
	Radio Al-Fajr	Sunni
Palestine	Radio Amwaj	Commercial
	Radio Ajyal	Commercial
	Radio Bethlehem 2000	Commercial
	Radio Isis	Commercial
	Radio Hebron	Commercial
	Radio Marah	Commercial
	Al-Horiyya-Hebron	Commercial
	Al-Nawras	Commercial
	Radio Nablus FM	Commercial
	Al-Manar28	
	Radio al-Shabab	
	Mood FM	
	Play FM	
	Mazaj FM	
	Radio Beat	
	Sawt Al-Ghad	
	Radio Rotana	
Jordan	Amman.net	Online
	Al-Hayat FM.	Independent
	Sawt Karak30	Commercial
Egypt	Nugum FM	Commercial
	Nile Radio 1	Commercial
Syria	Al Madina	Commercial
	Al-Arabiya	Commercial
	Syria Al-Ghad	Commercial
	Style FM	Commercial
	Melody FM	Commercial
	Farah FM	Commercial
Morocco	Radio Yabiladi	Online
	Radio Casablanca	
Algeria	Algerian Radio	

as production facilities in Algeria were too limited to meet around-the-clock broadcast demands (Boyd 1999, 205). In Morocco, radio transmissions began in February 1928 from Rabat with a 2-kilowatt medium-wave transmitter. Amateur transmissions were launched from Tunisia in 1924, catering to French colonists in and around Tunis (Boyd 1999, 263). The BBC Arabic Service was launched from studio facilities in London in January 1938 to counter German and Italian political propaganda directed at the Arab region (Ayish 1991).

Broadcasting systems in colonial times were modeled on existing structures in both France and Britain, where strong state control was defining radio operations. This feature was especially evident in countries falling under French colonial rule, where centralized structures were set up to run radio services as part of state information departments. The British public service broadcasting tradition was never reflected in radio systems in British-colonized territories in Egypt, Jordan, Iraq, and Yemen, as local authorities seemed keen on subjecting radio broadcast services to their direct political controls. Radio services launched in the colonial phase seemed to have dodged the commercial American broadcasting tradition for numerous reasons, the most outstanding of which is the inadequacy of local advertising markets to sustain private radio operations and the entrenchment of authoritarian traditions in Arabian societies, although a few private stations opened in Egypt, Morocco, and Tunis. At that time, radio broadcasting was catering to an elite who could afford radio receivers. In many Arab countries, bulky radio sets were set up at public places such as restaurants and coffeehouses where customers could listen to news and music as part of their outdoor experience. In rural areas radio was almost absent; traditional interpersonal communication networks were the news of the day.

The post-colonial era

After independence, radio was entrusted with a leading role in socioeconomic development by national governments. In the majority of Arab countries, radio broadcasting continued to be a government domain, serving as an official mouthpiece for state policies. Most radio operations were subordinated to ministries of information with limited administrative and financial independence. People saw that radio could play an influential role in national development, especially in remote areas marked by high rates of illiteracy and strong oral communication traditions. In this sense, radio was the incubator of what came to be known as the "developmental or modernization" paradigm, by which broadcasting could be harnessed to promote national development objectives in social and cultural fields (Lerner 1958). A study of broadcasting systems in the Third World (including some Arab countries), suggested an influential role for radio programs in promoting mainstream political views, fostering cultural and national pride, and supplementing grassroots oral communication networks (Katz & Wedell 1977). Based on this sense of success, governments were keen on launching radio operations on medium and short-wave frequencies to reach out to listeners in far-flung places. Countries such as Sudan, Egypt, Algeria, Libya, and Saudi Arabia used microwave booster systems to ensure the delivery of signals to target audiences.

The authoritarian nature of Arab political systems in the postcolonial era (except for Lebanon, Kuwait, and Morocco) was bound to generate a broadcast system drawing heavily on unidirectional and personality-centered discourse with little affinity with political and ethnic diversity. Pan-Arab nationalism and the fight against Western colonialism were two defining concepts of most Arab radio broadcast systems (Ayish 2001a). In Egypt, James (2006) notes that the first *Voice of the Arabs* program, launched on July 4, 1953, included an anticolonialist short statement by leaders of Egypt's July Revolution. Newly inexpensive transistor radios were being acquired by the illiterate poor in cities and villages across the Middle East, thus ensuring more accessibility to *The Voice of the Arabs*. James (2006) notes that *The Voice of the Arabs* became a major radio station in its own right, broadcasting the revolutionary opinions of the regime 18 hours a day across the Arab world. Boyd (1999) also observes that radio broadcasting in Egypt was used as a political mobilization tool by President Nasser as well as by leaders of republican governments in Libya, Iraq, Syria, and Yemen. Radio programs in this era featured news, propaganda political talk shows, religious materials, entertainment, social and agricultural awareness programs, and sports programs. While some radio services sought to engage local audiences in their live discussions, the issues addressed in radio shows were mostly service-oriented, with less attention paid to political issues of democratization and participation (Ayish 1990).

Arab governments always were concerned about seeing their national audiences fall victim to the entrapments of international and regional broadcasters, especially in the Cold War era. Ayish (1991) noted that listeners across the region were always able to gain access to international radio transmissions from international broadcasters in Western Europe and North America to verify the accuracy of news carried by state-run radio. The BBC Arabic service, launched in January 1938, was an important source of news and information for Arab audiences for almost six decades. With its fairly balanced and objective political programs, the BBC Arabic service provided Arab listeners with exposure to diverse views and opinions on matters bearing on their lives. The Voice of America, on the other hand, was failing on the Arab world front primarily because audiences associated its biased broadcasts with hostile US policies in the region (Ayish 1987). Other international radio broadcasters in the Cold War era included Radio France International and Radio Moscow (Ayish & Hijab 1988).

The globalization era

The globalization era started in the early 1990s with huge international political, economic, and technological transformations sweeping the region. Radio broadcasting was bound to be affected by those changes in different ways. From an institutional point of view, radio was no longer dominated by the state; private broadcasters sought a chunk of this expanding sector. Private radio stations became household names in countries such as Palestine, Lebanon, Saudi Arabia, the UAE, Morocco, and Egypt. The launch of radio operations as part of broader corporate media and nonmedia business initiatives secured adequate financial sustenance. The main implication of this trend has been reflected in program formats rather than in contents, with the introduction of more entertainment and Western-style radio shows. Live talk shows addressing public issues have become standard formats on Arab radio, especially in FM transmissions, in light of the proliferation of mobile telephone systems and the development of telecommunications and Web-based operations.

In the 1960s and 1970s, radio diffusion density was measured in terms of conventional receiver availability (Inkeles & Smith 1974). In the early decades of the twenty-first century, radio programs could be accessed via satellite broadcasting, Web-based media, and mobile telephony. This suggests that as much as new information and communication technologies have posed serious threats to radio, they have also offered new outlets for access to radio programs beyond the traditional radio receiver.

The radio landscape

By the end of the twentieth century, media convergence was already taking root in most of the Arab communications landscape, with varying effects on media channels and institutions, including radio. Not only have Arab radio transmissions gone international with their local and national coverage, but they have also developed broader orientations in their program offerings, with more open and liberal shows and more entertainment-oriented content featured on the airwaves. In the meantime, the institutional character of radio broadcasters has come to undergo significant changes in terms of ownership patterns, with more private players. According to Arab States Broadcasting Unit (ASBU) data, government radio broadcasters continue to dominate the broadcasting scene (ASBU, 2007). On the other hand, commercial broadcasters are emerging in Lebanon, Palestine, Jordan, Egypt, Saudi Arabia, United Arab Emirates, and Morocco. The following section describes the radio broadcasting scene in the mainstream state and emerging private sectors.

ASBU data (2007) demonstrate that there are over 250 government-operated radio stations in the region. Most draw on medium-wave transmissions to local and national audiences with official programs in news, culture, religion, social development, and the economy. Radio broadcasters, to some extent, operate as part of official or semi-official or independent organizations with varying financial and administrative autonomy. While many of those stations depend on advertising and sponsorship to finance their operations, they draw substantially on state subsidies to cover staff salaries and program production costs in addition to equipment acquisitions. According to recent data, advertising money is contributing increasingly to state broadcasters' budgets as governments come under harsh financial crunches to meet growing operational needs (PARC 2006). Many government radio stations have established some form of advertising and commercial business units to handle external revenue generation through commercial advertising or corporate sponsorship. The rigid and protocol-oriented outlook of radio broadcasting has long been a limiting factor in this sector's development in light of audiences' growing disenchantment with state policies at local and foreign levels. Several studies have confirmed that audience exposure to government radio has been highly selective, focusing more on cultural and entertainment content while being evasive of political programs as evident in newscasts and commentaries.

Except for Lebanon, private radio broadcasting had been a novelty in the Arab world in the pre-globalization era. Lebanon led other Arab countries in initiating private radio broadcasting ventures, drawing on entertainment content to address mostly young audiences. Non-state broadcasters in Lebanon also included services affiliated with national politicians and groups, thus serving as official mouthpieces for those actors in the national Lebanese public sphere. It should be noted here that when we talk about private radio broadcasters, it does not mean that we are talking about a political medium of communication that is totally disengaged from dominant political interests. It has been found that owners of private radio broadcasting operations are either politicians in power or businessmen with vested interests in supporting established political systems (Sakr 1999). But in terms of funding, these services do not depend on state subsidies to finance their operations.

Egypt and Tunisia were the first countries in the Middle East to allow private radio stations under a legal framework. Egypt launched Nile FM and Negoom FM in July 2003, which were followed by Tunisia's Mosaique FM in November. The Ministry of Information in Kuwait began granting licenses to private radio and television stations in the same year. Consistent with the liberalization trend, Oman next offered licenses to private TV and radio stations. Syria has been the last country to pursue liberalization. Saudi Arabia is currently planning to privatize some public radio stations. In the UAE, the Arab Radio Network (ARN) in Dubai and the MBC Radio Network have been effective players in the private broadcasting landscape. ARN started Al Arabiya 98.9 FM, a round-the-clock Arabic music and news station, in 2001. Soon afterwards, the network launched an English Radio Service, Free FM (96.7 FM) and City FM (101.6). In January 2003 the network launched Al Khaleejiya, thus creating a new platform for Khaleeji (Arabian Gulf) music and giving it a wider reach reflective of the UAE's inherent roots and traditions. HIT 96.7 FM followed and was designed to serve the interests of the largest expatriate community in the Gulf, the Malayalees from Kerala, India.

The broadcasting field is one where technologies are constantly changing and improving. Various strategic alliances ensure that UAE stations keep abreast of these developments. ARN recently created a strategic tie-up with KLOTZ, the leading radio system, to enhance ARN's hardware solutions (UAE Interact 2007).

According to a 2008 study conducted by Jordan-based Arab Advisors Group, the number of frequency modulation (FM) radio stations in the 18 Arab countries has increased to 316, compared with 211 stations in February last year. Palestine, Iraq, and Lebanon have the highest number of private radio stations, while Bahrain, Kuwait, and Oman have allowed private radio stations only in 2003, 2004, and 2006 respectively (AME Information 2008a). The regional landscape varies in the number and ownership of FM radio stations: Algeria and the UAE have the highest number of local government-owned FM radio stations while Palestine, Iraq, and Lebanon have the highest number of private local radio stations. The research revealed 9 regional radio stations that broadcast on FM frequencies in multiple countries. These regional stations raise the total of FM stations to 316 in the 18 covered countries.

Liberalization in several Arab countries was a key factor behind the boom in private FM radio stations. For instance, Libya and Oman had private FM radio stations broadcasting for the first time in 2007. In addition to the liberalization of the sector, the need to broadcast in multiple languages to cater to expatriates enhances the number of FM radio stations, even in countries where private FM radio stations do not exist. The UAE is a clear example of this, as it hosts FM radio stations broadcasting in Arabic, English, Malayalam, Hindi, Urdu, and Filipino (AME Information 2008a).

Continued government domination of radio broadcasting in the globalization era, according to Rugh (2005), is grounded in several factors. First, Arab governments regard radio and television as potent domestic political instruments because they reach most of the population regardless of literacy and income levels. Moreover, Arab broadcasting underwent its first major expansion during the period after World War II, when Arab nationalism and anticolonialism were strong, and governments were very eager to use them for purposes of political nation-building and national defense. Governments justified controls on the basis of the alleged need to protect the country against its enemies, old and new. By the same token, radio and television facilities have been prime targets of revolutions seeking to take power, and therefore the governments took special measures to protect them. Third, broadcasting is not lucrative for commercial investors because commercial advertising in the Arab world, and especially in the electronic media, is relatively limited, and generally advertising revenues do not cover costs. Fourth, governments are concerned about their image as conveyed to other countries through broadcasting, so they want to control the programs. There are a few exceptions, especially in Lebanon and among the new satellite television companies, but the norm is government control of electronic broadcasting.

Radio broadcast regulation

Transformations in the broadcast environment have induced debates about the regulation of the audiovisual sector. The question of broadcast regulation in the Arab world has been widely addressed in recent years in light of accelerating technological and sociopolitical developments in the region. Traditional arguments pertaining to spectrum scarcity and government monopoly came to a dead end with the introduction of digital radio transmission and production techniques that brought on further abundance in broadcast resources. Satellite broadcast systems have also contributed to the radio revolution with the integration of radio signals into these systems, allowing listeners exposure to radio programs around the world.

By early 2008, over 340 Arab radio broadcasters were transmitting their programs using satellite systems (ASBU 2008). The Web has become an arena used by thousands of radio webcasters to reach audiences in different countries. In March 2008, the writer identified over 143 Web-based radio broadcast services, some launched by private persons using normal portals. Mobile telephones have also turned into effective carriers of radio signals, either as digital receivers or as Web-connected systems. Arab societies have experienced dramatic social and political turmoil, which in time has given rise to more efficient civil society institutions and more liberal participatory arrangements (Lynch 2006; Ayish 2008).

Although regulation seemed to be a priority in dealing with radio broadcasting in the Arab world, domestic regulatory approaches to the radio sector have been plagued with serious problems. A study of radio broadcasting regulation in four Arab countries reveals that neither Egypt nor Syria have public legal frameworks for regulating the medium, while Jordan and Lebanon have developed more solid audiovisual laws (PANOS Institute 2006, 19). The prime objective of the law has been to reorganize Jordan's media by authorizing private investment, notably from abroad, in the country's radio and television stations. The law makes it possible to launch a radio station once a license has been obtained from the Audiovisual Commission, a new body created under law n°71. In Lebanon, radio and television broadcasting are under the jurisdiction of a 1994 law that aims "to regulate radio and television broadcasting, as well as regulating all questions relative to such broadcasting." A license is required before any radio or television media can be established on Lebanese soil, accorded "in virtue of a decree passed by the Council of Ministers after consultation with the National Audiovisual Council." The law further specifies that "the license is valid for a period of 16 years, renewable in virtue of an application submitted three years before the expiry date." This license is granted to radio and television media according to their capacities and the technical characteristics of their transmitters and broadcasting equipment (PANOS Institute 2006). In June 2001, the Lebanese Audiovisual Council asked the Legislature to pass other laws and decrees, pointing out that most category 1 and 2 stations were not adhering to the specifications laid down by the law. However, the most common infringement, according to the 2001 report, is a disregard for the legal arrangements concerning program schedules and the assignment of themes to certain times of day. The most recent Audiovisual Council report came out in September 2005. It brings attention to program content, where it found several cases of violations.

At the pan-Arab level, the 2008 document on satellite broadcasting regulations endorsed by Arab information ministers created heated debates about its potential threats to freedom of expression (Arab Media & Society 2008). Proponents of the document argue that the unprecedented numbers of new satellite broadcasting outlets in the region require some form of regulation to ensure conformity to internationally established standards in radio and television work. They assert that the document is meant to be integrated into national regulatory regimes to stem the negative effects of some satellite television content on individuals and communities (Amin 2008). On the other hand, the document has been criticized by some international and Arab world human rights groups, who label it an encroachment on freedom of speech to promote government policies (Kuttab 2008). Al Jazeera Satellite Channel devoted a good number of its talk shows to aspects of the document perceived to reflect hostility to private broadcasters. Qatar, which hosts Al Jazeera Channel, has refrained from endorsing the document.

Financing radio broadcasting

While state-controlled radio operations receive most of their backing from government subsidies and some supplementary advertising, non-state radio stations draw on advertising and corporate sponsorship as well as partisan funding to cover their expenses. According to available data, radio share of the Middle East advertising pie has been shrinking with the expansion of satellite television and Web-based communications. Ad spending worldwide neared 486 billion USD in 2008, or 6.7 percent more than in 2007, while ad spending in North America totaled 195 billion USD, up 4.1 percent, according to a market forecast (ZenithOptimedia 2008). Meanwhile, internet advertising is poised to reach three major milestones in the next three years, according to the forecast. Internet ad spending is projected to grow to 44.6 billion USD from some 36 billion USD, or a gain of 29.9 percent. Radio share of ad spending rose from 35,377 billion USD in 2006 to 37,782 billion USD in 2008 and is expected to reach 41,032 billion USD in 2010. Advertising spending in the UAE increased from 869 million USDS in 2005 to 1.3 billion USD in 2007, the highest in the Middle East, according to Spencer Felix, exhibition manager for Signage, Imaging, and Media (AME Information, 2008b), which takes place at the Abu Dhabi National Exhibition Centre from November 25–27. The bulk of the money – about 64 percent – went to Arabic and English newspapers. Television accounted for 16 percent while magazines got 13 percent. He predicts that advertising spending in the UAE will exceed 2 billion USD by 2010 (Gulf News 2008).

According to the Arab Advisory Group (2006), the average local FM station's ad rates have increased from 88 USD in 2005 to 101 USD for a 30-second spot in 2006. Pan-Arab average advertising rates supersede both the local and the regional average advertising rates. This could be attributed to the fact that these pan-Arab stations are the only way to target the Saudi Arabian market. The regional average advertising rate represents the mean for a 30-second commercial spot for the countries discussed in the report. There are three peak times – 7:00–8:00, 13:00–14:00, and 18:00–19:00 – when the advertising rates are at their highest in the region. Furthermore, the analysis in the report shows that the pan-Arab average advertising rates (especially on shows broadcasting music and entertainment) are usually higher, due to regional coverage and the audience targeted. For example, MBC Group's FM stations are the only FM stations that offer advertising targeting Saudi Arabia (the Arab world's largest consumer market), which is surely a reason for their higher advertising rates.

Radio audiences

It has been widely argued that information and communication technologies have expanded access to more diverse sources of information. Satellite television and the World Wide Web are seen as bearing on radio audience size and quality, with more people accessing the internet and getting satellite television content than ever before. But as the experience of the past two decades shows, radio broadcasting remains a credible source of information for audiences across the region, especially in areas where the Internet and satellite television are still uncommon. Even in media-rich cities like Dubai, Cairo, Riyadh, Amman, Beirut, and Baghdad, radio seems to be a favorite, especially for motorists who might spend hours entangled in traffic jams. On the other hand, there is a clear shortage of solid and periodic data on radio audiences as market researchers spend more time on satellite television and Web-based media.

Paucity of data on radio audiences seems to be generated primarily by the dominance of conventional perceptions of radio in the context of radio-set reception. Reporting on radio listeners and their sociology is more or less nonexistent, because independent survey organizations and specialized research centers are not interested in these subjects (PANOS Institute 2006, 18). Available data is based on research commissioned by radio stations in order to convince sponsors or businesses that they are competitive, and often respond to advertising imperatives, as is the case in Lebanon. But despite this paucity of data on radio listening realities, there seems to be a broad agreement that the medium is here to stay as it finds itself niches in an evolving media market. While traditional radio listenership findings have drawn on calculations of numbers of radio receivers per total population, new radio-enabled communications gadgets have come to embrace satellite receivers, the internet, and mobile telephony systems. In crowded cities across the region, motorists have turned into avid radio listeners to deal with their long commutes. All these technological developments should call for new and innovative ways to document radio listening realities. On the other hand, one has to admit that radio continues to face new challenges emanating from the same technological revolution that has given it a boost: television and multimedia-based Web are attracting more young fans away from traditional media such as newspapers and wireless radio.

The 2004 UNDP Human Development Report noted that in Jordan, where 10.3 percent of the population is officially illiterate, only 6.3 percent of homes have their own internet access, 79.7 percent possess a radio, 97.2 have a television set, and 46.9 percent have a satellite dish (UNDP 2004). In Egypt, almost two-thirds of the population listens to the radio every day, especially to news and religious broadcasts. In Palestine, Bir Zeit University carried out an opinion survey with a sample of 1,184 Palestinians living in the West Bank and Gaza, on the perception and coverage of the intifada by independent radio stations. According to the results published in June 2001, 36 percent of those interviewed said they could not express an opinion on the content of radio broadcasts, because they either do not register or do not pay attention to the way events are treated; 46 percent trust the information given out by these stations; 15 percent only believe in them moderately and 5 percent do not trust them (Olof Palme International Center 2001). In another survey carried out by a private company in Lebanon in August 2005 on a sample of 600 listeners, the following percentages show how different listenership varies across radio services in Arabic: *Sawt Al-Ghad* (40.3 percent), *Radio Delta* (20.5 percent), *Radio Strike* (20 percent), *Sawt Al-Mousika* (12.7 percent). On the other hand, the following foreign-language stations were associated with varying listenership percentages: *Nostalgie* (18.7 percent), Radio One (8.5 percent), and *Mix FM* (1 percent) (PANOS Institute 2006).

Radio programs

It is difficult to account for all program formats aired on radio in the Arab world; however; a survey of radio program schedules over 50 radio stations suggests the following findings: entertainment (43 percent), news and public affairs (23 percent), religion and culture (8 percent), family and children (7 percent), sports (4 percent), community development (11 percent), and others (4 percent) (ASBU, 2007). As for formats, prerecorded music and entertainment have been dominant while live talk shows are taking on additional significance. Topics discussed on call-in shows are mostly relevant for young generations while talk programs address issues relating to living concerns from an Islamic perspective; social problems, day-to-day living problems, and others. Service-oriented radio programs continue to dominate program offerings with programs addressing day-to-day problems and concerns. (PANOS Institute 2006). Official figures on the nine state radio stations in Egypt show that, between 1 July 2000 and 30 June 2001, news made up 0.6 percent of general programming, political programs 9.1 percent, religious programs 15 percent, entertainment programs 33.2 percent, and educational programs 1.2 percent. Religious programs are more important on local stations, with over 10 Quran-dedicated radio programs observed by a researcher in early 2008.

Religion is a central component of social values and traditions in the Arab world and is likely to remain so. Radio broadcasting has been an integral carrier of Islamic-oriented programs in the forms of talk shows, interviews, direct address shows, sermons, Quran recitations, and live coverage of prayers, pilgrimage, and other events. Some Arab countries have launched radio services dedicated to Quran recitations. In many shows, listeners normally address questions about Islam's position on contemporary living experiences as well as generic normative teachings. Religious programs are more common on state-run radio than on private services, though all operations seem to carry calls for prayers live to audiences. Governments' control of radio broadcasting has been useful in ensuring a rationalist and balanced religious discourse on the air in an era marked by religious extremism. Entertainment remains the dominant program category on Arab radio services. Arabic music and songs, as well as some plays, are common on state-controlled radio services, while private players seem to give preference to Western-style music, which has high appeal to listeners. Some stations have been dedicated to classical music while others have chosen Western-style musical shows.

Roles

One of the enduring questions often addressed by media researchers in the Arab world is how much radio contributes to the establishment of governance systems in the region. In dealing with this question, researchers have noted that radio could not play an active role in democratic reform as long as it is subject to both state political controls and private commercial manipulations. It is true that radio broadcasters have managed to establish nongovernmental institutional structures that are not subject to state administrative and editorial controls. Yet they seem to have failed in charting for themselves an independent course of adversarial journalism that could empower them to stand up to government excesses in public life. It takes only a pool of resources and some legal frameworks to make radio broadcasting possible, but to make it an effective part of the political transformation we must build up a broad political culture of diversity and media independence that seems to be lacking in much of the Arab world.

As noted earlier, in the postcolonial era, radio broadcasting was entrusted with a national development role to contribute to new nations' endeavors to build up their national capacities in cultural, social, and economic spheres. This traditional role continues to define broadcasting services in all Arab countries, especially state-sponsored broadcasters who see themselves as promoters of state development orientations and projects. Traditionally, this approach was quite effective in governments' attempts to reach out to masses in remote areas marked by massive illiteracy rates. However, as national economic production began to move toward urban centers with industrial and service-oriented sectors, the rural masses were losing some of their appeal as the prime targets of state-run radio services. Issues of urban crime, unemployment, inflation, social services, and environmental pollution were gaining new ground in national discussions across the Arab world, and radio was an appropriate arena for such exchanges (James 1979).

The role of radio as a tool of political communication varies from one Arab country to another. Many radio services serve propaganda functions for their governments. On the other hand, some radio stations in Palestine, Jordan, and Lebanon have taken on new political roles as voices of emerging civil societies, carrying programs critical of their governments. AmmanNet is a case in point. Maddison and John (Maddison 1971) surveyed 50 countries, including Algeria, Sudan, Tunisia, and Egypt, in the early 1970s to explore radio broadcasting conditions and roles. The study concluded that all the various ways of using radio and television should be fully exploited in all countries that have a sizeable illiteracy problem; this should be done as part of an overall plan to develop the new techniques of communication for economic and social (and especially educational) advancement. Research that aids in planning, and further research into "methods" and "materials," is called for; and training centers and programs for broadcasting personnel are also needed.

Radio has commonly served as an instrument of cultural enrichment in the Arab world, with key broadcasters carrying programs on national culture and heritage. Radio shows seeking to reinforce cultural and national identity among members of the population by drawing on ancient and contemporary history have been noted in all Arab countries. They cover a wide range of cultural issues such as social values and traditions, crafts, traditional sports, literary (especially poetic) works, folkloric arts, and more. In the mid-1970s, another study on broadcasting in the Third World concluded that radio was instrumental in mass communication, in the areas of education, cultural development, and capacity-building efforts (Katz & Wedell 1977). They even carry live broadcasts of cultural events such as camel and horse races, art festivals, and poetic competitions. Most radio programs draw on prerecorded and talk-show formats to deliver their messages.

Despite the technological expansions in radio broadcasting in the Arab world, as marked by digital production and transmission techniques, and the use of the Web and satellite systems and telecommunications channels for content delivery, radio's role in public life remains rather foggy. Research data is scarce. If the 1960s and 1970s were the golden years of Arab radio broadcasting, as per the expansions in radio operations and the harnessing of the medium to serve national development goals, the globalization era is the time for technological convergence as well as democratization in the Arab region. Yet the question that needs to be asked here is the extent to which radio broadcasting plays a viable role in promoting participatory governance and freedom of expression and human rights. It is true that radio remains largely under government control and is bound thus to reflect dominant state views, with little access for other voices. But as the experience of the past decade has shown, radio broadcasting, with its unique capacity to reach out to audiences in remote and scattered areas, continues to be a force to reckon with in the emerging Arab public sphere. The airwaves are full of bold and critical discussions of public issues in radio stations in Lebanon, Jordan, Iraq, and Palestine. To speak of the role of radio in the public sphere suggests that radio will not be turned into an instrument of effective political communication unless a truly democratic environment is created in Arabian societies.

AmmanNet, an FM and Web-based radio service in Jordan, has emerged as an outstanding example of how the convergence of new technologies and political democratization could bring about changes in media roles in society. In the fall of 2000, using the opportunities that the internet provided, its founder, Daoud Kuttab (with a group of independent media practitioners in Amman, Jordan) launched AmmanNet as the Arab world's first internet radio. With funding from the Open Society Institute, Amman Municipality, and UNESCO, the new Web-based station launched on November 15. AmmanNet began its first year under the patronage of UNESCO and the Greater Amman Municipality. AmmanNet began broadcasting terrestrially on 92.4 FM in the Amman metropolitan area in the summer of 2005 (AmmanNet 2008). According to the license, the content included general programming, excluding politics and news. But in September of the same year, it became the first independent radio station to broadcast news. According to one of the service's founders, AmmanNet has scored concrete success in handling public issues in Jordan, including the scrutiny of Amman Municipality's attempts to close down shops in a poor district (Mdanat 2008). A campaign on AmmanNet to free Jordanian prisoners in Israeli prisons has drawn wide public participation and created pressure on the Jordanian government to prioritize this issue. Most prisoners were set free and sent to Jordan to continue their prison sentences. AmmanNet is embarking on another campaign to free some 215 Jordanian prisoners in Syrian prisons, some of whom have been jailed for 30 years. Another example is the plight of refugees on the Iraq border; this issue had been marginalized amid more urgent national issues. A report carried out by the service's reporter was followed by a change in the camp's director, and civic society became more involved.

International radio broadcasting in Arabic

International radio broadcasting has been around for the past seven decades: radio transmissions emanate from the United States, the UK, France, Canada, Russia, and Germany to the Arab world. It was noted earlier that international radio broadcasts started as early as 1937 as part of colonial rivalry and turned into an instrument of cold war politics from the 1950s well into the mid 1980s. The BBC Arabic Service remains the most eminent broadcaster, and it has sustained huge audiences through its medium-wave and short-wave transmissions (Boyd 1997). Over seventy years the BBC Arabic service has built up substantive relations with audiences through adherence to professional broadcast journalism standards and appreciation of Arab-Islamic culture, including the Arabic language. In the postcolonial era, the BBC was offering itself as a viable alternative to national broadcasting services such as the Voice of the Arabs and other regional broadcasters. Along with the Voice of America, Radio Moscow, Radio Monte Carlo, and Radio France International, the BBC was creating a new public sphere in which Arab listeners found precious opportunities for expression unattainable in their national media systems (Ayish 1991).

In the past decade, the concept of international radio broadcasting began to change with the advent of satellite television and the World Wide Web. Few people could afford to listen to shortwave transmissions, but they could access programs via satellite receivers or the internet and mobile telephony. Broadcasters have adapted to the new technological developments by integrating their radio services into the new multimedia setting. They have also started to broadcast their programs on local FM stations to ensure good quality programming to their audiences. This has been the case with the BBC Arabic Service, Radio SAWA, and Radio Monte Carlo. Arab governments have granted international broadcasters rights to use local frequencies for a fee as part of a licensing procedure. While the BBC Arabic Service has beefed up its news and public affairs shows, Radio SAWA remains an entertainment-oriented medium with Western-style talk shows and music with 30-minute newscasts. As some market research has revealed, Radio SAWA continues to suffer from the same problems inflicted on the former Voice of America Arabic Service: credibility (el Nawawy 2006). Arab listeners continue to view Radio SAWA as an organ of the US State Department, which carries out what are perceived as "unjust and biased" American policies in the Arab World.

Conclusions

New information and communications technologies have brought about an unprecedented abundance in radio offerings; this chapter asks whether such huge transitions have generated larger social roles for radio in a media landscape defined by strong political authoritarianism and global commercialism. Although lack of empirical research on this matter seems to preclude the development of solid conclusions about radio contributions to democratization and social justice, it is clear that radio in the Arab world has turned into a forum for conventional and nonpolitical discussions of public issues; a tool for foreign public diplomacy in the region; and a venue for commercial income generation for private broadcasters. As a 2006 report by the Cairo Center for Human Rights Studies concluded, radio broadcasting is more likely to stay afloat in the evolving public sphere; however, its future contribution to democratization in the region will continue to be a function of the nature of social and political transformations in Arab societies. In a few countries like Palestine, Lebanon, Morocco, and post-Saddam Iraq, the rise of public-affairs shows as compared with entertainment and cultural programs has signaled a more vibrant role for radio in public life. But as the experience on the ground seems to suggest, radio has contributed to perpetuating political and sectarian divisions rather than to fostering a sense of national unity. This debacle is symptomatic more of Arab politics than of radio broadcasting per se. A new course should be charted for radio broadcasting based on more engagement with civil society; more government detachment; and more independence from commercial interests.

5   Television Broadcasting in the Arab World

Political Democratization and Cultural Revivalism

Muhammad Ayish

Until the late 1980s, television broadcasting in the Arab world was a local government-monopolized terrestrial operation with limited reach, serving as a mouthpiece for the state on issues of national and international concern. From 1991, however, when the first private Arab-world television station went on the air from studio facilities in London, to the present date, television broadcasting in the Arab world has experienced a real revolution: not only in terms of global reach, channel diversity, and program quality, but also in terms of the increased involvement of the private sector in broadcast operations. Arab States Broadcasting Union (ASBU) statistics show that over 500 free-to-air television channels are available to Arab viewers across the region, in addition to scores of channels furnished by cable and digital satellite TV systems (ASBU 2007). ASBU data also shows that over 65 percent of television channels in mid-2009 were privately controlled and operated, while governments maintained varying numbers of services ranging from 1 in Mauritania to 8 in the UAE to 22 in Egypt. For many researchers, the broadcasting revolution of the early twenty-first century echoed dramatic social, cultural, and political transformations taking place in the Arab public sphere since the mid-1990s (Lynch 2006; Ayish 2008). But as the television experience of the past decade reveals, this television abundance in the region seems to have fallen short of advancing either democratization or cultural fulfillment in Arab societies. This chapter argues that the so-called democratic and cultural transformations in the region were induced more by global developments than local ones, and hence were not durable enough to substantially affect television structures and roles. The emergence of a private broadcasting sector was seen as a purely commercial development, simply because it was not matched by an emergence of viable pluralistic and independent political structures with adversarial functions.

This chapter surveys the development of television broadcasting in the Arab world since the mid-1950s, with a focus on its contributions to political democratization and cultural fulfillment in the region since the mid-1990s. Television broadcasting in the Arab world has historically developed within patriarchal and authoritarian traditions that militated against its professional

Table 7: Program Categories Aired on Arab Satellite Channels

Channel Categories	Private Sector	Public Sector	Approximate Number
General (varied programs)	90	41	131
Music / varieties	117	2	119
Cinema / Drama / Serials	55	3	58
Sports	40	11	51
Commercial / Economic / Shopping	24	1	25
News	23	3	26
Children	20	1	21
Cultural / Educational	13	10	23
Documentary	12	0	12
Interactive	11	0	11
Religious	10	3	13
Touristic	3	1	4

Source, Arab States Broadcasting Union (ASBU 2007)

independence. In order for state and private television broadcasters to realize their envisioned roles as instruments of cultural and political development, they need to be politically and socially empowered through the institution of sustainable democratic structures and practices.

Historical developments

Television broadcasting in the Arab world has been around for the past six decades, launched in most Arab states in the immediate postcolonial era to serve as an instrument of national development. Its most dramatic transition took place only in the early 1990s with the advent of satellite broadcasting media technology trends. Ayish (2003) identifies three phases of television development: formative, national, and globalized.

The formative phase (1954–1976)

This phase dates back to the mid-1950s, when most Arab countries were either subject to European colonial rule or were just experiencing their early years of independence (Boyd 1999). Although Arab governments had long perceived television as an effective tool of national reconciliation and a symbol of cultural identity, pioneering efforts to introduce television broadcasting into some Arab countries – Kuwait, Morocco, Lebanon, Iraq, and Jordan – were initiated by private players for purely commercial purposes

(Boyd 1999). The commercial start of television in the Arab world was hindered by a combination of factors that included low receiver-set diffusion, absent national independence, and full preoccupation with radio as the most powerful medium of communication.

By the late 1960s, the promise of television as a powerful tool of communication seemed to have motivated Arab governments to step in to keep it as a state-controlled operation. Egyptian President Nasser's effective use of radio to promote pan-Arabist ideology seemed to drive the use of television as a tool of political mobilization (Hale 1975). The issue of television control by governments was never debated in Egypt at a time when the private sector had a limited role in the country's socialist-oriented economic and social system. But when the issue of financing a television broadcasting operation came up, the Egyptian government had no choice but to go with Radio Corporation of America (RCA) to carry out the project (Boyd 1999). In 1961 the Kuwaiti government took over television broadcasting by subordinating it to the Ministry of Information. In the post-independence period, television in Morocco was subordinated to the Postal Ministry and was controlled by the office of the Prime Minister (Boyd 1999). In 1962, Radiodiffusion-Television Marocaine (RTM) was set up as part of the Ministry of Information. Sudan Television was started in 1961 with assistance from Germany while Jordan Television went on the air as a government service in April 1968.

In a few Arab countries, the formative years of television development came late in the 1970s in concert with statehood development. In the United Arab Emirates, television was established in Abu Dhabi in 1969, in Dubai in 1974, and in Sharjah in 1989. In Bahrain, Qatar, Oman, and Yemen, television was introduced in 1975. Following the British public service model of broadcasting, television in the Gulf region was established as a government-run operation, mostly subordinated to ministries of information. Television's stated missions in those countries provided for serving national development goals, including fostering cultural identity. But once those services went on the air by political decree, they had to face a host of challenges that ranged from staff and program shortages to inadequate production and transmission facilities (Boyd 1999). With the flow of oil-generated income to their national economies, the Arabian Gulf states managed to establish some of the most technologically advanced television systems in the Arab region.

The rising popularity of television as a medium of communication, especially its ability to mobilize and educate Arab masses, presented governments in the 1960s and 1970s with the dilemma of having to manage a potentially effective broadcasting medium without adequate human and technical resources. To surrender television to private hands – which could have solved some of the resources problems – raised a new set of issues relating to the transmission of politically and culturally sensitive materials to generally conservative communities. While some argued that television was basically an entertaining medium, and was therefore inappropriate for governments to patronize, others highlighted the political and sociocultural role of television, arguing that these aspects warranted its subordination to government controls (Boyd 1999; Dajani 2001; Jarrar 1999). The second argument gained the upper hand in the Arab world in the 1960s and 1970s for three reasons. First, post-independence governments in the Arab countries of North Africa and the Middle East found centralized British and French public-service broadcasting systems to be convenient models to emulate in their national broadcasting structures. The Arab region was not familiar with the commercial American model of broadcasting, due to minimal U.S. geopolitical influence in the area in the immediate post-war period. Second, Arab governments in the 1960s and 1970s were sole players in leading national development efforts. The launch of government-controlled television as a tool of national development was highly valued. Third, political ferment in the region in the mid-1950s and in the 1960s created heightened tensions that warranted full government control of television systems to ensure program homogeneity across national broadcasting operations.

The national expansion phase (1976–1990)

Arab governments sought to build up their national broadcasting capabilities through training national staff during this period. They increased local production, pooled inter-Arab state production resources, and extended transmissions to cover national territories. The Arab States Broadcasting Union (ASBU), an Arab League organization based in Tunisia, and the Saudi-Arabia-based Gulfvision were instrumental in realizing collaborative efforts. In larger countries such as Saudi Arabia, Algeria, and Sudan, satellite and microwave links were used to carry terrestrial television signals to remote areas. Arab viewers had access to a range of one to three TV channels depending on reception locations. In many cases, the use of home videocassette machines was a major popular response to "bad government television" (Boyd et al. 1989). Imported materials from the United States, Britain, France, and Egypt dominated programming schedules. Egypt, with a long tradition of cinematic production, often referred to as the Hollywood of the Arab World, was a major source of drama serials for television stations throughout the Middle East and North Africa, where viewers could understand colloquial Egyptian Arabic.

In this national development phase, television broadcasting was overshadowed by long-operational radio services that gained extensive popularity in orally oriented Arabian communities.

The emerging television broadcasting model in the region suggested a perpetuation of structural arrangements and editorial practices initiated in the formative phase. Television organizations continued to have no administrative or financial independence, as their funding almost exclusively came from annual government subsidies and limited advertising revenue. Heads of television services were appointed by their nations' leaders and were directly accountable to prime ministers or ministers of information. This situation seemed to have created numerous problems. It deprived television organizations of programming and news editorial discretion by setting red lines and self-censorship practices in tune with national media policies. That required top broadcast managers to continuously resort to senior political or information officials to clarify state positions on handling sensitive developments. This subordination of television services to ministries of information had also deprived television operations of opportunities for technical and human development to cope with accelerating changes in the broadcast industry. With limited or nonexistent advertising income to supplement government funding, many broadcasters in the Arab world found themselves lagging behind in technical infrastructure or professional staff standards. As part of government information bureaucracy, television broadcasters were steered by official government orientations rather than by viewers' preferences. This trend has not only adversely affected programming content, but it has also damaged television's credibility among national viewers who perceived broadcasting as a mere propaganda machine for the ruling elite.

One exception to the total government monopoly of television broadcasting in the Arab world is found in Lebanon, where multisystem broadcasting dominated the national expansion phase. In the pre-civil war period, there were two private television services in the country: Compagnie de Television du Liban (CTL), and Proch-Orient (Tele Orient), which was launched in 1959 by a group of Lebanese businessmen with backing from the American Broadcasting Company (ABC) (Dajani 2001). In 1974, the Lebanese Cabinet approved a new broadcasting agreement seeking to institutionalize and formalize government control over broadcasting. The agreement allowed the Lebanese government to purchase and lease transmission equipment to CTL, have two censors at the station to gatekeep programs, have a daily one-hour program show, and levy 6.5 percent of net advertising revenue. Both companies suffered heavy losses during the civil war (1975–76) and were forced to dissolve under a new cabinet rule that brought about a new company in which the government had a 50 percent share. In late 1977, a legislative decree legalized the formation of Tele Liban "to manage, organize and utilize the various television transmitting installations and to undertake all commercial and television production tasks" (Dajani 2001). By doing so, Lebanon had joined other Arab states in placing part of its television system under government control.

The globalization phase

In 1991 the widely acclaimed CNN coverage of the first Gulf war raised Arabs' awareness of the need to diversify television ownership by allowing the entry of private players into the television broadcasting business. This phase was marked by the launch in 1991 of the Middle East Broadcasting Center (MBC) from studio facilities in London as the first private Arab-world television operation. According to Arab States Broadcasting Union data (ASBU 2007), by mid-2009, more than 400 television channels were operational, most of them owned by private broadcasters. Those channels range in their affiliation from foreign broadcasters to national state-owned services to private operations, all seeking to address Arabic-speaking audiences in their native language. The following section provides overviews of major television broadcasters in the region.

Al Jazeera Satellite Channel (JSC) was launched in 1997 from Qatar in the aftermath of the discontinuation of a BBC Arabic Satellite Channel's joint venture with Saudi-owned Orbit Television and Radio Network, following editorial disagreements over the airing of an interview with a London-based Saudi dissident. Over the past few years, JSC has evolved as part of Al Jazeera Network, an umbrella broadcaster that houses, in addition to the Arabic channel, Al Jazeera International, Al Jazeera Documentary Channel, Al Jazeera Children's Channel, Al Jazeera Direct Channel, and Al Jazeera Sports Channel. In addition, the Network also operates an Arabic-English Web portal featuring live broadcasts, news, knowledge, and other information bases.

Since its launch, Al Jazeera Arabic has presented itself as a forum for "the Opinion and the Other Opinion." Funded by advertising revenue and subsidies from the Government of Qatar, JSC has marked a major transition in Arab world broadcast media with its critical talk shows and live coverage of regional and global events. The channel's critical reporting of domestic political and religious affairs in several Arab countries has led to a series of diplomatic incidents as well as to the closure of some of its offices abroad (Da Lage 2005: 56). The channel's daring approach to political issues and developments has also generated misgivings about its journalistic performance, even within the Bush administration, which on several occasions asked its staff to shun the channel on the basis of its anti-U.S. reporting of the Iraqi conflict (Hudson 2006).

But regardless of the debate over the circumstances giving rise to Al Jazeera or to conspiratorial thoughts about its connections with global and regional powers and groups, it is inarguable that JSC has brought about a dramatic transformation in the long-stagnant Arab world media sphere. Lynch (2004, 2006) notes that Al Jazeera has presented itself as an alternative to state-run television, providing a forum for political views that are not likely to be positively received by government-operated media in the Arab world. He cited the example of the preeminent Egyptian journalist Muhammad Hassanayn Haykal, who was summarily banned in the spring 2004 from appearing on Egyptian television after he broached the deeply sensitive topic of Gamal Mubarak's aspirations to succeed his father as president. In response to the ban, Haykal signed a blockbuster deal with Al Jazeera, to air a weekly show entitled *With Haykal: A Life Experience,* devoting the first episode of the show to exposing the Egyptian government's efforts to silence his dissent. From Lynch's point of view, the experience of the venerable Haykal demonstrates how, by shattering state control over public debate, Arab satellite television "is building the foundation of a more democratic Arab political culture" (Lynch 2004).

Al Jazeera Satellite Channel has attracted a wide range of research on how this pan-Arab television channel contributes to the transformation of the traditionally state-controlled media environment. Miles (2003) notes that as a result of Al Jazeera's critique of many Arab governments, it has been labeled by some observers as a virtual political party. But he remarks that media can surely not compensate for the lack of civil society organization and the weakness of the existing opposition. Another volume edited by Zayani (2005) took a more critical approach to Al Jazeera while recognizing its impressive contributions to the emerging Arab public sphere. Zayani notes that in spite of its relatively short history, this Qatar-based news network seems to have left an indelible mark in the Arab world that has changed the face of the otherwise parochial Arab media – although in the West it is largely perceived as a channel that is set on countering Western ideologies. In an earlier book on JSC el Nawawy and Iskander (2002) also spoke lyrically of the channel's pro-democratization orientations in the Arab region and its role in preempting traditional Arab state media censorship by providing alternative perspectives on issues relating to politics, religion, and other sensitive cultural aspects of contemporary Arabian societies. Seib (2009) notes that Al Jazeera has emerged as a democratizing voice in the Middle East, but its civic role has been hindered by complex regional and global realities in the post-September 11 era.

Al Arabiya Channel is a 24-hour television channel launched in Dubai in January 2003 on the eve of the Anglo-American invasion of Iraq. The channel is backed by MBC, Lebanon's Hariri group, and other investors from Saudi Arabia, Kuwait, and other Gulf states. As part of what some call the "Saudi media empire" (Sakr 2006) Al Arabiya has risen to prominence in the past three years in the context of covering the conflict in Iraq, tending mainly to promote the new political developments in the country. On the eve of its establishment, some views circulated that the channel was intended to counterbalance the growing JSC popularity as a media outlet critiquing Saudi Arabia. During the pilgrimage season in early 2006, Al Arabiya was carrying live coverage of Saudi handling of the stampede in which over 300 pilgrims died. JSC, by Saudi law, was banned from covering the pilgrimage for the third year in a row. With no correspondents based in Mecca to report on the tragic incident, JSC used live video from Saudi television accompanied by views and observations of individual pilgrims who witnessed the accident. Satellite and telephone technologies made it impossible for Saudi authorities to circumvent coverage of the pilgrimage disaster by channels banned from operating on Saudi soil. Lynch (2004) noted that Al Arabiya, since its launch in early 2003, has offered a platform to liberal reformers with a tone tempered by greater restraint and sensitivity to the concerns of major Arab states.

Middle East Broadcasting Center (MBC) was first launched from London in 1991 as the first Western-style television broadcaster transmitting to Arab audiences. The channel's launch was met with much fanfare across the region. Researchers deemed it more professional in its program offerings than state-owned television programs (Ayish 1997). In 2002, MBC moved its operations to Dubai Media City before turning into a multiple-channel television service with news, Arabic and Western drama, and children's programming. In addition to MBC1, which carries Arabic entertainment and news, the network has MBC2 (Western drama), MBC3 (children's programs), MBC 4 (light Western talk shows), MBC Action (Hollywood action movies), and MBC Persia (Western movies and talk shows in Persian).

New TV(NTV) was launched in Lebanon on October 4, 2001, as a variety channel with a focus on news and current affairs. The channel's slogan is "respecting the public and being respected by the public." Since its inception, NTV has been embroiled in successive controversies. In December 2003, channel owner Tahseen Khayyat was arrested by Lebanese authorities on charges of having links with Israel. Earlier, NTV's satellite transmissions were suspended for a few days following its airing of a show critical of Saudi Arabia. With Syrian forces out of Lebanon in the aftermath of the assassination of the late Lebanese Prime Minister Rafiq al-Hariri in mid-February 2005, NTV's critical tone toward Syria has been on the rise.

Al-Manar TV was launched in Lebanon in 1999 as a media organ for the Lebanese Hizbullah Party. The channel's stated goal is to "preserve the Islamic values and to enhance the civilized role of the Arab and Islamic community." The channel also plays a significant role in Hizbullah's struggle against Israel. Its program offerings consist of news and current affairs, talk shows, cultural and religious segments, and historical drama. Al-Manar is distributed also via cable networks in Europe and North America. In March 2006, Al-Manar was banned from local U.S. cable networks on charges of fomenting anti-Israeli sentiments. During the 2006 Israeli war on Lebanon, Al-Manar studios were bombed, but transmission continued from underground makeshift facilities.

Future Television was launched on February 15, 1993, with eccentric, funky-looking, family-oriented programs that drew on a blend of Western and Arabian lifestyles. In 1996, in compliance with the new Lebanese audio-visual law, Future Television restructured its ownership to embrace about 90 shareholders in addition to the late Lebanese Prime Minister Rafiq al-Hariri, whose family remains the majority owner of this channel. Since Hariri's assassination in February 2005, Future Television has been engaged in a drive to expose the perpetrators, with a lot of fiery coverage directed at suspected Syrian involvement in the atrocity.

Al Hurra Channel (Arabic for "The Free One") is a commercial-free Arabic-language satellite television network for the Middle East devoted primarily to news and information. In addition to reporting on regional and international events, the channel broadcasts discussion programs, current affairs maga-zines, and features on a variety of subjects, including health and personal fit-ness, entertainment, sports, fashion, and science and technology. The channel is dedicated to presenting accurate, balanced, and comprehensive news. Al Hurra endeavors to broaden its viewers' perspectives, enabling them to make more informed decisions. The channel is operated by a nonprofit corpora-tion: The Middle East Broadcasting Networks (MBN). MBN is financed by the American people through the U.S. Congress. MBN receives this funding from the Broadcasting Board of Governors (BBG), an independent and autonomous federal agency. The BBG serves as a firewall to protect the professional independence and integrity of the broadcasters.

BBC Arabic Channel. Launched in early 2008, this BBC Arabic Channel has turned into a 24-hour television service with a range of news and documentary programs covering the region and the world. Drawing on the experience of BBC World Television, this Arabic channel caters to educated middle-class audiences.

Impact on state-run television systems

By the mid-1980s, the winds of change were already blowing in the Arab region as a result of global and local developments that included increasing literacy and education rates, urbanization, and privatization. The 1991 Gulf war, credited with the acceleration of those transformations, also served as a catalyst for further political reforms, privatization programs, and communications technology diffusions (al Umran 1996). These three factors, growing, more or less, out of broader global trends, seemed to have had an enduring impact on the Arab broadcasting scene. They have contributed to relaxing government broadcast controls; abolishing some information regulatory bodies; granting more airtime access to diverse political views; enabling communication with international audiences beyond national frontiers; and allowing more advertising on state television. These conditions created favorable attitudes on the part of both Arab governments and private businesses for the launch of fully commercial television operations alongside government-controlled services (Ayish 2002).

Regional and global television expansion has been a major feature of the 1990s in the region. Boukhnoufah (2001) notes that the audiovisual sector in the Arab world has developed outside national boundaries in its coverage of local arenas because national audiovisual policies are lacking, there has been little openness to local forces, and centralized regulatory frameworks have been absent. The traditional model of a national television system drawing on a government-controlled and -operated service began to experience major cracks in the early 1990s in the face of global technological and political pressures. This transformation is marked by the institutionalization of a "mixed television system" model; the restructuring of television organizations into more financially, editorially, and administratively autonomous bodies, and the opening up of airwaves to accommodate a wider spectrum of views. These trends stemmed from wider global developments pertaining to the changing status of public service television around the world. Achilles and Miege (1994) note that since the mid-1980s, public service television in Western Europe has had to confront competition from new commercial and (for the most part) generalist television channels. They noted that the resultant financial crisis was heightened by states' inability to draw more revenue from exhausted national budgets. Financial constraints have brought about a strategic reorientation on the part of public channels, leading to a sweeping restructuring of their organizational resources. Karthigesu (1994, 20) notes that changes in the Asian broadcasting scene are driven by an identity crisis in public service television. This crisis seems to be exacerbated by the introduction of new media technologies, the subordination of television to industrial policy considerations, the application to broadcasting of principles of economic and political liberalism, and the rise of production costs beyond the financial capacities of public service broadcasters.

The restructuring of state television organizations in numerous Arab countries in the 1990s has led to the creation of more autonomous entities, as evident in Jordan, Bahrain, the United Arab Emirates, Syria, Qatar, Kuwait, and Lebanon. In 1985 Radio Jordan and Jordan Television were merged into a single corporation. In early 2001, three channels in the indebted and overstaffed Jordan Radio and Television Corporation were combined into a single channel to save on resources (Digital Studio 2001a, 6). Six months later, Jordan Television reported its superchannel successful in terms of regional television competition (Digital Studio 2001b, 8). In the United Arab Emirates, Emirates Media Inc. was created in 1999 as an umbrella organization housing numerous broadcast and print media activities, including the highly reputed Abu Dhabi Satellite Channel and Emirates Satellite Channel. In 2005, Dubai Media Inc. was established as part of local media restructuring arrangements. These moves have been initiated both to enhance performance and cope with spiraling television production costs.

The introduction of satellite television to the Middle East in the early 1990s has presented viewers with diverse television contents. In the pre-1990s period, terrestrial television broadcasting covering national territories and border areas was the main feature of the broadcasting landscape. The diffusion of satellite television reception equipment and cable delivery systems expanded audiences' choices to include program offerings from the United States, Western Europe, and Japan. According to 2000 data, Arab viewers were able to receive up to 200 television channels from around the world (Labib 2000). The launch of regional satellite systems such as ARABSAT, NILESAT, HOTBIRD, and THURAYYA provided government and private broadcasters new outlets to reach audiences around the Arab world. On the other hand, international satellite systems like EUTELSAT, PANAMSAT, and ASIASAT have served as platforms for global television networks targeting the Middle East and North Africa. Arab Radio and Television Network (ART) and ORBIT Television and Radio Network are two examples of global digital broadcasters catering to viewers in the Arab region and around the world with encrypted packages.

Contributions to democratization and cultural revivalism

In February 2008, Arab information ministers adopted a satellite television charter that sought to control and regulate broadcasting operations by bringing them into closer alignment with state policies and orientations. Provoking angry reactions from some private broadcasters and human rights organizations, the Charter provided for legal actions against television channels that show materials offensive to religious figures and political leaders or that carry programs subversive to national traditions and cultures. The Charter underscores a growing uneasiness among governments in the region with the potential effects of satellite television on Arabian societies in the age of globalization. Arab states are becoming more uncomfortable with transnational television addressing sensitive political and cultural issues that they see as crucial to community cohesion and national security.

The nonbinding nature of the Charter did not increase its implementation. In the context of the evolving public sphere, satellite television presents itself as the promised arena for public discussions of politics, religion, and other issues. Talk shows such as Al Jazeera's *Opposite Direction, More Than One Opinion,* and *Without Frontiers* have offered Arab audiences a wide range of unorthodox views and perspectives on issues and events affecting their lives. Al Arabiya, Al Mustakilla, Abu Dhabi, Dubai, and New TV feature daring interviews with controversial personalities and political figures. The rise of some of these channels is driven by divergent political visions associated with different players. Occasional tensions between Qatar and Saudi Arabia were believed to have induced the launch of Al Jazeera in 1996 to counter "Saudi-affiliated media" (Sakr 2006). In January 2003, Al Arabiya Satellite Television Channel was launched from Dubai Media City to provide Arab viewers with alternative perspectives regarding the conflict in Iraq, the U.S.-waged global "war on terror," and political reforms in the region. Television channels were also launched by non-Arab governments as part of ongoing political rivalry in the region. Examples include U.S.-sponsored Al Hurra Channel, Iran's Al Alam Channel, France 24, Russia Today, and the BBC Arabic television channel that launched in late 2007.

The proliferation of satellite television in the Arab region has given it the largest share of the public sphere. Arab States Broadcasting Union statistics (2007) noted that there were 47 television broadcast organizations in the Arab world that included 20 government and 27 private bodies. They operated 75 variety channels and 65 specialized channels distributed among: children (6); sports (6); news (12); drama (12); music (11); documentaries (5); and cultural affairs (13). Free-to-air programs are on 78 channels, while 59 channels require subscriptions (ASBU 2007). Arabic is the language of

81 broadcast television channels, while 40 are in English and 11 in French. Imported Arabic programs amount to 70 percent while foreign programs reach 60 percent. Local production ranges from 30–100 percent. By early 2007, there were over 300 satellite television channels with diverse news and entertainment content accessible to viewers across the region. The numbers do not seem impressive in an Arab world of 250 million people or more, but they represent a more diverse platform for news and opinion, comparable to the traditional print news media. Al Jazeera, with its Western-style news programs, has had a marked effect on other region-wide satellite channels, such as LBC and Al-Mustaqbal (Future Television) of Lebanon, Abu Dhabi and Dubai channels of the United Arab Emirates, the Saudi-owned MBC (Middle East Broadcasting Center), and Egypt's Nile and ESC (Egyptian Satellite Channel), as well as others (Ayish 2003). New satellite channels are also marked by some interactivity with viewers around the Arab world, as evident in audience participation in live television shows. The following section surveys major satellite television broadcasters in the Arab World.

Television and political reforms

Ayish (2002) noted that the advent of Western-style television channels in the Arab world has brought with it new visions of journalism that drive daring and inquisitive investigations for the sake of creating an informed public opinion. As mentioned above, the Qatar-based Al Jazeera satellite channel has led television services in critical discussions of the region's issues and developments through its range of live talk shows. One of those programs, *Opposite Direction*, is a weekly live political *Crossfire*-style talk show that has created numerous diplomatic incidents between the state of Qatar and other countries targeted by the show. Along with other shows carried by Al Hurra, Al Arabiya, and the BBC Arabic channel, political programs aired by private television in the region have contributed to building civic consciousness among Arab populations. Programs about human rights, democratic politics, and religious moderation, dialogue with the other, peaceful coexistence, and human dignity and freedom have been frequent topics taken up by those programs. Although those shows allowed average citizens and dissident voices to be heard in the public sphere, television's role in politics seldom goes beyond civic education. People are becoming more conscious of the dynamics of national, regional, and global political developments bearing on their lives; yet they are rendered helpless when it comes to concrete actions for reform.

The perceived political role of leading television broadcasters like Al Jazeera, Al Arabiya, Al Hiwar, BBC Arabic Television, and New TV has led some researchers to describe these channels as forces of democratization in the region. The Qatar-based Al Jazeera channel has attracted an outstanding amount of scholarly attention in light of its coverage of military and political developments such as the 9/11 attacks, the war in Afghanistan, the U.S. invasion of Iraq, the 2006 Israeli attack on Lebanon, the war in Somalia, and the early 2009 Israeli offensive in the Gaza Strip. Research on Al Jazeera has spawned wide-ranging perspectives about the channel's contribution to creating and sustaining an Arab public opinion on those developments. While some researchers framed Al Jazeera's handling of those issues as reflecting genuine pluralistic journalism that contributes to building up true civic consciousness in the Arab world (Seib 2009; Lynch 2006; El-Nawawy & Iskandar 2002), others portrayed the channel as no more than a mouthpiece for Arab and Islamic radicalism. Al Arabiya, on the other hand, has been viewed as taking a less sensational, lower-profile approach to political developments that resonates with its generally moderate media discourse. When it comes to foreign broadcasters like Al Hurra and BBC Arabic Television, researchers have analyzed the two channels within public diplomacy traditions, where media outlets are perceived to fulfill foreign-policy goals.

Apart from the channel-centered research, few attempts have been made to investigate television's bearing on public opinion in the region. The problem, of course, is intrinsically methodological, suggesting the difficulty of establishing causal relationships between television content and political developments. A wide range of public opinion polls have been carried out in the region by national and international polling agencies to identify perceptions of major political and social developments, but none of them seemed to study how public perceptions were shaped by media exposure. The fact that multiple variables – different media, social traditions, and legal frameworks – are brought to bear on audience values and attitudes seems to have added more complexity to discussions of political television in the Arab world. Surveys have shown that a channel such as Al Jazeera commands huge popularity in the region, especially in times of crisis; yet, we are not well-informed about how that popularity trickles down into the political attitudes and behaviors of Arab publics. That gap has unfortunately given way to political speculations about how those channels shape public opinion. One of those relates to how Al Jazeera contributes to alienating Arab populations from their political leaderships, which are presented on the channel as authoritarian and undemocratic. Another speculation relates to how Al Jazeera fosters a sense of disenchantment with American foreign policies in the Middle East by highlighting U.S. support for Israeli and the so-called moderate Arab states.

Television and culture

As much as Arab world television was faltering on the political front, it seems to have also failed to make solid advances on the cultural front. As noted earlier in this chapter, television was entrusted with a central role in cultural integration and revivalism. But with the proliferation of literally hundreds of satellite channels since the mid-1990s, rising expectations about a constructive role for television in national cultural development were turning into agonizing frustrations about television turning into a conduit for global cultural hegemony. Television programs, especially those on commercial channels, have triggered heated debates across the region with respect to their role in promoting cultural hegemony and eroding national cultural systems. An increasing number of research works, public discussions, and policy orientations have come to view satellite television as playing a subversive role in community development, especially for children and teenagers (Ayish 2001b). Reality television has attracted a good deal of this attention. In 2004, Bahrain was associated with this genre when a show styled after the Big Brother program was supposed to be produced in Bahrain. But because the show was believed to promote "immorality" among Arab youth, hundreds of Bahrainis took to the streets to protest against the shooting of the show, which was produced by MBC. Finally, MBC caved in and cancelled the show. Other reality television shows such as *Super Star* and *Star Academy*, both produced by the Lebanese Future Television and the Lebanese Broadcasting Corporation (LBC), provoked negative reactions for their their potential effects on the young (Kahki 2008).

The showing of foreign programs on Arab satellite television channels has also received critical treatment in media research and public discussions. Though the issue goes back to the 1970s and 1980s, when state television services resorted to foreign television imports to fill air time, extensive use of mostly Western programs in the 1990s and beyond was creating greater uproar. Since 2007, some Arab television channels have come under fire for carrying Arabic-dubbed Turkish soap operas that presented viewers in the region with liberal lifestyles and attitudes many found unacceptable to their relatively conservative communities. Some Arabic television networks have also launched Western-entertainment-dedicated channels that carried sit-coms, soap operas, and Hollywood movies on a 24-hour basis. Examples include Dubai Channel One and MBC's Channels 2 and 4, Action Channel, and MBC Persia. One of those channels carries globally famous shows like *Oprah*, *Dr. Phil*, and *The Doctors*. Similar Western entertainment offerings are also available through subscription television platforms such as Orbit and Showtime.

But Arab television does also have something constructive to offer on the cultural front. Recent program innovations have made a wide range of culturally oriented content accessible to Arab viewers in the fields of heritage, science and technology, edutainment, and drama. In 2008, one channel dedicated to the promotion of poetry as a fundamental ingredient of oral Arab culture was launched from Abu Dhabi to showcase the best poetic talents in composition in classical language and local dialects. The channel's stated mission is to explore poetic talent and foster public attachment to this form of Arab cultural expression. Another unique television channel was also launched in early 2009 from Saudi Arabia to promote the Arabian horse as a precious symbol of Arab cultural heritage. The channel, named Al Kheil, carries equestrian sports activities from the region and around the world in addition to talk shows about the moral and social values associated with the Arabian horse. In the fields of science and technology and edutainment, Arab television has carried general-knowledge contests taking the question-answer format in a studio setting with audience presence. Examples include MBC's *Who Wins the Million,* presented by Lebanese George Girdahi. In mid 2009, a new reality television show seeking to promote scientific innovation among Arab youth was launched under the title *Stars of Science.* The show features young Arab scientists working on their projects under the supervision of a panel of specialized judges in different areas of applied science and technology. As for drama, Syria has emerged over the past few years as a central television series production center in the region. Its soap operas are shown on multiple channels, especially during the fasting month of Ramadan. The most outstanding Syrian television series has been *Bab Al Hara*, which tells the story of traditional Syrian life in the 1930s and 1940s.

Like its role in politics, television's role in cultural development in the Arab world has remained more a subject of speculation and isolated observation than of systematic scholarly investigation. A good number of studies have been carried out to identify broadcast portrayal patterns and audience perceptions of programs (Ayish 2002), but the way in which content bears on viewers' attitudes and values regarding specific issues remains untapped. Most researchers have sought to study how television commercials, dramas, and religious and cultural talk shows handled issues of gender, children's needs, social relations, and religious values. But when it comes to how exposure patterns affect audience values and attitudes, studies have not generated significant findings. The problem here, of course, is methodological, pertaining to the multiplicity of variables bearing on audience attitudes and values aside from television. Educational and social institutions play a major role in defining how Arab publics frame issues of women, children, religious values, and social relations. In many ways, television's progressive cultural discourse on women's rights and religious values does not seem to resonate with long-entrenched conservative modes of thinking that continue to be sustained by complex political and religious socialization processes.

Conclusion

Television broadcasting in the Arab world has indeed experienced drastic changes in the context of the global information and communications revolution. From single terrestrial national television markets to regional and global ones, television has proven to be a credible communication force in Arabian societies. With over 500 channels available to individual viewers across the region, the question that stands out in any investigation of television broadcasting relates to how this media resource has been harnessed to promote democratization and cultural revivalism in a region long dominated by authoritarian political and cultural systems. While some continue to view television as a powerful force of national development, many others see broadcasting as a Trojan horse for Westernized cultural hegemony that threatens the basic premises of Arab Islamic social and cultural traditions and values. Some even continue to see television as a force of political and security disruption for Arabian societies seeking to achieve national integration and political stability in the midst of global turbulence. According to research findings, while television has raised civic awareness of democratic values and practices, it has fallen short of effecting concrete changes on the ground. This fits the nature of media power when it comes to real-life transitions; communications only play a supportive role in the process of change. They cannot lead that change as such. On the other hand, the role of television in cultural development has been part of many critical discussions. Some charge that broadcasting is turned into a tool for Western cultural imperialism, as evidenced in the showing of Western media. There are concerns that cultural and national identity is at risk of being annihilated in the face of alien cultures brought to us through television. Sweeping statements such as these may not be appropriate, since the region has already produced constructive cultural television, as evident in family and children's shows that seek to inform and educate on the basis of indigenous cultural and social premises. With the economic downturn deepening in the region, television broadcasting is likely to be affected as its advertising-generated revenues continue to diminish. Only television networks with solid and sustainable financial resources will be able to survive, which means the huge range of television outlets available in the early part of the twenty-first century may shrink in the future.

An important challenge facing serious scholarship on Arab world television in the twenty-first century is how to account for broadcasters' impact on the region's political and cultural development. The current situation seems to suggest that television is monolithic when it comes to these two areas. While television continues to serve as a mouthpiece for governments, it also contributes to democratic education and civic consciousness in communities across the region. Likewise, while television is perceived as a vehicle for globalized cultural hegemony, it also offers significant content with redeeming social and moral values relevant for cultural development. This dual television role is bound to create confusion as members of the public receive conflicting political and cultural messages. For both governments and progressive forces, the mixed messages of current Arab-world television could create disruptive effects on the region's development.

Yet our assumptions about television's role in creating concrete changes in political and cultural fronts is short-sighted. We are failing to grasp the basic dynamics of media relationships with society. Successive communication research traditions have informed us that media, including television, play a supporting role in social change, and unless they are used in a setting with a strong predisposition for change, change messages will be useless regardless of the message strength. This conclusion raises the issue of the need for concrete political and cultural transitions on the ground in order to enable more effectual television contributions to the change process. This suggests that television in the Arab world is more likely to remain captive to patriarchal and authoritarian political traditions that define how populations relate to society and the state.

6   Arab Cinema
Noha Mellor

There is no common characteristic that is unique to Arab cinema industries. That is, "there is not one school, form, structure, or style" (Ghareeb 1997, 119). Yet when critics refer to "Arab cinema," they usually mean Egyptian cinema (Morgan 2005, 3). The film industry that flourished in Egypt has had its roots in the music and theatre industry that has thrived there since the late nineteenth century (Shafik 2001, 711). It was the European colonial powers who introduced film screening in their former colonies, particularly in the Northern African countries of Egypt, Algeria, Tunisia, and Morocco. For instance, in 1896, films by the Lumiere brothers were shown in Egypt, Algeria, and Tunisia, and by the turn of the century Egypt had five film theatres (Shafik 2007, 10).

This chapter will focus on the cinema industry in Egypt and compare it with other Arab states, particularly the new entrants in the Gulf region, who now host a number of international film festivals.

The main thesis of this chapter is that cinema has changed its status from industry (as it was in Egypt and Lebanon) to modeling modernity and progress (as it now is in Gulf countries such as United Arab Emirates and Saudi Arabia). The industry has gone through difficult financial hurdles with the advent of video and satellite TV, which is why Arab cinema now depends in part on joint productions for survival. Cinema has played a significant role in exposing social taboos, particularly in Egypt, and filmmakers in the Diaspora have recently been breaking more taboos about life in their native societies as well as the societies where they now live. This role is likely to continue in the future, when joint production with European partners will be more common.

A brief historical overview of the development of the cinema industry opens this chapter, followed by two sections on the film industry's economics and regulations. Documentary film, which has flourished recently on satellite TV, is the subject of a third section. The last section is dedicated to the impact of cinema on breaking social taboos, and draws on recent examples of such films.

A historical overview

The former European colonial powers introduced cinema in North African and Arab countries. Theatres increased in number where Europeans lived. In Algeria, for instance, there were 150 theatres in 1933; in Egypt, 244 in 1945 (Ghareeb 1997, 120). The movie theatres as well as film production were in the hands of European minorities and immigrants (Shafik 2007, 11). The first full feature film in Egypt (with native crew) was *Layla* in 1927; Syria followed in 1928 (Ghareeb 1997, 120). Tunisia had its first full-length feature film in 1922, and Lebanon in 1929 (produced by native Arabs) (Shafik 2007, 12).

Film production began with the political independence of Arab states – except Egypt, which had a history of film production well before its independence in 1952. One reason for the flourishing film industry in Egypt at the time was the interest of native Egyptians in film as a medium, combined with the interest of financial entrepreneurs like Talaat Harb who saw in cinema a good investment (Shafik 2007, 13–14). The Egyptian banker Talaat Harb laid the foundations of the Egyptian cinema industry when he established the Studio Misr in 1934, and by 1949 six more studios were built. During that period Egypt produced 345 feature films, and the cinema industry was one of the most profitable in Egypt at the time (12). Egypt managed to produce around 48 films per year between 1948 up to 1952, the year of the Free Officers' Revolution and the end of monarchy. This should be seen in contrast with other northern Arab countries such as Algeria and Morocco, where the French colonial power did not allow the indigenous culture to flourish and hence no film was directed by a native until after independence in the 1950s and 1960s (Shafik 2007, 12–15).

Egyptian production reached 80 films per year in 1953–54, and remained around 60 for the rest of the 1950s (Ghareeb 1997, 120). Following independence, the Egyptian government expressed interest in folk arts as well as in progressive arts such as ballet, and in 1957 the Center for Folk Arts was established under the Ministry of Cultural and National Guidance. The Ministry of Culture established the Higher Film Institute in 1959, which has provided the industry with generations of technicians, scriptwriters, directors, and actors.

Where other Arab states have produced perhaps one hundred films following their independence; Egypt has produced more than 2,500 films (Shafik 2007, 9). Some conservative societies (Saudi Arabia, North Yemen) did not introduce film theatres until the 1960s and 1970s (Shafik 2007, 10). After independence, Arab states struggled to lessen their dependence on American and European films. National film production made up only 20 percent of distributed films (Shafik 2007, 20). Arab states therefore nationalized their cinema industry and the distribution channels, but this could not meet the increasing national demand for films (Shafik 2007, 21).

Although Iraq was the first Arab state to embrace TV, it lagged when it came to cinema production. In fact, its first production was in 1945: a co-production with Egypt, with an Egyptian director (Hillabuer 2005, 117). Iraq produced only one state-funded feature film per year in the 1970s with the help of Egyptian directors (Ghareeb 1997, 121). The repressive Saddam regime made it difficult for Iraqi film culture to flourish, as it was important to join the Baath party as a prerequisite to making films. This had compelled several directors to flee the country,and in the absence of such skilled personnel the state made only short propagandistic films (Hillabuer 2005, 119).

The nationalization of the Egyptian film industry led to the move of Egyptian and Arab producers to Lebanon, where there was an economic boom (Shafik 2007, 28). However, the outbreak of the civil war during the 1970s, coupled with that decade's privatization of Egyptian cinema, moved the production back to Egypt (29). The former Egyptian president Anwar Sadat worked hard on rebuilding Cairo to resemble Western cities and called for major state privatization. He became known for implementing the Infitah (Open Door) economic policy. The financial impact of the 1967 and 1973 wars combined with the mismanagement of the industry during the 1960s had paved the way for the new Open Door Policy in the cinema industry, which was re-privatized to offset public spending on this industry, which reached seven million Egyptian pounds (Shafik 2007, 32). This was the first step to commercial cinema in Egypt (Armbrust 1995, 103).

Films produced during that period tended to exalt the newly independent regime. The Algerian cinema, for instance, examined and praised the agrarian revolution in 1971 through a number of films, in what was called "agitational cinema." In this genre the filmmakers seemed less concerned with cinematic art than with informing the public about the impact of the revolution (Hennebelle 1976, 9). The exaltation of Arab unity and Nasser's socialist ideals, however, had shattered by the defeat in the 1967 war with Israel. There followed a period of self-realization; a group of filmmakers set up the Association of New Cinema (or Chabab Cinema) in 1968. Among their publicized aims was to "denounce the hybrid character and absence of real personality in Egyptian cinema . . . [and to replace it with] a new cinema with deep roots in contemporary Egypt" (Hennebelle 1976, 5). Thus, those artists wanted a new form of art that was not "copied from foreign examples." Following the 1967 defeat, some filmmakers used film as a medium to express their anger at the failure of Arab socialist ideals, particularly those related to the Nasser regime. One such film was *The Karnak* (1975), which associated

Nasser's regime with torture and rape (Shafik 2007, 110). The Egyptian New Cinema also critiqued the gap between social classes and the reduction of the old middle class, which had been the centre of pre-1970s films (Armbrust 1995, 105). The Realism movement had its roots in the 1950s with the Egyptian director Salah Abu Seif's films, such as *Master Hassan* (1952), *Muscleman* (1957), and *Beginning and End* (1960), which all focused on the struggle of lower classes in Cairo (Hennebelle 1976, 4).

The spread of video in the 1970s compelled the Egyptian film companies to sell their productions in the Gulf States, particularly Saudi Arabia, where there was an increasing demand, as well as an interest among Saudi investors in getting into the cinema industry. The Egyptian film industry thus grew dependent on the Saudi distribution companies (Shafik 2007, 27). The 1980s were a period of commercialization, with the majority of films produced by foreign (Gulf) investors who provided loans to film producers, the amount of which depended very much on the status of the leading stars. This has prompted a culture of stardom and secured the leading actors and actresses of the time fixed places in the industry while limiting the possibilities available for the new generation to build up their names (Shafik 2001, 713). The 1980s and 1990s were also seen as the epoch of "morality," in which stars' private affairs were publicly scrutinized. Films such as *Darb al-Hawa* or *Alley of Love* and *Khamsa Bab* or *Gate Five*, both released in 1983, stirred public anger due to the implicit sex scenes and superficial plots (Shafik 2001, 718), as will be discussed below.

The cinema as an industry

In the Arab world, leisure time usually means family time. The whole family gathers and spends their evenings and/or weekends chatting and watching television. Thus, television, and later video and DVD, has been an integral part of family life. One reason for this is that spending time in front of the television or video is by far cheaper than spending time outdoors. This is particularly so in poor countries such as Egypt where the prices of daily goods have skyrocketed recently, thereby reducing the family leisure spending. The availability of hundreds of satellite channels as well as DVDs of imported films has enforced this tradition and provided a vast range of variety and entertainment programs for the whole family.

Also, recent years have seen the launching of large shopping malls and hypermarkets which have mushroomed all over the Arab region. In Saudi Arabia, for example, shopping malls have become an embodiment of the Western lifestyle; likewise, Egypt has seen the building of several hypermalls over the past decade, visited by people of different classes and providing an elegant space for youths, even poor youths, to meet and flirt (Abaza, 2001). In fact, the sales at such hypermarkets grew by 14 percent in 2007 (Global Market Information Database Online). Such malls are usually located in large centres with luxurious cinemas and fun parks to provide a lifestyle experience for the young visitors.

The impact of this trend on the cinema industry is twofold: on the one hand, film production even in Egypt has decreased over the years. More and more consumers choose other kinds of outings, rather than going to the movies, and more viewers access hundreds of TV programs and existing DVDs, rather than attending new productions. The number of films produced in Egypt has been 40 films on average annually: an average of 20 films per year produced between 1927 and 1945, of 50 films between 1945 and 1990, and of 44 films between 1990 and 2000, followed by a period of declining production reaching a minimum of 16 in 1998 (Ghoneim 2004, 14). The emergence of satellite channels and media cities have also delayed the production of feature films, as studios would often be booked up for the production of TV programs and commercials (Hillauer 2005, 41). The revenues from feature films in the domestic market do not cover their production costs, and therefore Arab production companies depend on distribution in the greater Arab world to boost revenues (Ghoneim 2004, 15).

On the other hand, there is a revived interest in building new cinemas despite the fact that the number of functioning cinemas is in decline. For instance, the number of screens in Egypt increased from 110 in 1995 to 183 in 2001. Functioning cinemas numbered around 175. (Ghoneim 2004, 16). That figure rose again in 2006 to 250 (Global Market Information Database). Likewise, Lebanon had 25 screens in 1996, but this number increased sixfold to 150 in 2006. Gulf states, in particular, have introduced cinemas in their hypermalls; Emirates had more than 200 cinemas in 2006 and Oman increased its number of screens from only two in 1996 to 18 in 2006.

Other Arab countries, such as Morocco, have seen the opposite trend: more and more consumers who prefer to watch TV and video rather than visiting movie theatres. Morocco had 183 screens in 1996 but that figure was reduced to 96 in 2006 (Global Market Information Database). While the number of movie theatres in Morocco dropped to less than 100, video clubs have increased to more than 2,500 (Sabra 2005, 333). Many Jordanian movie theatres have also had to close down in recent years, putting film production at a standstill for years. Nonetheless, Jordan hosted a few film festivals (Hillabuer 2005, 416).

The following table summarizes the recent trend in cinema admission and number of screens in selected Arab countries:

Table 8: Cinema Admission and Number of Screens in Selected Arab Countries

	Egypt	Lebanon	UAE	Algeria	Morocco	Tunisia
Population (m., est)	73.6	3.8	4.5	34.0	30.7	10.3
Admission 2007 $ billion	26.8	2.1	6.3	0.7	3.8	0.3
Admission per capita 2006	0.36	0.56	1.41	0.02	0.12	0.03
Screens 2006	250	87	202	69	115	29

(Source, UNESCO statistics)

The high cost of production combined with the harsh competition of DVD and TV has led to the decline of feature film production, with more and more filmmakers seeking funds from abroad. France has been a major supporter of the Arab cinema industry and has co-produced various Arab films (Ghareeb 1997, 121). In fact, most of the Egyptian production is now dependent on foreign investors, particularly from the Arab Gulf States (Ghareeb 1997, 122). One example is *Dunia* (2005), which is an Egyptian-French-Lebanese production by the Lebanese Jocelyne Saab. It features a young Egyptian woman who wants to be a professional dancer in a country where dancers are regarded as whores; this is already controversial; more controversy is added by the mention of circumcision in the film. Tunisian films are also very much dependent on foreign subsidies, as the native market hardly pays for the cost of the films. Subsidies come also from the Tunisian Ministry of Culture, which contributes up to 30 percent of film budgets (Hillabuer 2005, 364). Moroccan cinema, moreover, hopes to increase its production in the future, judging by the creation of a film fund to subsidize Moroccan films; and, since 1988, the increase in co-production, particularly with France; and the cooperation between television and filmmakers in production and marketing of films (Sabra 2003, 333–34).

Another reason for the falling number of movie theatres in Egypt is the Gulf investment in Egyptian cinema, or what commentators call "Contractors' Cinema," with the release of productions on video targeting Gulf audiences, who used to have few movie theatres of their own. A large number of films were released during the 1980s, 95 in 1986 alone, mostly video-only. This led to the closure of several movie theatres (Hillauer 2005, 40). Added to this erosion in demand for film in theatres, Saudi distribution companies paid low prices for foreign rights. "The inflation of Egyptian films on the market also caused the sale prices of new Egyptian productions to crash" (Hillauer 2005, 41). Thus, film budgets are calculated according to the revenues they can bring from the Gulf market. An Egyptian producer explains, "in order to get the money for a product that does not yet exist, you have to say, for example, 'with this actress I'll get $50,000 from Saudi Arabia, $30,000 from Kuwait, $10,000 from Lebanon . . . and the sale of video rights will bring in

$250,000 in Egypt, so I'll make a film with a budget on that scale. You don't calculate a film based on an idea or a script, but only according to how much you can bring in" (cited in Hillauer 2005, 42).

Several distributors resort to film imports, particularly from the USA, to boost their earnings. The Egyptian film distributor Gabi Khorui sees the popularity of American films among Egyptian audiences in balance with the profitability of such films in the Egyptian market. An imported film, he said, costs around 100,000 Egyptian pounds (or roughly $17,750) in legal clearance, permissions, and publicity, and has to bring in 200,000 Egyptian pounds (or roughly $35,500) to ensure an appropriate profit margin. This means it has to be seen by at least 12,000 viewers. Any other imported film, whether Indian or European, he added, would be a risky affair, as there would be no guarantee that thousands of Egyptians would come to watch it. The Head of the Egyptian Cinema Union, Mamdouh al Leithy, justifies the popularity of American movies with the fact that a significant number of American and European expatriates live in Egypt, and they form a lucrative market for such imported films (al Leithy 2007). On the other hand, al Leithy is pessimistic about local film production in the future due to the recent global economic recession. He warns that revenues from foreign distribution have fallen and will continue to fall as many satellite channels face closure. Revenues from local distribution, he added, only cover 50 percent of production costs, which have skyrocketed thanks to the extravagant fees required by major stars – for their own services and their teams of personal assistants and stylists (Ibrahim 2009).

In an attempt to channel more funds to the national cinema industry, several Arab states, such as Egypt, Morocco, and Syria, impose a higher sales tax on imported films than on local films. The Cairo governor's recent decision to impose 10 percent taxes on cinema tickets compelled the Chamber of Film Industry to protest; they demanded that all movie theatres in Cairo be closed (*Al-Ahram Weekly* 2005). The protest was meant to point up the ill-considered policy of the government, which on the one hand seeks to encourage local production and on the other hand puts economic barriers on movie theatres. Movie theatres' traditional closure during Ramadan also reduces revenues, and audiences give in totally to the competition of TV. Ramadan is also usually the month of renovation for movie theatres, which means less profit for owners.

Regulations of the cinema industry

Egyptian cinema policy can be divided into three phases: during the 1930s and 1940s, policy can be described as liberal; this was followed by a protectionist policy during the 1950s and 1960s; finally, a period of mixed laissez-faire was pursued from the 1990s on (Flibbert 2001, 42). The Egyptian state stopped producing feature films in 1971, but maintained ownership of studios. Recently (2001) the state established a new body to re-engage in producing feature films (Ghoneim 2004, 4). There is no proper film archive in Egypt apart from the Egyptian Film Centre in Giza, which has a limited budget and archive of old movies (Hillauer 2005, 41). Moreover, Egypt imposes various restrictions on foreign companies shooting in Egypt in terms of taxes and charges on equipment (Ghoneim 2004, 7), not to mention the censorship and permission needed to shoot in the country.

Film production is concentrated, with five companies producing nearly half of all films produced in 1992; one company produced 27 percent of the total. The same can be said about distribution, 75 percent of which is controlled by five companies (Ghoneim 2004, 3). The main challenge facing the Egyptian cinema industry at the moment is piracy, despite the existence of copyright laws (Ghoneim, 2004, 8).

The state's direct support to the cinema industry has been in decline and indirect support has proven ineffective (Ghoneim, 2004, 8). For instance, the sales tax imposed on foreign films is higher than that on local films (10 percent and 5 percent respectively), yet imported films have been increasing. Egypt has had a quota of 300 foreign films a year since 1973, but the rule is not regarded as binding (Ghoneim 2004, 10). In an attempt to revive the cinema industry, the Egyptian government introduced the Investment Incentives and Guarantees Law in 1997 to encourage film companies to produce more high-quality feature films. Rather, film companies resorted to distribution of imported films, particularly American films, rather than investing in production. In principle, the Egyptian state set the ceiling of 300 films as the maximum number of imported foreign films but this figure has increased lately, to the dismay of filmmakers and actors (Essam El Din, 2000). Currently foreign films pay a duty of 20 percent while Egyptian ones are taxed at 15 percent.

Rachty and Sabat (1987) showed that during the period from 1965 to 1969, Egypt imported 80 to 90 percent of its films, mostly from the USA. The importation of these cultural products was reinforced by the advent of television (in the 1960s) and the increasing importation of foreign material to fill the empty programming slots.

Now, American films as well as Egyptian comedy films can run in theatres for months – such films as those by the young Egyptian actor Mohamed Heneidi, for example – while other genres have relatively short runs in theatres. The Egyptian film critic Samir Farid states that films now represent a mix of genres rather than one distinct genre, such as the genre of realist films which was dominant in the 1960s (Omar 2005).

In Syria, the state monopolizes film importation and prohibits raising prices in movie theatres. There were around 120 movie theatres in 1963, but now there are only 40, the majority of which are in Damascus and Aleppo, with a seating capacity of only 15,000. The state imposed a law in 1969 that restricted film imports, but this law has been repealed, making it easier for distribution companies to import foreign films. However, the tax imposed on imported films was prohibitive, as the state first demanded 150,000 Syrian lira (or roughly $3,220) on Arab films, 225,000 lira or $4,830 on Indian films, and 125,000 lira or $2,684 on any other. Upon the complaints of distribution companies, these fees were reduced by half; later they were set at 50,000 Syrian lira or $1,080 for any imported film, regardless of the country of origin (Azzam 2007). The restrictive policy has brought the Syrian film industry to a standstill while prompting new filmmakers to look for profits in making inexpensive videos for the lucrative Gulf market. Even Syrian public TV has competed in producing TV series for distribution in the Gulf; some of these have bettered the Egyptian productions and scored huge popularity among Arab audiences. Features production, however, has been progressing very slowly. The future will very much depend on the current government's policy toward art and culture (Hillabuer 2005, 248–49). Also, the popularity of Turkish TV soaps has become a new market for Syrian actors, providing voiceovers in Syrian dialects.

In Tunisia, the film industry is governed by the Ministry of Culture and not the Ministry of Information, which governs press and broadcasting. This, according to some Tunisian filmmakers, has made it easier for Tunisian filmmakers to tackle taboo issues in their films: homosexuality in *Man of Ashes*, 1986; and sex tourism in *Bezness*, 1992 (Hillabuer 2005, 361).

In Saudi Arabia, the conservative Islamic rules have suppressed the set-up of movie houses or the launch of a native film industry. To satisfy the ever-demanding and lucrative Saudi market, Arab films have provided the Saudi home cinemas with all kinds of film formats: videos, 35mm. films, even pornographic films are sold in the black market. The latter is usually "tolerated for home use as long as it does not undermine 'public morals'" (Hillabuer 2005, 418). Due to the large number of Asian expatriates in the Gulf region, these rich states have become a lucrative market for imported Bollywood and South Asian productions, which have then gained currency among native Arab audiences as well. This could be because such films deal with topics similar to those in Arab films, that is, ideal family behavior. One of the Bollywood stars, Amitabh Bachchan, was invited to the Cairo Film Festival in 2001, and has attracted a large base of fans among Egyptian women, some of whom dream of marrying him (*Times of India* 2005).

New markets, new entrants

Cinema was an industry in Egypt, and also in Lebanon, "a business and entertainment, and cinemas were also used as a means of information and of cultural contact with the rest of the world" (Dajani, K. 1980, 90). The Egyptian export of films to other Arab countries has helped spread the Egyptian dialect. The success of Egyptian cinema was mainly due to the fact that their films are in Arabic and reach a wide range of Arab audiences, of which a large percentage is illiterate (Dajani, K. 1980, 90). The difference in dialects of the various Arab nations has been the reason used by film distributors to ensure the spread of Egyptian films and hence the Egyptian dialect as the pan-Arab cultural code, rather than accustoming Arab audiences to following films in other Arab dialects (Farid 1998). Some countries (Syria, Iraq and Libya), however, refused to import Egyptian films that deal with political themes, which was why a significant percentage of the films produced in the 1970s were nonpolitical (Dajani, K. 1980, 92). Particularly upon signing a peace treaty with Israel in 1979, Egyptian production was boycotted in some Arab states, although film distribution remained about the same, but suffered minor delays in orders (Dajani, K. 1980, 92f).

Film export to Saudi Arabia has increased steadily throughout the years. In 1961, the total Egyptian film export to the Gulf kingdom reached 42 films, while in 1965 this figure was 176 (Dajani K. 1980, 94). Egypt also exported films to other countries, such as France, Russia, Canada, Greece, Australia, and Indonesia (Dajani, K. 1980, 95). Saudi Arabia imported those films to show in private screenings, for instance, in schools or clubs, as there were no film theatres in the kingdom.

Since the 1990s, the launch of satellite TV channels has meant more sluggish film production, particularly in Egypt, where feature film production fell from 60 a year during the 1980s to slightly over 20 during the mid-1990s (Shafik 2007, 43). The Egyptian film critic Samir Farid also argues that the artistic features of the Arab film industry have been sidestepped by the commercial interests of production companies. He sees this as a weakening of the film industry. He criticizes the Arab governments for caring only about issues of taxation and censorship, rather than the establishment of national film archives to preserve the original negatives (Farid 1998). Not only has satellite TV pulled Arab consumers from film theatres, but it also offers fierce competition to the film industry, with more and more television production screened in film theatres (Shafik 2007, 43). Most of these satellite channels were owned by Saudi business tycoons who have found in media a new investment and a culturally prestigious field (Mellor 2008). Middle East Broadcasting Corporation (MBC) was established in 1991 by wealthy Saudis related to the royal family, followed by Arab Radio and Television Network (ART) in 1993 in Rome with funds from one of the MBC founders. Italy also hosted another Saudi satellite adventure, namely Orbit, in 1994. One of the Saudi tycoons in this field is Prince Al Waleed Bin Talal, owner of the Rotana channels (Rotana Music, Rotana Clip, Rotana Cinema, and Rotana Zaman). Rotana Film and Rotana Zaman are dedicated to old and new movies, mostly Egyptian, and they own an impressive archive of Egyptian films, thereby assuming the responsibility of preserving a valuable cultural heritage, which should be the state responsibility. When the Egyptian TV host Hala Sarhan assumed her post as regional manager of Rotana Cinema, she insisted that her job entailed a national duty of preserving the wealth of Egyptian Arab movies in Rotana's library. (A February 2007 interview with Hala Sarhan can be seen at www.arabtube.tv.) There is fear, however, that the Saudi investors would reshape the Egyptian film industry by imposing their own censorship of themes or scenes that do not match their market or culture.

Saudi Television empires such as Rotana and ART have now moved to cinematic production (Hammond 2007, 152). According to the Saudi historian Khalid Rabiae Assayed, Saudi film production began in 1977 with a film called *Ightiyal Madinah* or *Assassination of a City* by Abdallah Al Mohaisen, and it told the story of the destruction of Beirut following the Lebanese civil war. The film scored a prestigious prize in the Cairo International Film Festival for the best short film. There followed a period of silence during the 1980s when conservative Islamic groups managed to suppress the film movement in its infancy, close down cinemas, and prohibit foreign embassies from screening films to Saudi citizens in an attempt to keep the native moral code intact (*Arabian Business*). Imported Egyptian and other Arab films were usually shown in homes, private clubs, or schools. However, the past few years have witnessed a revolutionary shift in film policy in the Kingdom with the opening of the first movie theatre in Al Riyadh in 2005, followed by the release of a couple of Saudi films, with Saudi actors but usually Egyptian and Lebanese crew.

The first Saudi production was *Zelal Assamt* (2006), followed by *Keif al Hal*. The conservative kingdom launched the first Saudi Film Festival in 2006. It was called Jeddah Visual Productions (to avoid using the word "cinema") and a year later the Saudi Ministry of Culture launched a contest encouraging Saudi youths to enter the film field and form their own film society. Rotana produced *Menahi*, and launched it in Saudi Arabia in December 2008 in public theatres and cultural clubs. The film tells the story of a Saudi young man of Bedouin origins who travels to Dubai and faces a series of funny situations due to the different lifestyle in Dubai. In the press conference that preceded the premier, a Rotana official said that the film would not be the last production but the first of many to come, and promised that Saudi productions would never offend the social norms and traditions (*Al Sharq* 2008). Despite the lack of a Saudi film industry, the Saudi female filmmaker Hizam Al Kilani, a graduate of the Higher Film Institute in Cairo, made a documentary for Saudi Television called *al Diriya* (1991). Another Saudi female filmmaker is Haifaa Mansour, who has directed three films, mostly about Saudi social problems. One of her films received a special mention at the 2004 Rotterdam Film Festival (Hammond 2007, 140).

Other Gulf states have entered the film industry, although they lack the necessary film talents. For instance, Abu Dhabi Media Corporation dedicated one billion dollars to producing Arab and international films through the production company Imagination, in an attempt to promote a new industry and lessen dependence on the oil industry. Abu Dhabi wants to become a regional and international centre for filmmaking and therefore it also introduced its Middle East Film Festival in 2007. These efforts addressed Emirati youths who are encouraged to access the film industry and to join the contest "Films from Emirates," which urges native youths to produce feature, documentary and animated films. A number of scholarships to learn film production are also available. Some of the films address local problems, such as one written by the Emirati woman Aliya Ashamsy, about an Emirati woman who managed to penetrate the labor market and fulfill her dream of becoming an engineer. To connect filmmaking students in Abu Dhabi with film internationally, a film academy was built in Abu Dhabi, New York-Abu Dhabi Academy, which is a cooperative venture between Abu Dhabi Culture and Heritage Organization and New York Film Academy (Adousry 2008).

A number of regional film festivals have attracted filmmakers to showcase their work and ensure their exposure regionally. Among the most prestigious is the annual Cairo International Film Festival, held since 1976, and the Carthage Film Festival, held every other year since 1966 in Tunisia. Recently, the United Arab Emirates launched Dubai International Film Festival in 2004. Its fifth edition (2008) was attended by a number of international stars, such as Goldie Hawn and Salma Hayek. The recent encouragement in and by rich Gulf cities such as Dubai to young people to enter the field has attracted many youths from the whole Gulf region to create amateur productions to show in the youth contests, whether in Dubai or Saudi Arabia.

In Oman, film theatres were launched in the 1970s with Oman Arab Cinema Company launching City Cinema Ruwi in 1971, which is the largest theatre in Oman. In 2002, the company opened a modern cinema complex with a capacity of 640 seats (Film City Oman). In Bahrain, a Bahraini company set up in 1968 owned the six movie theatres in the country and has a monopoly on film imports, of which the majority were Indian (Cinematech Haddad).[1] This could be due to the fact that Indian and Southeast Asian expatriates form a significant part of the workforce and population in the Gulf States.

Documentary films: another story

Documentary production is not new. It dates back to 1924 in Egypt and was a means of documenting government development projects and informing the public about them. This role was particularly important during the 1967 and 1973 wars. Thus, most of the documentaries of this era were produced by the public sector rather than by private sector and independent filmmakers (Al-Hadidi 1982, 13–75). Arab states do offer support for documentaries, albeit sporadically, such as the support announced during the festivities of Damascus as Cultural City 2008, which is part of the Annual Arab Culture Capital initiative launched in 1982, and organized by UNESCO. The Syrian young filmmakers and literary talents were called to submit proposals for short documentaries as well as fiction and short plays.

Documentaries are regarded as a tool with which to debate and critique sociopolitical problems. For instance, Palestinian documentarists have found in filmmaking and creativity a new means to express Palestinian daily life, particularly in the occupied territories, in an attempt to offset what they see as distortion of their image in Western media (Burwell 2003, 33). Renowned among these documentarists is Mai Masri, a Palestinian-American filmmaker who directed several documentaries about Palestinian refugee children, and whose work has gained international recognition. One of her films is *Ahlam al Manfa* or *Frontiers of Dreams and Fears* (2001), about two Palestinian girls in different refugee camps who manage, despite the distance, to communicate and develop a unique friendship.

Moreover, the demand for TV documentaries has grown remarkably with the explosion of the numbers of satellite and terrestrial channels available to Arab audiences within and outside the region. The Arab Media Outlook report released in 2007 (Arab Media Outlook 2007) estimates that there are around 500 pan-Arab satellite channels, most of them managed by private corporations. Of these, it is estimated that news channels constitute approximately 22 channels, while the majority of the remainder are music and entertainment channels.[2] (Also, new agencies such as Ramattan News Agency help increase the demand for political documentaries.[3]

According to Mohamed Hashem, founder of Beirut DocDays festival, "Arab television stations were purchasing foreign documentaries to fill up their broadcasting slots . . . but now all that has changed. Today, stations like Al Jazeera and Al Arabiya produce their own programs."[4]

For example, the MBC group which owns Al Arabiya has set up O3 Production Company to produce documentaries for Al Arabiya as well as MBC. It is said that during its first year of operation, O3 managed to shoot over 60 hours of documentary material on current political issues. The production director of its doc film department, Mohamed Soueid, once said, "Since 9/11 we have been increasingly looking at the relationships between people in the Arab and Western worlds as well as the debate on terrorism[5]". Since 2007, the O3 Production Company has sponsored an annual competition to submit proposals for documentaries to be funded and "supervised" by the company and broadcast on Al Arabiya. In its 2008 competition, the company states its willingness to help "Arab documentary filmmakers – and those who don't have previous experience in documentary filmmaking achieve their first short production and to air it on its screen."[6] Also, the competition targeted Arab professional filmmakers who were invited to submit proposals for co-production with international broadcasters, production houses, and international NGOs. Such competitions are open to Arab filmmakers and journalists but are usually confined to reportage-style documentaries shot within four days and limited to 15–20 minutes.[7]

In addition, Al Jazeera launched its specialized Documentary Channel in 2007 to "become a leader in the field" focusing on political themes of importance to Arab audiences.[8] Examples of such documentaries include a film on life in the Jewish state (*Israel from the Inside*) and another on the Druze community in Lebanon. The channel is said to produce approximately 10 percent of its production locally and to import the rest.

Although the market for documentary films is expanding, particularly among production companies in the Gulf States, there is little interest among those companies in financially supporting educational/training programs for aspirant filmmakers. Also, independent Arab filmmakers see as an obstacle the current demand for films on political themes dictated by each channel's political agenda and ideology. Direct intervention of the production companies in the content of documentaries is not welcomed. The only option, then, for such filmmakers is to "look abroad for opportunities."[9] There is a strong demand for Arab documentaries in international festivals.

In summary, the independent Arab documentary industry is relatively new. Most of those produced used to "consist of interviews that are illustrated with random images."[10] Now, the documentary industry is said to be booming, because, as the Jordanian documentarist Sawsan Darwaza said,

> documentaries ... [are] the more democratic way of keeping records of modern history from the point of view of the people and not by the political regimes. This is also related to the less expensive and more accessible equip-

ment and cameras that are more available for young directors, professionals and documentaries. And probably that is why it has become a trend, along with the online short documentaries available on the internet.[11]

Most documentary themes, however, still centre on political issues and the documentarists could get themselves in trouble if they cross the red line with regards to religion, politics, or sexual orientation.[12]

Role of cinema in the pan-Arab public sphere

Following their independence, Arab states, in particular Egypt where the film industry flourished, focused on producing films that exalted their ideals of pan-Arabism and unity. For instance, the historical film *Saladin Victorious* was produced in 1963 by Youssef Chahine as propaganda for Nasser's regime through the analogy between Nasser and Saladin, who is regarded as the Arab hero against European crusades. Like Saladin, Nasser wanted to be seen as the Arab leader who was capable of unifying Arabs and defeating the Western colonial powers. This was apparent in the recurring slogans uttered by Saladin in the film, such as "Religion is for God, the Nation for all" or "there can be no victory without unity" (Halim 1992, 79).

Some films with political overtones were either banned or limited in some Arab countries. In 1971, the Egyptian Tawfik Saleh had directed *Al-Mukhaduun* or *The Dupes*, which is an adaptation of Ghassan Kanafani's novella *Men in the Sun*, but the film was limited in Syria where it was produced, and banned in Egypt and Iraq (Rosen 1989, 35). The film tells the story of three Palestinian men from three different generations who come together with a common goal of escaping poverty and finding jobs in Kuwait. The Palestinian issue has also been the theme of numerous Egyptian and Lebanese films. In fact, a group of Palestinian intellectuals formed a Palestinian Film Group in the early 1970s with the aim of producing films by creative Palestinians that supported the Palestinian cause. Many Palestinian filmmakers live in exile, so several of them would not be able to travel to Israel; they might have arranged for a foreign crew to shoot in Israel and the Palestinian territories (Neidhardt 2005, 207). The Palestinian territories have not had any film school but Palestinians have set up a Film Foundation following the Al Aqsa Intifada in 2000 to co-produce with foreign institutions short films and documentaries about daily life in the region (Hillabuer 2005, 196).

Overall, taboo themes in Arab cinema were religion and sex (Shafik 2007, 34), but these taboos have been challenged lately, particularly by daring female directors and actresses. In fact, female artists in the early twentieth century in

Egypt were either Jews or Syrian Christians and the entertainment profession had a bad reputation. The cinema industry, however, improved the image of female entertainers, paving the way for more women to enter this profession (Fahim 2008). To attract families to the movie theatres, a positive image of Arab and Egyptian women was enforced in the 1950s and 1960s, particularly in works of the Egyptian actress Faten Hamama, known as the Lady of the Arab Screen, through a series of films that gained her broad public respect (Morgan 2005, 4). The commercial cinemas of the 1980s and early 1990s, however, showed promiscuous women characters, compelling a wave of veiling among prominent Egyptian actresses who denounced the *haram* cinema business and offered to wear the veil and withdraw from public life (Morgan 2005, 4).

A new trend of films released over the past decade, called *cinema nazifa* or *clean cinema,* avoided offences against cultural and religious sensibilities (Morgan 2005, 4). Although several recent films have been, using this term, "clean," there were others whose plot and characterization challenge religious and social taboos. One recent example is the Egyptian *Sahar El-Layali* or *Sleepless Nights* (2002) which stirred a hot debate in Egypt. It features four couples wrestling with problems of adultery and sexual dissatisfaction, in a society that exalted the image of mothers and wives as devoted to their husbands and families rather than women seeking sexual pleasure (Morgan 2005, 5). Another example is *Baheb El-Seema* or *I Love Cinema* (2004). This film tells the story of a conservative Coptic man whose wife, disheartened by her husband's chastity, becomes involved in an affair. The film caused demonstrations among the Coptic minority of Egypt, and a series of lawsuits against the director and scriptwriter, who are both Copts (5). The Egyptian female director Inas el Degheidi stands behind several daring films that deal with sensitive social issues such as AIDS, homosexuality, and virginity. Her film *Muzakarrat Murahiqa* or *Diary of a Teenage Girl* (2001) stirred a huge debate for presenting an Egyptian teenager's rebellion against the notion of virginity as a prerequisite for marriage.

Two recent Algerian films portray Algerian women breaking social restrictions; these are *Le Harem de Mme Osmane* (2000) and *Viva Laldjérie* (2004) by Nadir Monknèche. This second film dared to show an Algerian woman completely naked (Aberrezak 2007, 348). Also, the Lebanese director Nadine Labaki's film *Caramel* (2008) was a co-production with France. It featured five women who meet regularly in a beauty salon, and exchange intimate conversations about men and sex. Labaki justified the film's daring theme by the double standards in modern Arab societies, or as she put it,

> I live in a country that is very modern and exposed to Western culture, and at the same time I'm confused between this culture and the weight of tradition,

religion, education and there's always a lot of self-censorship, self-control. I'm a little bit lost between these two things, and I don't know who I am exactly. I looked around me and felt that all women around me were feeling the same thing, and that's why I decided to write this film, to talk about women now in Lebanon and what they are facing, and this contradiction between East and West and how we are trying to find our own identity.[13]

Back in the early 1990s, more than 20 Egyptian actresses wore the veil and left the industry to devote themselves to religious piety, but this trend slowed down after 1994, particularly with the government's slam on Islamist movements (Shafik 2001, 716). In Morocco, Islamist protests surrounded the Moroccan director Abdel Qader Laqtaa's films, such as *Al Hub fi al Dar Al Bayda* or *Love in Casablanca* (1991) and *Dam al Akhar* or *Blood of the Other* (1995) for scenes of lovemaking. In fact, some Egyptian films, such as Yousef Chahine's *al Muhagir* or *The Emigrant* (1995), were banned in Morocco for daring to depict the prophet Joseph (Hammond 2007, 143). On the other hand, a series of Egyptian films were launched in the 1990s with the apparent backing of the Egyptian government to depict a negative picture of the fundamentalists. Such films include *Al Irhabi* or *The Terrorist* and *Al Irhab wa el Kabab* or *Terrorism and Kebab* (1992) both starring the popular Egyptian actor Adel Imam.

Moreover, the recent political turmoil in the region, beginning with Iraq's invasion of Kuwait, the economic restrictions on Iraq, and the 2003 Iraq War has resulted in a wave of films critiquing the present political situation and outlining the Arab stance toward Israel and America. One example is the Egyptian star Nadia Al Guindi's *48 Hours in Israel* (1998). This film tells the story of an Egyptian lady who outwits an Israeli secret agent. Another example is *Laylat Suqut Baghdad* or *The Night Baghdad Fell* (2006), which was inspired by the Iraq War and which depicts an Egyptian schoolmaster's fear that the USA would invade Egypt following the fall of Baghdad. Some of the scenes drew on the Abu Ghreib prison scandal presenting "an allegory of impotence of a subordinated people in the face of a dominant imperial power" (Shafik 2007, 95). The Egyptian star Adel Imam starred in the popular movie *el Sifara fil Emara* or *The Embassy Is in the Building* (2005), depicting an Egyptian womanizer who returns from a long working life in the rich Gulf States, to find that the Israeli Embassy has opened its doors next door to his apartment. Imam's character finds it hard to lead a normal life when he's constantly subjected to body searching and questioning, and when he rebels, he becomes a national hero. The film comically critiques the Egyptian-Israeli normalization and ends with Imam leading a large demonstration against Israel's policy toward the Palestinians.

Other films show Arabs as hard to be spoiled by Western influences. For instance, Adel Imam featured in a successful blockbuster, *Danish Experiment* (2003). It tells the story of a Danish woman (perhaps an allegory of the West) who comes to Egypt to improve sex education and causes major chaos in the Minister's house where she stays, and where the Minister and his four sons are lured by her beauty. The young Egyptian comedian Mohamed Heniedi has been featured in other films that have a similar moral, such as *Saidi fi al Gamaa Al Amerikiya* or *An Upper Egyptian at the American University* (1998) which was a huge box-office success, showing that upper-class Egyptians have maintained their nationalist spirit (Hammond 2007, 140). Another one, *Hammam in Amsterdam* (1999), was also a hit, depicting a young Egyptian man pursuing the dream of many of his compatriots of immigrating to Europe. Heniedi managed to depict the native Egyptian values "uncorrupted by the Americanization of Egypt" or the modernization and privatization that have emerged since the 1970s (Hammond 2007, 151).

On the other hand, there are dozens of Arab filmmakers who reside and work in Europe. For many of them, the challenge is not necessarily to keep the native culture intact but to reconcile their native roots with the values of their host societies. Algerian émigré filmmakers in France have used film as a means to debate issues in their native Algeria as well as in their French home. Among such filmmakers are Merzak Allouache, Abdelkarim Bahloul, Okacha Touita, and Mahmud Zemmouri, whose works manifest the way émigré filmmakers negotiate their relationship to their native country and their new diasporic identity (Higbee 2007). Moreover, the Algerian female director Yamina Benguigui, a second-generation French-Arab, has launched her documentary *Mémoires des Immigrés, l'héritage maghrébin* or *Memories of the Immigrants* in 1997, giving a voice to the first generation of both male and female North African immigrants. She also made a feature film, *Inch'allah Dimanche* or *God Willing Tomorrow* (2001), which tackled the difficulty first-generation women had in adapting to life in France (Sutherland 2007, 12). Some diasporic filmmakers feel drawn to their home country's affairs when in Diaspora, such as the Lebanese-French Borhane Alaouie who once said, "The more time I spend in France, the more I feel myself preoccupied by the problems of Lebanon" (cited in Rosen 1989, 36).

Conclusion

The cinema developed as a profitable business, particularly in Egypt up to the 1970s, when the industry was privatized and faced a series of economic hurdles. During the 1980s, the cinema industry had to endure the harsh competition of video for distribution in Gulf markets, particularly Saudi Arabia, and since the 1990s, the competition has become even fiercer with the advent of satellite television, whose productions can now feature in major film theatres. However, there is a revived interest in the cinema as an art and an industry; for instance, Emirates and Saudi Arabia have produced their own films and encouraged their native talents to penetrate this industry as part of the modernist image of these Gulf States. In general, the cinema has contributed to the breaking of social taboos, perhaps more than any other medium. This may be because the cinema, at least in Egypt and Lebanon, is privatized – unlike TV, which is largely under the direct supervision of the Arab governments.

The future prospects for the cinema industry point to continuous growth but on new premises. The lack of sufficient funding may drive a push for more joint productions, not only among regional producers but also involving international funders, particularly from Europe. This could also affect the themes addressed in future films, as more daring themes could be tackled. Although the Arab regimes can, in theory, impose new strict regulations and censorship to restrict the freedom of filmmakers, this power is now challenged by the globalization of the medium, which has both positive and negative impacts on Arab cinema.

On the positive side, the films are now shown in international film and documentary festivals, which encourages filmmakers, particularly the new generation, to present new and daring productions in the context of such gatherings. Also, the Arab Diaspora communities form new markets for the Arab film industry abroad as well as a breeding ground for a new generation of filmmakers who grew up in these communities. On the negative side, the cinema industry remains in the hands of a few players with significant financial resources, making it difficult for newcomers to access the industry, thereby compelling many of them to seek funds from abroad when producing feature or documentary films. Finally, the fierce competition from satellite television will only add more pressure on feature film production, which makes film production a financially risky business, and makes joint production one crucial means of securing enough funds for such production.

Notes

1 http://www.yabeyrouth.com/pages/index3401.htm
2 For an overview of these channels, see ASBU tables, http://www.asbu.net/www/ar/directdoc.asp?docid=117
3 Source: http://english.ramattan.net/Profile.aspx

4 www.qantara.de/webcom/how_article.php/c_310/_nr-153/ihtml
5 www.qantara.de/webcom/how_article.php/c_310/_nr-153/ihtml
6 www.o3productions.com/arabiya08.htm
7 www.o3productions.com/arabiya08.htm
8 http://english.aljazeera.net/documentary/2007/02/200852519224757854.html
9 www.qantara.de/webcom/how_article.php/c_310/_nr-153/ihtml
10 www.qantara.de/webcom/how_article.php/c_310/_nr-153/ihtml
11 www.onculture.eu/story.aspx?s_id=193
12 www.onculture.eu/story.aspx?s_id=193
13 Source: *Filmmaker Magazine*, 1 February 2008, http://www.filmmakermaga-zine.com/directorinterviews/2008/02/nadine-labaki-caramel.php (accessed on 23 April 2009).

7   Arab Internet

Schizophrenic Trilogy

Khalil Rinnawi

We firmly believe that technology adoption from a governmental, social and economic point of view is essential to the growth and stability of the Jordanian economy and society. This agreement with Microsoft is a step towards our vision to transform Jordan into a knowledge-based technology center.

King Abdallah of Jordan, in "Jordan Wants to Be Tech Mecca," *Wired News*, March 6, 2000.

The city is already imposing censorship on the internet. This is to be praised because we are not supposed to leave the internet open for all because there are immoral websites which violate the rights of Muslims to apply the rules of their religion.

Saleh Ben Abdullah Al-Azlz, manager of King Abdul Aziz City for Science and Technology.

The two quotations that open this chapter reflect the schizophrenic situation of the internet in the Arab world. On the one hand, Arab governments are attempting to be current in the field of telecommunications and the internet. On the other hand, they have restrained, and are still restraining, the development of the internet in their countries. Thus, they deal with the internet in an ambivalent way. At the same time that they are aware of its importance to their economic development and its vitality in attracting foreign investments, they perceive it as a factor that affects the political and social stability of their countries. Governments who use Western cultural imperialism as a reason for their restrictions take pains to control this information highway: through governmental control on suppliers, limiting the number of internet suppliers, using filtering and control software, establishing supervision and controlling bodies on internet use, as well as revising regulations to control access to the internet. These techniques, which differ from one country to another, turn the internet, like traditional media, into a public sphere subject to the usual censorship and sanctions.

Surveys from 2009 on the internet, which has been evolving for the past two decades, estimate the number of users around the world to be more than 1.9 billion; that is, 28.7 percent of the world's population are internet users, in comparison to 1997 estimates of 70 million – an 18-fold increase (according to the latest statistics from the website internetworldstats.com).

The most wired Middle Eastern countries are Bahrain (88 percent) and UAE (75.9 percent), as the largest number of internet accounts in the region is in Iran (33,200,000 accounts) (internetworldstates.com). However, the rest of the Arab countries are far behind the other non-Arab countries such as Israel, Turkey, and Iran.

As we see from Table 9, the percentage of the world's population that is Arab was 4.87 percent in June 2010; yet Arabs represent only 3.32 percent of the total number of internet users.

The real number of internet users in the Arab world could be higher than these figures, as most of the internet users in this region have access through public computers in universities, internet cafes or collective usage, and not through private accounts. Despite the rapid and huge penetration rates of the internet in Arab societies, which is continuing to rise, the percentage of internet users ranks as one of the lowest in the world, except for the Arab Gulf countries where it is relatively high (around 30 percent and more). However, in the rest of the Arab countries it does not exceed 10 percent of the general population.

Why, with such a young population, is the Arab world still lagging behind when it comes to the digital revolution? Several factors, such as the limited knowledge of the English language, the high cost of IT facilities, problematic media infrastructure, and limited access in rural areas to the internet, all contribute to restricting the spread of the internet and keeping it as a luxury available to specific social groups and classes in Arab societies, namely, highly skilled professionals from the middle and upper social classes.

Despite these figures we cannot ignore the importance of the Internet as an information source and research instrument in the Arab world, because of its interactive nature, which shapes the collective identity and community solidarity – and also because of its potential as a social and political power, both for religious fundamentalist and human rights groups, which may indeed push for changes in the Arab world. The outcome was reflected in the recent rapid growth of this medium among Arab societies relative to other parts of the world, and the world average growth, as can be seen in Table 9. This shows that the growth in internet use in the Arab world was 2170 percent between 2000 and 2010, while the growth in the rest of the world was only around 357 percent.

This chapter addresses the emergence of the internet and its current level of penetration and use in Arab societies. The chapter also discusses the main obstacles facing the diffusion of this medium in this part of the world, and

Table 9. Internet users in the Arab world and in the World

World Region	Population (2009 Est.)	% Pop. of World	Internet Users, June/2010	% Population (Penetration)	User Growth (2000–2010)	% Users of World
Arab World Total	332,171,543	4.87%	65,134,200	19.6%	2170%	3.32%
Rest of the World	6,513,438,417	95.13%	1,901,380,616	29.2%	357%	96.68%
World Total	6,845,609,960	100.0%	1,966,514,816	28.7%	467%	100.0%

NOTES: (1) Internet Usage and Population Statistics for the Middle East were updated as of June 30, 2010. (2) Population numbers are based on data contained in the US Census Bureau (3) Data on this site may be cited, giving due credit and establishing an active link back to InternetWorldStats. com. Copyright © 2010, Miniwatts Marketing Group. All rights reserved.

the use of the internet as a virtual public sphere, examining use patterns and internet culture in this region. The chapter elaborates on the reaction of the Arab governments and regimes to this medium and its spread through internet cafés.

Internet in the Arab world

The first internet connections in the region date back to the early 1990s, when it was only available in government offices, universities, and research institutes. With the passing of time, its use started to grow and today there is public access to the internet by local suppliers in all Arab countries.

Tunisia was the first Arab country to link to the Internet (1991). However, it only became widely used from 1996, when the main provider, the Tunisian Agency for Internet, was established to administer and market internet services and technology and to monitor exchange of information (Eid 2006). Tunisia attempted to spread technology in a manner that would attract foreign investment. Internet services are done via 12 providers; these include 7 that provide public institutions and agencies, and 5 private companies providing the service to the wider market.[1] Internet services are provided using dial-up and DSL lines. According to statistics from June 2010, the number of users reached 3.6 million, which is 34 percent of the total Tunisian population, while the growth in usage between 2000 and 2010 was 3,500 percent. Finally, there is a large difference between the number of internet users and websites browsed because Tunisian internet users prefer to use foreign email accounts to avoid government censorship.

Egypt followed Tunisia by linking to the Internet in late 1993. This was done by the Information and Decision Making Support Center affiliated to the Egyptian Cabinet. At the beginning of 1997, the Center started to privatize internet services by licensing Internet Service Providers (ISPs). Following this, these ISPs sold the service to other clients. In 1997, the Egyptian market had 16 private ISPs connected with each other via the Telecom Egypt web portals. The Government launched the ADSL service in May 2004, through an initiative established by seven companies.[2] With these huge efforts, the number of internet users has increased significantly. The current number of users in Egypt is just over 17 million, which is 21 percent of the total population, while the usage growth was 3,691 percent between 2000 and 2010. All receive the service through 211 ISPs; Link and TEData[3] are the largest in the Egyptian telecommunications field.

Algeria got internet service in 1993 via the state-owned CERIST research center. Five years later, the monopoly of the service provision by the state ended, and private-sector companies were allowed to provide services. By 2000 there were 18 private service providers (Eid 2006). However, the telecommunication market is still dominated by the Algeria Telecom Company, the state-owned parent company that provides telecommunication services in Algeria. One of the major obstacles to the widespread use of the internet in Algeria is this monopoly held by the Algeria Telecom Company. In 2005, however, two private companies acquired a license to construct a terrestrial phone line network and also to launch an ADSL service; the monopoly has ended. As of June 2010 there were some 4.7 million internet users in Algeria, which is 13.6 percent of the entire population. The growth in users was 9,300 percent between 2000 and 2008. Despite the liberalization of the telecommunication sector, internet services and use are still under the level of other neighboring countries.

United Arab Emirates (UAE) next connected to the internet through the Etisalat Company, which until 2006 had a monopoly over telecommunication services in the UAE.[4] In that year, another national internet service provider (DU) was launched to boost diversity in the national telecommunications market. The UAE was considered the first Arab country in the spread of the internet in the level of users as well as infrastructure. Besides corporate and commercial websites, which are numerous and of high quality, all government offices maintain sophisticated websites in Arabic and English. In order to attract local and foreign investment in the field of information technology (IT), the UAE has also established an internet city, one of only two in the Arab world. The 2007–2008 Human Development Report issued by the UNDP ranks the UAE at the top of all Arab countries in internet access, with 308 users per every 1,000 people (Hancock 2008). According to statistics from June 2010, the current number of internet users in the UAE is nearly 3.8 million, which is over 75 percent of the total population – the second highest rate in the Arab world. The increase in usage was 414 percent between 2000 and 2010.

Jordan and Sudan connected to the internet in 1994. Since the internet became available to the public in Jordan, it has had strong backing from the Kingdom's authorities. The service was provided by the Public Institution for Wireless Communications, which was turned into a state-owned company by 1997 and was operating on a commercial basis under the name of the Jordan Communication Company. Until 2004, it was the only company offering national and local telecommunication services. Then the Government sold its shares to France Telecom which became the dominant player in the communication sector in Jordan (Middle East Online, 2005). These steps have contributed to an increase in the number of internet users from 127,000 in 2000 to 630,000 in 2004, a total of 117 users per 1000 citizens; this is a high rate in comparison to other Arab countries.[5] Currently many companies provide internet connection services. This rapid development has led Jordan to stand among the best Arab countries in this field. According to statistics from June 2010, there are over 1.7 million internet users, 27 percent of the total population, with a growth in usage of 1,268 percent between 2000 and 2010.

Nineteen ninety four was also the year when the Internet first entered the Sudan; prior to that, the Sudanese Government dominated the telecommunications sector. However, this ended when the State announced the foundation of the National Telecommunication Corporation and its intention to open the telecommunication market to the private sector.[6] In addition to these measures, the state-owned Public Wire and Wireless Telecommunication Corporation was turned into a joint-stock private company known as SudaTel, which constructed a new telecommunication network (Bab Website, 2005). Afterward, the construction of the network, SudaNet, a state-owned company was founded to provide internet services in Sudan (Sudanet Website, 2006). SudaNet remained the sole provider in Sudan until 2005 when its monopoly was eliminated for the purposes of decreasing telecommunication costs, increasing the rate of development in the field of IT, and to narrow the digital divide between rural and urban areas (Maktoob Moheet Network, 2007). Currently there are six companies providing internet services in Sudan. By June 2010 there were around 4.2 million users in Sudan, which is 10 percent of the total population. The rate of usage growth was 13,900 percent between 2000 and 2010. These are low in comparison with regional or global usage and adoption rates.

Bahrain connected to the internet in 1995. The sole Bahraini ISP is Bahrain Telecom, or Batelco, a state-owned and -operated company. Despite the fact that in 2002 a decision was passed to free the market, Batelco is still the only Bahraini ISP. The monopoly it enjoys has generated criticism, especially concerning the high prices of internet services, which has encouraged some subscribers to establish a specialized site to protest against the company's policies (Batelco 2007). This monopoly is considered the main obstacle to increasing internet usage in Bahrain. Although Batelco offers ADSL, it is very expensive. Press reports say that the reason for the policy is to limit internet use because of the fear of political empowerment (Asheihaby 2005). By June 2010, there were 649,300 internet users in Bahrain, which was 88 percent of the total population, which is the highest percentage in the Arab world and the Middle East. The usage has grown by 1,523 percent between 2000 and 2010.

Morocco also first connected to the internet in 1995. Initially there were few users, but this changed when King Muhammad VI came to power in 1999, declaring his support for a new educational decade through 2008, during which all schools would connect to the internet (Browna 2006). The main reason for this newfound importance was to attract foreign investment. The Morocco Communication Company, supplier of internet services, dominates the market in Morocco. The company was fully government-owned until 2000, when a resolution privatizing it was issued. The market changed enormously in 2006 when the Mid Tel Company won a license for fixed phone service, which means it is providing services which Morocco Communication had monopolized (Bozbani 2006). Official statistics from June 2010 estimated there to be nearly 10.5 million users, which is 33 percent of the total population, and the growth in usage was 10,342 percent between 2000 and 2010.

Yemen, characterized by miserable economic circumstances, started using the internet in September 1996, when it was well accepted in spite of limited access due to the high cost of computers, modems, and subscriptions. Yemen has two ISPs, Tele-Yemen and Yemen Net. Both numbers of users and rate of growth in Yemen are much lower than in other states in the region. The social and economic situation does not allow for a massive increase in the number of clients.[7] At the beginning of 2006, due to the lack of infrastructure, Yemen only had some 110,000 internet subscriptions (El-Bahry 2007a). Until recently, when Tele-Yemen launched an ADSL service, only dial-up or ISDN service was available. Despite the great advantages ADSL offers Yemeni citizens, the economic situation means that only very few are able to take advantage of it; there are less than 2,000 ADSL service subscribers (El-Bahry 2007). Therefore the current number of internet users in Yemen is only 420,000, which is only 1.8 percent of the population, while the growth in usage was 2,700 percent between 2000 and 2010. Furthermore, the economic situation also prevents Yemenis from spending long periods of time engaged in activities on the Web, which significantly limits the impact of the internet on its political and social life.

Oman, Qatar, Kuwait, Saudi Arabia and Syria: these nations were connected to the Internet in 1997. Omani people could first access the internet in the beginning of that year; that sector is dominated by the Oman Tel Company, which is a closed joint-stock company wholly owned by the government. The Sultanate of Oman is striving to catch up with modern telecommunications through its ambitious e-Government project, which led to a rise in internet use. Despite the rapid rise, Oman still has relatively few users in comparison to other countries in the region. The monopoly of internet services, high prices, and technical problems have deeply affected the spread of the service and the number of users there. As a result, the June 2010 number of internet users in Oman is over 1.2 million, which is 47 percent of the total population, while growth was at 1,274 percent between 2000 and 2010.

Internet services have also been available in Qatar since 1997. This nation now has one of the best telecommunication infrastructures in the world. The private Q-Tel company controls the Qatari telecommunications market (Reporters without Borders, 2006). It provides both terrestrial and cellular phone services in addition to providing an internet service through its affiliate company, Internet Qatar.[8] Q-Tel, which has a monopoly until 2013 (*Al-Watan* 2005), provides a wide range of services, including ADSL and Wi-Fi. It also exploits its market position and charges very high fees. Despite the fact that Q-Tel is nominally a private company, its chairman is a member of the royal family. This means that the state is still able to control the internet. In 2003 there were some 70,000 internet users (Reporters without Borders 2006), though this number has more than doubled since then, and at the end of 2006 it stood at some 165,000 users.[9] According to 2010 statistics, there were 436,000 internet users in Qatar, which is nearly 52 percent of the total population, and growth in use was 1,353 percent between 2000 and 2008.

Kuwait, at the beginning of 1997, privatized the telecommunication sector to provide internet services. The most prominent among these are Quality Net and Fast Telecommunication Company. These companies provide a wide range of service and products including dial-up service, leased lines, ADSL, and prepaid cards.[10] Because of the extensive telecommunication structure, high level of literacy and economic prosperity in Kuwait, access to the internet is relatively easy. Internet services are provided by a number of private companies. Therefore, the number of internet users in Kuwait has grown rapidly: from 150,000 in December 2000 to some 600,000 in March 2006 (Internet World Statistics Website). Based on June 2010 data, there were 1.1 million internet users in Kuwait, which is over 39 percent of the total population, and growth in user numbers was 633 percent between 2000 and 2010. The 2007–2008 Human Development Report issued by the UNDP put Kuwait second among the Arab countries in internet use during that year, with 276 users per 1,000 people (Hancock 2008).

Saudi Arabia has been connected to the internet since 1997, but due to the prevalent skeptical view toward all things Western, it took a long time to gain acceptance. It was not broadly available in the Kingdom until December

1998, when individual Saudis for the first time were able to acquire internet access accounts within the Kingdom. This made it one of the last Arab countries to gain access, despite its enormous financial resources. For more than five years, King Abdul Aziz City was, with the help of the Saudi Telecommunications Company, the authority responsible for the internet; it also provided external telecommunication lines through the city. This situation continued until 2004, when the Telecommunications Company had the responsibility for licensing ISPs; supervising the filtering of the service; implementing security controls; and registering Saudi domains. Despite the increasing importance of e-mail and information access to the business community, the Kingdom was slow to open up access because of concerns about unsuitable material being available to ordinary citizens. As a result all Saudi connections are routed through a single government-controlled server, and they are filtered. Despite the sustained increase in users, the complaints of the citizens are endless because of increasing subscription prices, bad service, and weak technical support. Technical problems and social blockades suffered by users in Saudi Arabia have not prevented them from using the internet or benefiting from it. The June 2010 number of internet users in Saudi Arabia was 9.8 million, which is 38 percent of the total population, while growth in usage was 4,800 percent between 2000 and 2008.

Syria officially began operating connections to the internet in July 2000, shortly after the passing of President Hafez Al Assad and the takeover of his son Bashar, who served as Chair of the Syrian Computer Society, and had often advocated public access to the internet. Before that, internet connectivity was illegal in the country, although it had been available since 1997. The Public Telecommunications Foundation has exclusive rights to provide wire and wireless services all over Syria,[11] where the first two ISPs still dominate the market. They are the Public Telecommunications Foundation and the Syrian Information Technology Association, both of which are run by the state. In the first two years after it became legal, use of the internet increased drastically from a mere 30,000 users in 2000 to 226,000 users in 2002 (UNDP, 2002, 2004). By the end of 2004 there were some 800,000 internet users.[12] These figures are low, indicating the weakness of the spread of the service in comparison with other countries in the region. Security forces objected to internet use from the very beginning, and this resistance to it has slowed its spread (Marmarita Forum, 2006). Some of these restrictions have been lifted during the last few years. In 2005, a private service provider appeared, Aya Company, followed by the Computer Engineering Company (Bafel, 2006). Although the state is attempting to develop the telecommunication sector and increase access, it is doing so without any attempt to liberate the market itself. According to statistics from June 2010, there are 3.9 million internet users in Syria, which is almost 18 percent of the total population. The growth in usage was 13,016 percent from 2000 to 2008.

Libya has had access to internet services since 1998. The state-owned Libya Telecom and Technology company, founded in 1999, has a monopoly over both telecom and internet services. Although this has changed recently, the monopoly on internet services remains. The state still fully controls the company. This is due largely to the role played by Mohamed Gaddafi, the son of the Libyan President,[13] who is able to extend enormous control over the telecommunication sector. According to HRinfo's statistics from the beginning of 2006, there were almost one million users in Libya (Arabic Network for Human Rights Information, 2004). June 2010 statistics record 353,900 users, over 5 percent of the population. The percentage increase from 2000 was 3, 439 percent.

Palestine, Iraq, Lebanon: These three countries can be considered special cases. Each has unique circumstances that inflect the internet realm in their countries. The internet began operating in Palestine in late 1990s under the semi-regime of the Palestinian National Authority (PNA) after the Oslo Accord. By 2001 there were 13 companies providing internet services. The Palestinian National Authority for the Internet (PNAI) was founded in 2005 to administer internet services. Telecommunication service in Palestine is expensive in comparison to neighboring countries. The main reason for this is the relationship between the Palestinian telecommunication company Pal-Tel and the Israeli network, as the Palestinian company has to purchase the service from Israel and then resell it in Palestine.[14] Besides that, there are political problems affecting the telecommunication sector in Palestine. Despite these obstacles, the Palestinian internet market is growing strongly and the Ministry of Information is dominating all (*Al-Ayam* e-newspaper, 2005). Despite the difficulties, the International Telecommunication Union reports that there were up to 160,000 internet users in Palestine in 2004.[15] Based on data from June 2010, there are 356,000 internet users in Palestine, which is 14 percent of the total population, and the growth in usage was 917 percent between 2000 and 2010.

The internet began operating in Iraq in the late 1990s under strict central control under Saddam Hussein. Despite the obstacles and difficulties under the strict regime of Saddam Hussein, internet diffusion continues slowly to increase, especially at the governmental level. At that time individuals were not allowed access to the internet through a private provider; the only permitted access was through public institutions under the regime's control. The situation changed after the fall of Saddam's regime. Although the internet may now be used from private homes, the prices are still so high that the ordinary citizen cannot afford it. Besides that, the political chaos in Iraq has deeply influenced the internet market. There is no official information about the companies who provide private internet service, their relationship with the Ministry of Telecommunication, or the acts and laws regulating their work. Some foreign companies have capitalized on this situation and have established a hold on the satellite dish market and have started to sell internet access service to the flourishing internet café market. The subscription cost of these companies is much higher than the official service provided by the government. However, they are widely used because of the high quality of their devices and regular maintenance (Elwan 2004). The number of internet users in Iraq increased from 21,500 users in 2001 to approximately 325,000 users in 2010. In all cases, these figures show serious weaknesses in the current infrastructure of the Iraqi telecommunications network, which is to be expected due to the current situation.

Lebanon's internet and telecommunications infrastructure was largely built in the early 1990s, as it was rebuilt after the civil war. The Lebanese Ministry of Telecommunication supervises the telecommunication sector and allows free competition. The state only has the right to provide local and international telephone call services. All other services are provided by private companies under the supervision of the Telecommunications Regulatory Authority, which is affiliated with the Ministry of Telecommunications. Lebanon is the only Arab country that did not use the ADSL service before 2006. Now, there are 11 licensed ISPs.[16] The problems faced by internet users in Lebanon are mainly technical and related to the high costs of access, especially in poor areas (Eid 2006). Some small ISPs illegally supply houses with internet connections to get around the high costs of official access (*Al-Mostaqbal*, 2007). Despite these difficulties, the 2007–2008 Human Development Report from the UNDP ranks Lebanon in fifth place with 196 users per every 1000 people (Hancock 2008). According to statistics from June 2010, there are one million internet users in Lebanon, which is 24.2 percent of the total population, and growth in user numbers was 233.3 percent between 2000 and 2010.

The following table sums up the current use of the internet in the Arab world.

From Table 10 we can conclude the following: First, except in Iraq, Lebanon, and Palestine, which are special cases due to political or military crises, the process of the development of the internet in most of the Arab countries was similar. Second, we notice that in most Arab countries the state was the main supplier of internet access, and that the state had that monopoly

Table 10. Arab World Internet Usage and Population Statistics

Arab World	Population (2010 Est.)	Usage, Dec/2000	Usage, June/2010	% Population (Penetration)	% User Growth (2000–2010)	(%) of Table
Bahrain	738,004	40,000	649,300	88.0%	1,523.3	0.99
Iraq	29,671,605	12,500	325,000	1.1%	2,500.0	0.498
Jordan	6,407,085	127,300	1,741,900	27.2%	1,268.3	2.67
Kuwait	2,789,132	150,000	1,100,000	39.4%	633.3	1.68
Lebanon	4,125,247	300,000	1,000,000	24.2%	233.3	1.5
Oman	2,967,717	90,000	1,236,700	41.7%	1,274.1	1.8
Palestine (W.Bnk.)	2,514,845	35,000	356,000	14.2%	917.1	0.54
Qatar	840,926	30,000	436,000	51.8%	1,353.3	0.66
S. Arabia	25,731,776	200,000	9,800,000	38.1%	4,800.0	15.0
Syria	22,198,110	30,000	3,935,000	17.7%	13,016.7	6.0
UAE	4,975,593	735,000	3,777,900	75.9%	414.0	5.8
Yemen	23,495,361	15,000	420,000	1.8%	2,700.0	0.64
Total M. East	126,455,401	1,764,800	24,777,800	15.65%	10,800.0	38.0
Algeria	34,586,184	50,000	4,700,000	13.6%	9,300.0	7.2
Egypt	80,471,869	450,000	17,060,000	21.2%	3,691.1	26.19
Libya	6,461,454	10,000	353,900	5.5%	3,439.0	0.54
Morocco	31,627,428	100,000	10,442,500	33.0%	10,342.5	16.0
Sudan	41,980,182	30,000	4,200,000	10.0%	13,900.0	6.48
Tunisia	10,589,025	100,000	3,600,000	34.0%	3,500.0	5.5
Total AFRICA	205,716,142	740,000	40,356,400	16.95%	5,700.0	61.95
Total A. World	332,171,543	2,504,800	65,134,200	16.45%	2,066.0	100.0

NOTES: (1) Researcher's calculations based on The Middle East and North Africa Statistics which were updated for June 30, 2010. From internetworldstats.com Copyright 2010, © Miniwatts Marketing Group. (2) The demographic (population) numbers are based on data from the US Census Bureau. (2) For growth comparison purposes, the usage data published by ITU for the year 2.000 is furnished. (3) Data may be cited, giving due credit and establishing an active link back to InternetWorld Stats. Copyright © 2010, Miniwatts Marketing Group. All rights reserved.

from the beginning. Only recently have regimes opened the market to private or semi-private suppliers. Third, there is a big difference between the number of internet users and the websites browsed in some countries such as Tunisia, Syria, and Saudi Arabia. This is due to the fact that internet users in these countries prefer to use foreign email accounts to avoid government censorship. Fourth, each ADSL line is used by three people on average. However, in some Arab countries such as Egypt, Morocco, and Lebanon, 10 to 12 people use one line. Egypt, Palestine, and Lebanon witnessed a unique phenomenon in respect to ADSL networks. Some people subscribe to the service and then sub-distribute it to others (neighbors participate in paying the cost of one line and then distribute sub-lines to each other). This has made it harder to determine the number of ADSL service users.[17] Moreover, the real figures for internet users in the Arab world are likely much higher than those shown here, since most have access through public computers, universities, internet cafes, or collective users, and not through private accounts.

Finally, while estimates of the number of internet accounts vary from source to source, there is no doubt that in the last few years, especially in 2007, there has been an exponential growth in the numbers of Arab citizens and businesspeople online. Some countries have doubled the number of accounts in the course of one year. However, the internet remains the province of the elites – Egyptian *fellahin* and Yemeni mountaineers are unlikely to have their own web pages soon – and English and French remain more common than Arabic as the linguistic code of communication.

Obstacles to internet diffusion in the Arab world

Despite the rapid spread of the internet in the Arab world, especially in the last few years, it has been slow to plunge into the traffic on the information superhighway for the following reasons:

Political and cultural censorship: As mentioned above, the main obstacle facing the widespread use of telecommunications in general, and the internet in particular, comes from political and socio-religious elites. Formal and informal regulations prohibit uncontrolled free expression (Rinnawi 2003; Abdulla 2007). This political and cultural censorship is used by governments to minimize the effects of this global and interactive medium that challenges the existing political rules. The political public sphere is controlled, and religious and traditional values are kept intact.

Expense: The second reason is the high cost of internet use relative to the economics of daily life in most of the Arab countries. Some researchers argue that the high costs of internet services in the Arab world are one way of controlling internet use in some Arab countries (Eid 2007). For instance, although Batelco in Bahrain offers ADSL, it only does so at a very high cost. Press reports say that the reason for the policy is to limit internet use because of the fear of its political empowerment (Asheihaby 2007). Despite the already relatively high cost of telecommunication services in Syria, the state – represented by the Ministry of Telecommunications – imposed a new tax on terrestrial and cellular phone lines of 2 percent and 3 percent respectively and called it an "entertainment" tax (Sultan 2006). This arouses suspicions that the state is not truly interested in increasing the spread of modern telecommunication facilities.

Poverty: Except for the oil-wealthy Gulf States, most of the Arab countries in the Middle East and North Africa are considered developing countries, with very low Gross Domestic Product and very low standards of income. These include Yemen, Syria, Sudan, Morocco, and Egypt. With such poor populations it is normal to deal with the problems of supplying necessities such as food, health care, and accommodation before dealing with other needs such as education, science, and new technologies, including the internet. In most of the Arab countries, the internet is very expensive relative to the local average income. This fact hinders its widespread use in the Arab world.

Illiteracy and in particular digital illiteracy: The levels of illiteracy that characterize most of the population in all of the Arab countries are high. Literacy is crucial to the development of the internet. Not only does the Arab world need to reduce illiteracy, it also needs to illuminate digital illiteracy: people's ability to deal with digital and new media technologies.

Infrastructure: We have seen that physical infrastructure – fiber optics and other networks that allow internet distribution – is very problematic in the Arab world. This situation prevents the diffusion of the internet, especially in the rural areas and regions far from the capital. Not only is the expense of modern computers problematic, but, more important, the uncertain quality of some of these countries' telephony has been an impediment in the penetration of the internet in the Arab world (*The Estimate*, 1998).

Language barriers: Unlike Southeast Asia or Latin America, where efforts are made to adjust vernaculars to the internet and to make it popular in this way, the internet in the Arab world remains English-language-dominated. An even greater challenge is posed for speakers of languages that are not written in the Roman alphabet. The World Wide Web and Arabic browsers have ameliorated that problem somewhat, but text-based areas such as email remain problematic.

The main players

In the Arab world, governments were the first to begin to use the new media technology, especially the internet, for their interests. Their websites, which were very impressive relative to their traditional media, gained free effective access to elementary resources with high credibility. These included formal texts of documentations, speeches, and news articles that the regime wanted accessed and emphasized. For instance, since 1999 the formal website of the Egyptian Presidency is the biggest archive of all the documents related to the regime, including speeches, conference press releases, and other important documents. This is also relevant to the formal websites of different Arab countries, and the websites of their government offices. Even the Arab League and other pan-Arab organizations have become very active through the internet.

Despite the efforts made by the Arab regimes to control the public sphere, the internet turned out to be an alternative virtual public sphere (cyberspace). In this public sphere the main players are the different political, ideological, economic, ethnic, national, cultural, and religious powers and minority groups. These groups used to be marginalized by the mainstream discourse, and used to face obstacles in traditional media, which is heavily controlled by the regimes. The internet, as a virtual public sphere, is used as an alternative media channel; as an instrument for gaining solidarity and for creation of dialogue and more open discourse; a podium for exposing different attitudes and new discourses and activities that were denied by the traditional media. Also, and more important, it is used as an instrument for cultural and civil participation in the public life of Arab societies (Rinnawi 2003).

For researchers, the websites run by these powers and organizations become on-line archives. From the websites, we can learn about the conceptual framework within which the regimes operate, their agendas and strategies, and besides that, how they use the Web to bring about the structural, normative, and value changes they seek.

The Islamic fundamentalist groups are the most effective players on the internet. Through their Web presence they create the social and economic capital needed for solidarity and mobilization; also their websites target well-defined communities that have an interest in their message. The most important example is the Islamic Brothers websites, of which the most significant is ikhwanonline.com. This was established in Egypt in 1995 in order to be the mouthpiece of the fundamentalist Islamic group el-Ikhwan (Moslem Brotherhood), and represent its ideas and activities.

The moderate form of Islam, which was and continues to be represented by the mainstream media of the Arab regimes, also has its websites, which aim to strengthen perceptions of existing Islamic practice by the regime and the religious elites. The most famous example is the Qaradawi website, owned by Al Qaradawi, a religious leader highly respected by the Arab regimes. He has been also the religious "expert" of Al Jazeera. His website is very impressive, comprehensive, up-to-date and includes all of his works, sermons, and fatwas.

Besides the huge numbers of these websites belonging to the radical Islamist movements on the one hand, and to moderate mainstream Islam on the other, there are also a huge number of websites that represent more moderate Islamic movements. These use the internet in order to present an alternative point of view, different from the monopoly of the state system on defining the social and political public agendas. They also present an alternative for the different interpretations of fundamentalist Islam (Bunt 2003). One important example of such Islamic moderate websites is Islam-online, which has Islamic contents with universal messages in Arabic and English. It is funded by Qatari money and operates from Egypt. It targets ordinary people as reliable references for understanding Islam and its practice in modern daily life. The website provides consultancy to people online and open discourse, which characterizes the new generation, which is called "al-wasat" (the middle).

Other important Islamic websites are those of Hezbollah, the militant Shia'a Party from Lebanon. This represents more moderate Islam compared to the fundamentalist one, but at the same time it is different from the websites of liberal Islam. It is also a very special kind of political Islam, where it is used as a part of a larger media system to represent a certain ideology, not only on the Pan-Arab level, but also on the international level, especially among Muslim communities in Diaspora.

Other groups that use the internet heavily are the Arab and Islamic communities in the Diasporas, especially those immigrant communities in the West, who used this medium before it was accessible in the Arab societies in the Middle East. In these websites there is a very active and free discourse about what is going on in the Arab homelands. One of the famous websites is alhewar.org, which is considered a very open podium for Diaspora-homeland issues.

Ethnic, religious, and national minorities also are well-served by the internet, of which they make intensive use in order to present their cases and problems. Examples include Coptic websites such as copts.net or copts-united.com, which attempt to create a virtual community to communicate with other Copts and also to preserve the Coptic heritage and collective identity. More important, they use these websites to be in touch, connected, and updated about what is happening in the homeland, especially with the problems facing Copts in Egypt. It is the same with the Bahi', the Kurds, and Amazigh websites, which challenge many Arab regimes in Egypt, Syria, Iraq and Morocco.

Other important players are the human rights organizations. Most gain from this new media since they can now overcome the governmental restrictions and censorship on their publications and their use of traditional media. Almost all of the human rights organizations in the Arab world, especially the new generation of them, set up their websites in a way that helps them to introduce their reports, attitudes, and documentation on human rights violations in the Arab world quickly and cheaply by bypassing the regime obstacles. In this case, using the internet is turning these issues of human rights into global ones, meaning that they now attract international concern and are part of the international agenda. It also strengthens such NGO's role as instruments in the internal political, cultural, and social discourses. Therefore, most of these websites are bi-lingual: Arabic for the local public and English or other European languages for the international audience. In this context the website of the Egyptian Human Rights Organization, eohr.org, which is considered the most important website in the Arab world, covers the human rights violations in the Arab world through its annual reports and other publications in each Arab country. The Cairo Center for Human Rights Studies website, cihrs.org, has the most important and comprehensive archive of human rights violations in the Arab world and other reports and research related to human rights and democracy.

Women's organizations are also winners of the new media, as they use the internet to propagate their causes, for the internet works well in exposing their issues to the public, particularly with regards to gender empowerment and to act for obtaining women's rights. This is needed in a conservative patriarchal society, where women's activities and behaviors are under strict control by family, community, and society, and where anonymous use of the internet provides the protection and power to overcome these traditional restrictions. Many women's organizations have adopted internet forums for discussions to change ideas and experiences, as well as for the exchange of information and mutual assistance. On most of these websites they raise issues that are considered taboo in Arab society, such as violence against women and honour killings crimes. For instance, the website amanjordan. org, which operates from Jordan as the formal website of the Jordanian local branch of the International Institution for Solidarity with Women, is considered the main information center and resource on violence against women in the area. There is also the website of the Egyptian Center for Women's

Rights, ecwregypt.org, which concentrates on the political empowerment of women and publishes their roles and achievements in the political life of the Arab world.

The traditional media outlets, commercial as well as governmental or those related to political parties, are also very active in using the new medium in order to strengthen their role as widespread mass communication tools. This trend is relevant not only to print media such as big-city popular newspapers like *Al-Ahram* in Egypt, but also to electronic ones like Al-Jazeera satellite television. Some of these media outlets have long time Web presences and have grown to become credible among internet users, to the extent that some news websites have visitor hits much higher than the total readership rates of elite newspapers in any one country: Naseej, Elaph, Muheet, Islamonline, Masrawy, and AlBawaba are all examples. The internet in the Arab world is heavily used as a main media outlet to cover sensitive issues that are hardly covered or are ignored by the mainstream and traditional media. These include child abuse, child rights violations and sexual abuse of children as well as issues related to environmental quality and the preservation of natural resources and archeological sites. In this regard, it is important to notice that the spread of the internet in the Arab world has encouraged many newspapers and media outlets to resort to it by creating their own websites. Many organizations in the region have also set up their own websites.

Finally there are the bloggers: Out of the 37 million blogs on the Internet, there are almost 40,000 Arabic blogs (Casters, 2006). Although most were created in 2006–2007, their influence and popularity has exceeded all expectations. Despite the novelty of blogging in the Arab world, it has become an effective tool for Arabs to express themselves and reveal both public and personal grievances. Internet users in general, and youth in particular, are extremely interested in practicing their right to freedom of expression via this tool. One of the reasons why blogs have become so popular all over the Arab world is their use of Arabic colloquial language (as opposed to the more formal Arabic normally used in the media, which is different from the everyday spoken language that people use to communicate with each other in their homes and on the street). They also use the same expressions that are used in the streets and cafes in their writing. This has encouraged the youth to use their own spoken language in writing, which is normally discouraged. While reviewing Arabic blogs, one can see the wide range of issues that they deal with, including literary writings, personal issues, or technical tips. Many political issues are discussed; this is part of the reason for blogs' popularity, particularly their relationships with political movements supporting democracy in the Arab world.

Internet as a virtual public sphere

As we will see in detail in this section, the internet in the Arab world works as an open public sphere that enjoys a wide range of freedoms in contrast to traditional media and even satellite television, as shown in the content analysis study by Rinnawi (2003). The study argued that the discussion rooms on Arab websites are often used as an alternative medium. This then replaces the traditional media; it allows different groups to promote new ideas in public. For example, it can inform the public about demonstrations, petitions, or human rights violations committed by the Arab regimes.

In circumstances of developmental and tribal media, where the traditional mass media is controlled by the central regime and only flows one way (Boyd 1993), the internet is a significant medium expanding the public sphere. In this case, the inter-Arab discourse is altered by new positioning and new interpreters, despite it being a tool of a particular elite, who have access to this technology as well as the language skills and financial means to use it. Moreover, despite the unlimited borders of the internet as a public sphere, for most in the Arab world the borders of the internet are the borders of the Arabic language. Arabic-speaking users of the Web will also have certain issues of concern in the political, social, and cultural spheres.

Therefore, the dynamics of the internet have further created a sociopolitical vision of the Arab world shared among individuals. The internet has provided an opportunity for an open exchange of ideas and aspirations among Arabs, including intellectuals from different parts of the Arab world as well as Arabs in the Diaspora. This has led to the creation of a new generation of Pan-Arabists on the Web. New Pan-Arabism highlights not just new interpretations but also the multiplicity of views, settings, projects, and expressions of pan-Arabism today.

In sum, these developments initiate more desire, and perhaps increased demands for democratization and openness on the level of the Arab nation-state. Meanwhile, it is important to consider two aspects. Democratizing inter-Arab communication in the twenty-first century is closely related to the dialogue between people from the same culture. This sort of cultural dialogue impinges on individuals rather than on governmental initiatives, and is conducted through effective use of the internet.

Users' patterns and internet culture

Few studies have examined Web users and the different aspects of internet culture in the Arab world. Concerning users' perceptions about how they were affected by their internet use, these studies reached three main conclusions. First, the internet opens a new window onto the world, although it might not challenge traditional value systems and the basis of Arab culture. The second direction stands in sharp contrast and claims that the internet will eventually reshape Arab cultures through the internet's Western influences. This may endanger the traditional value system of Arab societies. The third direction, which is more sophisticated, claims that internet effects on Arab users vary from one country to another.

The first direction was salient in early research done among Kuwaiti students. All agreed that the internet presents a new window onto the world to them without being in strict alignment with the traditional tenets of their culture (Al-Mazeedi & Ismail 1998, Abbas 2001). Wheeler's (2003) findings continue this tendency, as was shown by her interviews with female Kuwaitis, in which they declared that they used the internet to communicate with males, and found it to be educational because "they did not generally have first-hand knowledge of how the opposite sex thinks." They valued this experience since it taught them about males within the relative safety of a computer screen. Taking into consideration that youths in Kuwait study in segregated schools for most of their lives, Wheeler concluded that "the most magnetic quality of the Internet, which draws Kuwaiti youths to the technology, is the way in which it enables the transgression of gender lines, which are otherwise strictly enforced in Kuwaiti society." She argued that such communication could lead to a better understanding of the males in general and therefore to better marriage and family relationships. She also noted that the traditional Islamic cultural norms that Kuwaiti students grow up with ultimately shape their long-term internet use, so that they refrain from usage patterns that strongly contradict these values, such as accessing pornography sites. Instead, even if they experiment, they eventually adapt their patterns of internet use to their upbringing, and to the societal norms and values they cherish.

Piecowye (2003) reaches similar conclusions in his study among female students in the UAE. His findings contradict the notion that the internet might reshape Arab cultures through unwelcome Western influences. The researcher noted that his interviewed students were active audiences on the internet, who knew exactly what aspects of global culture they wanted to expose themselves to and what aspects they turned away from. His main conclusion was that, while the UAE cannot ignore the internet as a technological revolution, female Emirati students are not helpless victims of globalization. Rather, they are conscious media consumers who are capable of determining what aspects of the local and global cultures they can accept, preserve, share, or reject. The researcher concludes that the internet is more likely to reinforce rather than challenge Arab culture, while providing an opportunity for sharing this culture with the rest of the world.

Another study by Wheeler (1998) provides some insights about the development of an internet culture in Kuwait. Wheeler claimed that while Kuwaitis are promoting internet use, they are worrying about the effects of foreign values and norms on their traditional Islamic society. Through investigating the practices of the Kuwaiti government as well as companies and individual citizens, she noted that the notion of cyberspace and its uses was bound to differ based on the local culture. Many other studies on this context conclude that information is regarded as a threat rather than an opportunity in some Arab societies, and that there is a feeling among ordinary people, as well as the elite, that having and/or verbalizing an opinion, particularly a political or social opinion, might badly challenge the society's terms of reference (Delwany, 2005). Wheeler finally concluded that local identity and cultural frameworks played a vital role in the way and the degree to which a society would adapt to a global economy or a global culture.

Another study, also by Wheeler (2004) examined Arab females' patterns of internet use in Egypt, Morocco, Saudi Arabia, Kuwait, and Bahrain to find out what this new medium means to them as Arab women. Her most important conclusion was that, despite the fact that Arab women from these countries stand to gain much from the internet in terms of general empowerment and as an educational and professional tool, their use of it varied from one country to another. For example, while the females she interviewed in Kuwait used it mainly as a means of socializing and entertainment, this was not the case in Egypt, where females mostly used the internet in work-related ways. The researcher gave a cultural explanation for this difference, pointing out the fact that in Kuwait there is segregation of sexes, and therefore the internet provides a virtual space for meeting members of the opposite sex.

Relying on the uses and gratifications approach, which assumes that audiences are active and goal-oriented, and that they are actually the ones to decide how to use the media in their lives, Abdulla (2007) in her recent interesting comprehensive study among Egyptian students addressing their patterns of internet use, concludes that Egyptian students are using the internet in accordance with their needs. Therefore, since they are active consumers, it is not affecting them as passive consumers. For instance, one of her findings was that the most important use of the internet for these students was to seek information (for research purposes). This was followed by keeping abreast of what is happening around them in the world. This indicated a more instrumental use, emphasizing that students here are active audiences who know what they want from their internet use.

However, one of the problematic points concerning these studies is that they try to examine only one small segment of the Arab world – for instance, students. They are not representative of the total population in the Arab world. Still, these findings are important to developing an understanding of the real picture of internet use and environment in the different Arab societies, and can clarify the huge differences among the Arab societies, such as those between the Gulf states and the rest of the Middle East, such as Lebanon, Syria, and Egypt on the one hand, and the differences between all these and the North African societies such as Morocco, Libya, and Sudan.

The rest of the research on internet use and culture has targeted other topics such as internet journalism in the Arab world. Hassan's 1996 study addresses the prospects and concerns of the Egyptian information superhighway through a survey of a purposive sample of media professionals. Here he pointed out the importance given by those professionals to the potential effects of the Internet and other new information technologies on Egyptian society and on the Arab world. His main conclusion was that this would lead to accelerating the exchange of information and modernizing the media systems in the Arab world. There would also be social effects, including more exposure to world cultures, and more democratization of Arab political systems. Concerns identified at the time included affordability, financial aspects, training of personnel, and the availability of the technological facilities needed.

Another study is Abdel Salam's 1998 research, in which he pointed out that Egyptian and Arab newspapers and magazines simply publish the same content online, instead of taking advantage of the interactive nature of the internet. This is a problem that is just as valid today as it was when the internet entered this part of the world. The second one, conducted by Ibrahim (1999) continued in this direction by studying internet use among journalists in Egypt. His main conclusion was that there was as yet limited internet access; the problem at that time was that journalists using it were mainly confined to those concerned with foreign affairs, translation, and technology. He concluded that the internet was used as a means of gathering information more than anything else.

We could not end this section without mentioning the distinguished study done by Nagib (2000) where she claims that since Arab users are utilizing new features on the Web, such as Arabic-language email access provided by the many Arabic portals, this should help in removing the language barriers between Arabs from different places. Therefore, the Arabization of the internet has a significant role in inter-Arab dialogue and at the same time the desire among Arabs to reach out to each other in their mother language has also affected the development of the internet in the Arab world.

144

Official approaches to the internet

Freedom of expression has always been a thorny issue in the Arab world. Some have argued that the relatively late and slow launch of the internet in some Arab countries is primarily due to a desire to control information on the part of the governments of these countries. For example, Iraq made it illegal for its citizens to access the internet from within its borders during 1997–2000. Syria and Saudi Arabia[18] did not allow its citizens to access local ISPs; citizens who wanted to access the web had to log on through an international phone call to an ISP in a neighboring country (Franda 2002). Almost all Arab countries took serious steps in order to regulate this new medium. Taking into consideration the complexity of such regulation, this was mainly to restrict use of the internet by groups and individuals who were not in line with the regime or the traditional order of the society. However, one can say that there is a clear legislative hole in the cases of electronic publishing and internet crimes.

Arab internet users are besieged by a triangle of social, religious, and political censorship, which prevents free access to the internet (Al-Saramy 2006). These three kinds of censorship differ from one country to another. In some countries such as Saudi Arabia and other Gulf states, the internet has been turned into a battlefield between liberals and extremists (Hardy 2005). In other countries it is a battle between the regime and the opposition groups, such as in Egypt, Syria, and Tunisia. In other parts of the Arab region, the internet has become a battle line between ethnic and religious sects, as is the case of the Sunni and Shi'a in Iraq, Bahrain and Lebanon. After September 11 it has also become a battlefield between Arab regimes and the fundamentalist groups, as is the case in Egypt, Algeria, and Jordan.

The legal frameworks governing control over the internet in most of the Arab countries are vague. Internet regulation articles in the UAE use vague terms, such as "disrupt morals," "social principles," "family values," and "crimes against Islam." One of the most famous cases is the "anti" websites in Syria, where such terms' definition is completely open to interpretation, and which include Israeli, Islamic, news, and even Syrian websites (Al-Awsteany, 2005). These terms, and others that exist in most of the Arab countries, are open to a wide range of interpretation and therefore abuse by prosecutors acting on behalf of the government to prevent dissenting views being aired to the public, and deny internet users their right to freedom of expression.

Besides the vagueness of the terms, arbitrary reasons for blocking sites are a very problematic issue. For instance, in the UAE, Tunisia, Syria, and Libya, censorship and blocking of websites seems to be arbitrary because of the number of factors that can motivate a decision about whether to block a site or not. These range from political and cultural considerations, which originate in the government, to economic considerations by internet suppliers. For instance, in a country like the UAE, the issue is further complicated by technological issues and the fact that there are dual standards in place with regards to Dubai Internet City and the rest of the country's internet users. Therefore when any individual case of censorship or blocking is considered it is not always clear exactly why it has happened.

In many Arab countries such as Kuwait and Saudi Arabia, censorship was also practiced on "anti-Islamic" websites, mainly during the period surrounding the controversial Danish cartoons of Prophet Muhammad. The Kuwaiti service provider Fast Telecommunication Company blocked all the weblogs affiliated with the Blogspot website, which hosts the majority of Kuwaiti blogs[19]. Extremist Islamic websites were also blocked in the vast majority of Arab countries by the governments, especially after September 11, in the framework of the "War against Terrorism." This was the case in Egypt when the government blocked all websites of the Muslim Brotherhood Group, which is one of the largest opposition groups in Egypt.

Many Arab countries block websites of ethnic, religious, or national minorities or groups within the country, such as the case of Bahrain where the "Bienat"[20] website was blocked. This belongs to one of the famous Shi'ite Muslim clerics, who publishes his discourse and answers questions received from his followers on it. Also, the Saudi government blocks Islamic websites that contradict the dominant Wahabism. These include the Shi'ite and Baha'i websites. On the other hand, the Saudi government allows the broadcast of many extremist websites that incite hatred (Eid 2006).

Finally, the Syrian authorities have blocked all Kurdish websites, especially after the bloody events of Qamishli (Bafel, 2006). Economic censorship includes restrictions imposed by the UAE Etisalat Company on websites that link to online voice call software, particularly Skype. The company fears that such online software will cause it to suffer financial losses, as it also runs the phone network.[21] At another level, the government of Yemen, for instance, monopolized service provision and kept the price of access to the internet very high so that many citizens cannot afford to use it (Human Rights Watch, 2002).

Many Arab countries practice censorship against Israeli websites. Syrian, Lebanese, and UAE authorities have blocked all websites registered within Israel that end with the suffix (.il)[22]. But the very interesting thing in this sense is that some Arab governments block websites that are against Israel, as in the case of the Jordanian authorities who have blocked the Qawem. net website, as it called for resisting Israel and boycotting American goods (Mara'i, 2006). Finally, websites which aim to overcome the blocking of the authorities of the websites in the Arab world are also blocked: UAE authorities, like other Arab states, blocked the boingboing.net blog, a foreign blog that discusses, among other things, technical tips to avoid the censorship imposed on web pages (Boing Boing 2006).

Finally, in most Arab countries, freedom on the internet was eclipsed after September 11, 2001, when the governments took measures to restrict this freedom. Most of these efforts came in response to pressure from the United States to crack down on terrorism (or terrorist communication) within the Arab world. This is because it was reported that the terrorists behind 9/11 attacks used email as the main channel of communication (Franda 2002). There were also pan-Arab efforts to enforce their control over the internet. This was the case when Egypt cooperated with the Saudis to draft a project proposal for the formation of a higher committee for electronic media that would operate at the level of Arab states (Al-Harethy, 2006).

Conclusion

Due to Arab society's traditional nature it is less permissive and less open politically and culturally. The internet thus provides a chance to express ideas that they could not do through traditional media. As discussed in this chapter, Arab governments attempt to do their best to be up-to-date in the field of the telecommunications and the internet while still struggling to restrain the use of the internet by their political foes and opposition movements. Two things will thus remain very relevant to internet development in the Arab world: first, internet penetration in the Arab world has increased very rapidly compared to other countries in the world and to other media; this will likely continue. Second, the younger generation, regardless of their social class, is likely to be the main consumers of new media in the Arab world.

Notes

1 Ministry of Communication Technology, http://www.infocom.tn/index.php?id=5
2 ADSL project initiative by the Egyptian Government, Ministry of Telecommunication, http://www.mcit.gov.eg/ar/app.asp?article_no=631.
3 TEData is a private sector company founded in 1992 with the name "In Touch". It was the first ISP in Egypt, while the latter is a joint-stock state-owned company.
4 Service provider in UAE, rehareal.tripod.com/isp.htm

5   The CS important indications,COA, http://www.trc.gov.jo/static_Arabic/mind icators.shtm (23/7/2006).

6   National Telecommunication Corporation, www.ntc.org.sd/ntc/ntc_func.htm

7   The Services of ISP Ynet Company. www.y.net.ye/arabicynet/ynet/background. htm

8   Internet Qatar website, www.qatar.net.qa/services/services.htm

9   International Telecommunication Union, Arab Regional Office, www.ituarabic. org/arab_country_report.asp?arab_country_code=15

10 www.qualitynet.net

11 Syria Telecommunications, a hint on the Foundation, www.ste.gov.sy/ ?act=about

12 International Telecommunication Union, Arab Regional Office, Syria, www. ituarabic.org/arab_country_report.asp?arab_country_code=10

13 Libya Telecom and Technology Company website, www.lttnet.com.

14 Minister of Telecommunication and Information Technology: we will offer soon a draft for a new telecommunication law, Ministry of Telecommunication and Information Technology, http: www.mtit.gov.ps/detalse.asp?id=57&tbl=all_ news&dep=reports

15 International Telecommunication Union, Arab Regional Office, Palestine, www.ituarabic.org/arab_country_report.asp?arab_country_code=14

16 The full bylaw is found on this link: www.mpt.gov.lb/isplist.htm

17 Egypt Information Portal, Digital Availability Seminar, www.idsc.gov.eg/Docs/ DocsDetails.asp?rIssueCategory=2&MainIssues=107&DocID=281.

18 Human Rights Watch also reported that the Saudi Kingdom has had access to the internet since 1994, but barred its citizens from public access until the Government ensured a good system for controlling what it referred to as "the bad things on the Internet."

19 kuwaitjunior.blogspot.com/2006/01/blog-post_21.html

20 www.bayynat.org.ib

21 The threat of skype, secret Dubai dairy, http://secretdubai.blogspot. com/2005/12/threat-of-skype.html

22 Libraries and Intellectual Freedom, IFLA/FAIFE, www.ifla.org/faife/report/ lebanon.htm

8   When Global Meets Local

Khalil Rinnawi

New global market

This chapter sums up the main trends underlying the globalization of Arab media industries as reviewed in the previous chapters. I will also review the role media industries play in enforcing a new pan-Arab identity. Despite the region's increasing nationalism, manifested in holding onto one's Arab dialect, arts, and cultural heritage, Arab media industries have consolidated a regional identity or a new kind of pan-Arabism, particularly manifested in the news coverage of *shared* political issues.

To start with, the most important four effects of globalization on Arab media firms are:

1. The privatization of mass media outlets
2. Cross-ownership
3. Trans-border ownerships
4. The regionalization of marketing and advertising.

Media privatization

While some may see the lingering Arab-state ownership of electronic media as a positive sign, others, including business tycoons, lament this as a sign of an outdated economic system. The privatization process of Arab media and telecommunication was kick started in the late 1990s, when the Arab world joined the global trend to privatize and liberalize electronic media (radio and TV) as well as telecommunications sectors (ITC). The privatization of Arab media stemmed in part from economic pressures that forced many Arab governments to invite foreign investors to finance the Arab media industry, particularly some projects beyond the capacity of governments, such as the Egyptian Media City (Sullivan 2001a). The new liberal economic wave has also opened the door to a new generation of capitalists who have sought to maintain political support for their economic projects by owning media outlets, especially television channels (Galal & Lawrence 2005).

The privatization of ITC has been more evident in mobile telephony services than in regular mainlines. Many Arab countries, such as the United Arab Emirates, Bahrain, Egypt, Jordan, Morocco, and Qatar, have spearheaded the privatization of their telecommunication services and infrastructure. The Emirates Telecommunications Corporation (Etisalat), for instance, is 40 percent owned by shareholders, serving the UAE population of fewer than 4 million. The Jordan Telecommunications Corporation (JTC) in Jordan is exactly like Etisalat in UAE and Batelco (Bahrain Telecommunications Company) is the key player for mobile and fixed mainline telephony services in Bahrain (Abdulla 2007).

Another group of Arab countries (Algeria, Kuwait, Lebanon, and Syria), has private mobile telephony operators while their fixed mainlines are still operated by government-owned organizations (Abdulla 2007). As for the internet, many Arab countries have taken the first steps toward privatization of this medium but to different degrees. In UAE, Qatar, Kuwait, and Lebanon privatization of the internet is well advanced, while in Syria, Saudi Arabia, Yemen, and Libya the privatization process is very slow and limited.

The popularity of CNN among Arab audiences during the Gulf War in 1991 triggered a series of developments that led to the launch of Arab private television, inaugurated in 1991 with the Middle East Broadcasting Corporation (MBC) channel from London, financed by a Saudi business tycoon, followed by ART and Orbit in 1993. When it comes to satellite TV, the Gulf States as well as Lebanon have spearheaded privatization while other Arab countries including Egypt lag behind. It was not until the end of 2001 that Egypt's first privately owned satellite network, Dream TV, was launched. Privatization of the Arab media is reflected in the increasing number of satellite TV channels and radio stations owned by Arab media moguls such as Al-Walid Ibn-Talal, the owner of Rotana channels, Sheikh Selah Kamel, the owner of ART, and Sheikh Walid bin Ibrahim al-Ibrahim, owner of the MBC Group, among others.

Moreover, the free media zones are a by-product of this privatization process, which was the rationale behind the three free media zones in three Media Cities, Dubai, Jordan, and Egypt (Sullivan 2001a). Modeled after duty-free zones in airports and duty-free repackaging and redistribution centers, these media-oriented areas offer special incentives and rules. It is attractive to businesses due to cost savings, reduced bureaucracy, modern infrastructure, lower labor costs, synergy, and one-stop shopping for skills and services. However, one fundamental issue here is the bureaucracy that has been an obstacle to media privatization in the Arab region, as can be seen in the case of two of the above three media cities: the Egyptian and Dubai cities. Because of bureaucratic obstacles, the Egyptian Media City was delayed, while Dubai Media City (DMC) was launched and quickly attracted media investors. The latter benefitted from Dubai's leadership, the Al-Maktoum Family and their business allies. Dubai is an absolute monarchy, where any law can be changed or altered by the ruler. The advantage is that bureaucracy is minimal and plans are executed swiftly. Clearly, there is also the risk that unilateral plans could result in negative outcomes (Walters & Quinn 2003).

Still, the main problem of the privatization of Arab media is political, and this obstacle has yet to be resolved. For instance, freedom of expression remains an important issue in the structure and form of media in the Arab world. As in other parts of the world, freedom of expression is a by-product of the overall political, social, cultural, and economic environments. All Arab constitutions recognize the right to communicate and preserve freedom of the press. But the reality is that all expressions are restricted by ancillary law and practice. Thus, media in the Arab world often finds itself either bound to the regime or walking a tightrope and highly dependent upon largely autocratic governments (Tawella 2002). For instance, a media free zone law that has been widely debated in Jordan's Parliament has never been passed. Companies operating television channels in Egypt's free zone will have to abide by the media code of ethics. As of early 2003, the Ministry of Information was still preparing that code of ethics. When it is completed, both Egyptian and foreign companies must abide by this code. On the surface, the situation is better in Dubai, but the press law regulates the operation of the DMC, as the general director of the DMC noted that "journalists were expected to exercise their freedom not to politicize society but to focus on issues such as education, health and economy" (Al-Bakry 2001). Consequently, each media city has capitalized upon what each does best within their own social and cultural context (Hamada 2008).

Despite the privatization of electronic media and the ITC in the Arab world, the link between private ownership and political freedom and cultural liberalization will need a reassessment. After all, many countries in the world have enforced measures of economic liberalization while keeping the political noose tight. In the Arab world, privately owned electronic media and ITC companies are still indirectly controlled by the ruling national elites, whether through family relationships (as in the case of MBC), or by shareholders such as the Lebanese satellite channel LBCI. Therefore, the privatization of media does not in itself insure political pluralism or cultural openness and liberalization (Kraidy 2002). Directly or indirectly, those rulers are still bankrolling the media, which is not entirely financed by advertising revenues, and hence it can still be used to communicate certain ideological or theological messages (Khalil 2006).

Cross-ownership

Arab regimes used to be the only owners of media outlets. In most Arab countries except Lebanon, the state owned the main TV channel, main radio station, and the main newspapers, which were all under the control of the governments. Now there is cross-ownership of different media by large corporations. For instance, the Arab media mogul Sheikh Selah Kamel, the owner of ART, also owns the Dallah Media Production Company, which has established and run the Jordanian Media City Company. In 2002, the newspaper *Al-Hayat* was partially owned by a Saudi media tycoon related to the Royal Family; LBCI TV is also partially owned by the Lebanese media giant Pierre Daher, who made this group one of the largest media corporations in the Arab world. Last but not least, Sheikh Walid bin Ibrahim al-Ibrahim, the owner of MBC, has created corporate structures that span continents, combining holdings in broadcast, print, and film companies while controlling distribution facilities such as satellites and cable networks (Ghareeb 2000). It is still debatable how this process of consolidating a few vertically integrated pan-Arab media giants would impinge on the creation, production, and distribution of media content. Al-Walid ibn-Talal of Rotana Company is an excellent example of that: Rotana Group is one of the biggest satellite TV channels, with more than 15 different satellite channels, dozens of radio stations and magazines, but more important, the biggest entertainment production company in the Arab world, with two hundred signed music artists.

Trans-border ownerships

Central to changes in ownership are the rise of global markets and the role of trans-border and transnational corporations in adapting to, producing for, and profiting from these changes (Bagdikian 2004). Unlike the post-independence period during which each Arab state owned its mass media outlets and hermetically controlled them, private Arab media corporations have grown regionally as well as globally since the beginning of the third millennium. The picture began to change as the Arab Gulf countries began to invest in telecommunications, and as Egypt and some other governments began to adopt technological development. Also, business tycoons from the Arab Gulf region now own transnational media outlets (satellite TV stations, radio stations, and newspapers and magazines) in other Arab countries and control telephony and internet suppliers.

Finally, most satellite media outlets used to be located outside the Arab region, and now most of the media firms have returned to the Arab world. The reason for their presence in London and Rome was the opportunity to access modem technology, information, and more freedom. Today, however, physical location does not determine such access, and modern technology has made it easy to receive and publish or broadcast information from anywhere (Rinnawi, 2006).

Regionalization of marketing and advertising

The conventional wisdom reflected in trade journals and general publications is that Arab satellite television offers unparalleled opportunities for media businesses and advertisers. At stake here are Arab audiences estimated at over 350 million people, most of whom had not experienced commercial television before the early 1990s, and thus were ideal targets for corporations wishing to shape consumer loyalties. In industry publications such as *Arab Ad* and *TV World*, the satellite industry is touted as the prime engine of the regionalization of marketing and advertising. This regionalist outlook is based on the fact that the Arab audience is united by language, and, to a large extent, by religion, which makes standardized advertising viable. According to some observers, regionalization facilitates Arab economic integration by embedding individual countries in a pan-Arab market.

The commercialization of the Arab media, especially the TV, however, results in the need for such stations to ensure a fair margin of profitability. Many stations in Egypt, Jordan, and Syria among others remain government-operated, and thus do not face the usual market pressures. Not enjoying the deep coffers of governments, privately owned stations face several financial hurdles (Kraidy 2002). First, there is reluctance in the Arab world to pay for television programs, which makes pay-TV extremely difficult to sell to Arab audiences. Orbit and ART, pay-TV pioneers, are challenged by the free services of MBC, LBC, and Future (Schleifer 2000). Second, the race for specialization and differentiation has made private media aim to target narrow segments of audiences; they appeal to a part of the market rather than to the whole market. This specialization is seen, for instance, in channels such as Al-Jazeera, which focuses exclusively on news, albeit sensational, while LBC, MBC, and Future TV focus on talk shows and variety programs, characterized by their scantily clad hostesses. Third, the efforts of satellite broadcasters to understand their audiences have been made even more challenging with the advent of the internet and related digital technologies that fragment the audience into myriad small segments (Kraidy 2002). Finally, due to the low socioeconomic standards across large parts of the region, the advertising industry has not fulfilled its potential, and advertising rates remain relatively cheap despite hikes up to 50 percent in 2000. Revenues come predominantly from wealthy Gulf States, whose populations constitute a small percentage of the region as a whole (Fakhreddine 2000).

Consequently, unlike regions such as Asia and Latin America, and despite the high socioeconomic standards of audiences in the Gulf region, the majority of Arab audiences do not have the income that would make them an attractive target for global advertisers. Therefore it is understandable that global media conglomerates are reluctant to buy into the privately owned Arab satellite stations. This leaves the pan-Arab satellite industry unintegrated into the global media economy.

Changing media roles

One of the most important features of globalization in the Arab media landscape is the transformation of media function. This transformation can be seen not only in media content but also in the reception of this content.

Arab media, especially broadcast and other electronic media, have long abandoned their traditional role of regime mouthpiece used mainly in mobilizing the nation behind the development plans of their regimes. Now, media serve as a means of information and entertainment. This does not mean that media are no longer manipulated by Arab regimes – in most Arab countries, main TV stations are still controlled by the government – but those outlets now have to fight to win their audiences, who have been attracted by the growing private and semi-private outlets. With the exception of Al-Jazeera, there is not a single example of a government-funded outlet in the Arab world that has changed its role from being a government tool. Other governmental channels have been compelled to increase their entertainment programs in order to attract larger audiences, as news production is rather costly.

While traditional media used to perceive their audiences as dependent and passive receivers of media content due to the lack of alternative media, now Arab media tend to perceive audiences as active and independent consumers who have the power to move from one channel to another using a remote control. The result is that media firms compete among themselves in offering attractive and credible content. The quantity of programs has increased, with the launch of 24/7 channels – a change from the past, when TV channels used to broadcast for a limited number of hours.

Also, several Arab media outlets perceive themselves as commercial ventures liable to their shareholders, rather than being an instrument for delivering public messages. This new role means that media promotes cultural products, as well as a range of necessities such as food and health products, often global brands aiming to reach potential markets in the region. This trend is referred to as the "consumerism of the Arab media and its audiences" (Kraidy 2002; Fakhreddine 2000). Advertisement time has notably increased within TV programs, which are seen as a tool to promote goods more than a tool to promote a certain ideology.

Khalil (2006) thus argues that television news in the GCC (Gulf Cooperation Council) is undergoing transitional currents with the increase of 24-hour news channels such as Al Jazeera and Al-Arabia. These channels have now to profile themselves as global ventures that are attractive for global investors. Government channels such as those in Dubai, Bahrain, Oman, and Saudi Arabia have changed their image radically to compete with the private channels. Moreover, broadcasting regulations, at least in Kuwait and the UAE, have allowed the launch of new channels dedicated to news and business (Khalil 2006). However, the traditional role of media is arguably similar to the new one: media as a mouthpiece of government aimed at brainwashing audiences and controlling them politically and ideologically perhaps does not differ as much as one might think from media put out by new private corporations, aimed at controlling the same audiences to serve the economic interests of their shareholders.

However, it can be argued that the audiences' trust in these media is still limited, for two reasons: first, despite the change of performance in several media outlets, the vast majority of Arab media still back the policy of their regimes. Second, the commercial channels can hardly deviate from the agendas of their owners, who are normally businesspeople with good relations to the ruling elites (Fundy 2000). For instance, Al-Arabia TV, which is a private channel, part of the ARA Group owned by Saudi Sheikh Walid El Ibrahim, who is a relative of the Saudi King. Thus, Al-Arabia claims to abide by the Saudi foreign policy, and the Saudi linkage has been instrumental in the editorial policy of that channel (Rinnawi 2009). In fact, the channel receives the support of Saudi businesses as long as its content respects the red lines of Saudi taboos and policies (Khalil 2006). The Lebanese LBC TV channel is another example. In addition, Al Jazeera claims to criticize all Arab regimes but when it comes to the Qatari regime, it runs short of critique. This makes it look like a tool in the hands of the Qatari ruling elites, at least because of its financial dependence for the past 12 years of operation on the support of the Qatari government. The channel has very little commercial advertisement to meet the costs of its operations (Khalil 2006).

Global media flows

The dominant direction of the changes in media flows in the Arab region is the massive flow of Western cultural products and media content, and specifically TV programming such as movies, TV series, and dramas, to the Arab world. This content fills a major part of the broadcasting time in almost all Arab state-controlled TV channels (Karam 1999). Since Arabian TV's establishment in the late fifties, the percentage of local TV productions by Arab state-controlled TV has been less than the imported ones of American movies and French comedies and Latin American telenovellas. Only a few national systems (as in Egypt, Lebanon, and to some extent Syria), have made major transitions to increasing their own program production. The rest of the Arab countries are still heavily dependent on imported TV programs.

This process has deepened and intensified in the last two decades. The growth of satellite TV broadcasting since the early 1990s and the ensuing need for Arab programs forced the new channels to increase their share of imported programs, notably from the USA. Today only 3,000 hours of annual programming are produced by Arab channels, which are a small fraction of the total air time (Ghareeb 2000). Because most of the imported global cultural and media products come from the USA, many commentators call this process the Americanization of Arab societies, thereby relating globalization to Americanization (Tunstall 1977). This argument also prevails in other parts of the world: in Latin America, despite the success of their media content in global markets, the major part of airtime is filled by US programs (Osava 1990). The majority of Arab satellite TV channels have also become more and more dependent on American content. They also tend to copy the American TV style, and adapt successful American TV concepts to Arab screens. This is in addition to the proliferation of American brands such as Coca Cola, McDonald's and Proctor & Gamble. Beside popular Egyptian films and Syrian drama, Syrian-dubbed Turkish telenovellas, are popular. These have become commercial brands like the American programs, and are interrupted by many commercials marketing all kinds of goods and encouraging a consumerist lifestyle, following the US example.

Arab governments have enforced several different measures in an attempt to balance the above imbalance of cultural and media content, some of which are "clothed in the garb of cultural measures ostensibly designed to protect the cultural sovereignty and artistic heritage of the country in question." (Ghareeb 2000) The first measure is to impose trade barriers on the imported cultural and media content, limit the amount of imported programs, and increase tolls on imported materials. This was done in Saudi Arabia, Libya, Syria, Egypt, and Iraq under the Saddam regime, as well as in other Arab

Gulf countries. Like Brazil, Korea, and other Third World countries, Egypt was noted for developing policies promoting homemade cultural production, which is evident from the experience of Time Warner and other corporations. Time Warner argued that it faced formidable trade barriers, "some of which are clothed in the garb of 'cultural' measures ostensibly designed to protect the cultural sovereignty and artistic heritage of the country in question." Egypt was not the only Arab country that developed policies subsidizing its local cultural productions. Other Arab Gulf countries, despite their high living standards, have spearheaded this trend. On the other hand, Syria, Iraq, and Libya have struggled to prevent access to foreign productions altogether, thereby protecting their local audiences from foreign content that challenges local political values.

Arab governments, to stem the continuous flow of Western cultural products, attempt to strengthen the regional exchange of media content. Since the establishment of Arab TV until the end of 1980s, a major part of regional content broadcast on all Arab TV channels has been produced in Egypt, Lebanon, and to some extent Syria. Now, TV programs such as dramas and movies as well as video clips and other forms of entertainment programs come from other Arab counties, whose production has greatly increased. Egypt remains the main factory for Arab movies and video clips funded by Arab Gulf production companies. In addition, Lebanon has become a leading exporter of video clips and reality TV programs, while Syria is now a leader in exporting TV dramas such as the popular TV series *Bab El-Hara* (The Gate of the Neighborhood), broadcast for Ramadan 2007 and 2008 on MBC and scoring the highest ratings among Arab audiences ever noted in Arab entertainment TV.

A new trend in the region is Islamization. The recent decade has witnessed the creation of Islamic TV channels, which reflects regional changes. Since the launch of TV broadcasting in the 1950s and 1960s, Islamic programs have been produced as part of the overall program schedule. Now, there are dedicated thematic Islamic channels – around 40 of them. This trend has developed as a response to the needs of certain audience segments who reject the "permissive media" and wish for alternative media that appeal to their socio-religious values. The strengthening of Islamic fundamentalism in the Arab region since the Islamic Iranian Revolution is one of the forces driving this new trend, which also crosses the borders of the region and targets Arab and Islamic Diasporas all over the world, who are attracted by a sense of belonging to a pan-Islamic identity while living in non-Muslim environments (Rinnawi 2009). The Arab satellite TV landscape has acquired a new kind of Islamic TV channel, with new and more attractive Islamic TV content. In an interview with Ahmed Abu Haiba, the manager of *Risala TV* (The Message

TV), he explained the vision behind his new Islamic TV channel launched in 2006, "as is part of a heavy dose of 'ethical' entertainment programs, . . . such as comedy, late-night talk shows, game shows, documentaries, soap operas, video clips and women's programs starring veiled pop stars and actresses, designed to compete with religious channels like Iqraa' with more liberal variety channels like Saudi-owned MBC and Beirut-based LBC" (Wise 2005). This niche for such value-based entertainment programming in the Arab satellite TV is not dominated only by Risala. According to MBC programming director Abdel-Fatah El-Masry, his network's reality TV has since 2006 offered a new trend of reality shows perceived as being more sensitive to Arab religious and cultural values (Wise 2006). He added, "These shows are doing well and they're feel-good type of shows so they have a better impact among viewers. It's a trend that now a lot of stations are moving into it. It has to do with making people feel good and creating something for themselves. Plus, you still have the reality element" (Wise 2006). Finally, the emergence of an "ethical" reality TV trend reflects a larger political and cultural negotiation taking place between socially conservative Islamists and more liberal secular elements in the Arab world.

It is also worth noting that foreign cultural products have now been developed and adapted for Islamic societies. Thus there has been an increase of imported media products which appeal to Arab and Muslim audiences by offering content that does not challenge Islamic religious and traditional values. In addition, most Arab countries, especially in the Gulf Region, have increased local production of television programming by their main national TV stations, in order to appeal to conservative audience segments. The rather permissive imported TV programs are limited to special TV channels that depend on imported content appealing to liberal audience segments that demand such programs. Therefore, such niche stations do not constitute a threat to the overall TV landscape nor constitute harm to Arab societies. The satellite channel MBC4 is 100 percent American TV: programs for teenagers and talk shows like *Oprah* and *Dr. Phil.* The TV channels MBC2, MBC Max, ONE TV, and Fox Movies broadcast 24 hours of Western movies (mainly American); MBC Action is action movies and TV series. Rotana TUNS and Melody Hits broadcast 24-hour Western video clips and music.

There is some evidence that domestic and regional production is preferred over imports. Turkish telenovellas and Syrian dramas garner larger audiences than imported American soaps in all Arab countries. The Turkish telenovellas *Noor* and *Asmar*, broadcast in 2008 and 2009, and the Syrian drama *Bab El-Hara* are examples of this trend. On the other hand, although audiences in some Arab countries, such as Egypt, Lebanon, and Syria, are more loyal to domestic programming, there is some evidence that audiences in other

Arab countries, like the North African and Gulf countries, prefer imported programs. Presumably a mix of demographic variables such as gender, education, urban dwelling, linguistic background, coupled with different patterns of work, leisure, and actual programming schedules, may all play a role in accounting for the diet of programs viewers actually chose when offered a mixed diet of foreign and domestic content. This makes generalizations about audience behavior difficult, and suggests that much work needs to be done to reveal Arab audiences' preference.

Now, different Arab satellite TV channels compete with each other to import reality TV programs from the West (Khalil 2004). It all started with *Who Wants to Be a Millionaire* on MBC in 1998: at that time one of the highest rated programs among Arab audiences. Later, the Lebanese Future TV channel imported the reality TV program *Super Star,* which became the most popular TV program among Arab audiences between 2003 and 2006. Most of Western reality TV has been imported and Arabized (Khalil 2004). The secret behind the success of these global media products in the local Arab arena is the Arabization of these programs, ensuring that they do not challenge existing Islamic and religious red lines or traditional Arab values.

The strategy here is to carefully prepare programs that fit the local Arab audience. This pan-Arab content is dependent on local and regional actors from different Arab countries, which gives the reality program the flavor of competition between these different countries. Each competitor then acts as their country's representative and usually is voted for by his/her country's audiences. This gives the program a pan-Arab flavor, which adds to the attractiveness of the program. Moreover, TV channels take out Western permissive components and other unacceptable features from the original reality TV concepts when Arabizing them, and replace them if possible with local Arab elements in order to abide by the religious and cultural values in Arab societies. The reality TV show *Big Brother,* adopted by MBC in 2002, is an example of this adaptation. MBC TV aired an Arab version of this show. Public pressure began with the Islamic religious groups and elites in Bahrain, which hosted the program, leading to a pan-Arab public protest against the program. The MBC channel had to face the criticism that the program harmed Islamic values. The final outcome was to cancel it shortly after its airing date (Wise 2005). Khalil (2006) argues that *Big Brother's* failure was partly due to a lack of Arabization – the show failed to strike a balance.

Another example is the public campaign started in Egypt in 2006 calling for the boycott of a certain fruit juice because the advertisement for this product was considered harmful to Islamic and Arab traditions. The Anti-Star Academy campaign during 2005 is another example. The demonstration against the reality TV program aired by Lebanese satellite TV LBCI was not only run in traditional media, but was intensified on the internet, where a website under the name "Anti-Star Academy" spurred great protest against the program (Al-Dakhil 2005). It is important to mention that such protests were different from traditional censorship policies as practiced by main TV stations. These recent public campaigns were very effective in leading to the removal of targeted content from Arab TV screens. However, in some other cases the public anti-campaigns led to the opposite effect. *Star-Academy's* campaign became a good advertisement for the TV show, bringing new audiences to watch the show.

In order to understand the above mechanism, Khalil (2006), who used to be a director, executive producer, and consultant with many Arab satellite TV channels, explains the considerations of Arab reality TV producers when adapting an international reality TV program to the taste of Arab audiences.

> Structural needs for respecting Islamic, particularly Saudi, values [remain] because of the powerful influence of sensitive and conservative Gulf-based advertisers and viewers. Creatives and advertising personnel working on reality TV programs in the Arab world cautiously interpret and continuously rewrite the rules of what can and cannot be broadcast. The dilemmas of how and whether creative producers should or should not faithfully adhere to original formats, suggests that sociocultural elements, specifically Lebanese and Islamic, are at the centre of format adaptation for the Arab World – its Arabization. The Arabization of an international format involves as much adherence to a Lebanonization as does Islamization. My use of Arabization refers to the repackaging of Western formats to Arabic-speaking audiences. The process of Lebanonization involves the staffing, the aesthetic and editorial treatment of the format, while Islamization refers to the various codes that producers apply in evaluating their stories. In other words, Lebanonization is not a reductionist notion; rather it helps explain the introduction of words like the French *nomine* for nominee in *Star Academy*, and the Western looks and language on *Al Wadi*. At the same time, Islamization justifies the prayer rooms in *Big Brother*, and the taboo subject of religion in *Star Academy*. In the Arabization of an international format, both programmers and advertising salespersons have a vested interest in balancing Lebanonization and Islamization. In doing so, they achieve a Pan-Arab audience appeal while maintaining an Islamic "safe margin" that guarantees continuous advertising support" (Khalil 2006).

To sum up, the Arab region, like many other Third World regions and countries, has seen the flow of media content from the West, especially the USA, to the Arab region. The latter, however, has not managed to penetrate global markets with, for instance, Egyptian movies, as was the case with the Latin American telenovela or the Indian Bollywood movies. As a response, Arab governments enforced a set of rules to circumvent this flow that was seen as harmful to traditional values. However, unlike most Third World countries that did not export news globally, some Arab channels such as Al Jazeera have been able to export news and images to the rest of the world.

Media effects

Except for some research on the internet, there is a paucity of studies on the impact of global media, especially satellite TV, on Arab audiences, despite the heated debate over the influence of globalization in the media field and the new information technologies on Arab youths. While the transnational media might be likely to make the world more of a global village, some Arab scholars still approach it with caution as they try to assess whether this will result in cultural imperialism or a multicultural world characterized by understanding and tolerance. Cultural imperialism sees the information revolution as a process dominated by the West, as a result of the preponderance of Western cultural products. Thus, local languages, cultures, religious beliefs, and values are threatened by the increased monopolization and conglomerization of the global media, and by the homogenizing nature of its instruments. Many Arab media observers claim that satellite media may not be a threat to Arab culture whereas the internet may be a threat; Amin (2002) for instance argues that that open access to the internet and other transnational media may indeed be a threat to Arab culture, values, and traditions.

Others, however, believe that this development is here to stay, and unless the Arabs master the new technologies and become full participants, not merely consumers, they are likely to be left by the wayside (Ghareeb 2000). Nagib (2000) for instance, argues that the transnational and satellite media would provide Arabs with a chance to "diffuse their culture and heritage worldwide." The new technologies are crucial for businesses and their competitiveness in global markets, and to spread political and social ideas. Consequently, technology may also change the decision-making process in the region, by weakening hierarchical systems, reducing the power of the state, and redistributing power downward (Ghareeb 2000).

When studying media globalization in the Arab world, most scholars have focused on the universalism of technology and ignored the particularity of Arab histories, cultures, and societies. There is a lot to be said about the way in which individuals engage with new media. For example, local cafés have historically played an important role on the consumption of new media, starting with radio during the 1940s and spanning TV during the 1960s and satellite TV during the 1990s. Now internet cafés are widespread. It is important for future research to analyze not only access to internet cafés but also the social structure that makes cafés a site of mass communication, where Arabs meet and collectively engage with a media product.

Fandy (2000) argues that new structures, means, and processes of modernity, enhanced by the global media, are usually absorbed into the local context. Some technologies may remain simply grafted onto the society and may not take root, in at least certain segments of these societies. Fandy (2000) argues that the main issue in the Arab world is not the diffusion of new information technologies but other cultural implications such as trust. Thus, Arab state-controlled media have failed to win the trust of the populace, while a transnational media such as Al Jazeera TV has won that trust based on its coverage of Desert Fox from inside Iraq. Another example is the way consumers use the internet as a market where they purchase and sell goods. It is still problematic in the Arab world to purchase on the internet, not because of lack of access but because of lack of trust in the internet as a marketplace. Exposing sensitive information such as credit card numbers seems too risky. While consuming news on a television channel requires trust in that particular channel, selling and buying on the internet requires trust in the whole system. Therefore, it is not enough to trust the medium or the message, but also the whole social, economic, and political system (Fandy 2000).

Moreover, one can analyze the media effect on Arab consumers drawing on reception theory or "the active consumer theoretical approach." For instance, Leibes and Katz (1990) argue that meaning is not exported in global media content but is created by consumers themselves according to their already formed cultural attitudes and political perceptions. Another example is Abu-Lughod's (1993) ethnographic study, which addresses the impact of what she calls "technologies of public culture" among western desert Bedouin in Egypt. Although these Bedouins have been quite marginal to the mainstream Egyptian culture, they were still affected by global cultural and technological changes. Abu Lughod examines the impact of tape players, radios, and television on these Bedouins' lives, arguing that their use does not eliminate sociability but in fact brings people together for long periods of time. Such usage does realign social relationships, mixing the sexes and tempering age differences at home, while video shows in local cafes keep young men away from home and give them greater exposure to media. Abu Lughod also argues that these technologies do not destroy distinctive cultures because "it is not just that people themselves seem to embrace the technologies and actively use them for their own purposes, but that they select, incorporate and redeploy what comes their way."

Moreover, Alterman (1998) argues that with a multitude of information sources available to Arab audiences, Arabs would have to be selective and evaluate the credibility of their sources. Rinnawi (2006) argues that the new media technologies such as Arab satellite TV channels have led to the creation of a new kind of pan-Arabism he calls "McArabism." This kind of instant nationalism is a direct outcome of the simultaneous exposure to these transnational channels among Arab audiences living in different places inside as well as outside the Arab world. Finally, Abdulla (2007) argues that an important function of the internet is that it has managed to connect Muslims worldwide, facilitating their communication and discussion on an unprecedented scale, and in a manner that overcomes obstacles of time and geographical boundaries.

Moreover, the transnational media have the potential of strengthening cultural ties among Arab countries, who could capitalize on their cultural commonalities in order to bring their national diversities in contact (Rinnawi 2006). Regional festivals, exhibitions, competitions and production cooperation are seen as some of the desirable consequences on the cultural front. In that respect, satellite television has brought about a pan-Arab consciousness. The depth and significance of this regional identification have not been empirically researched, but anecdotal evidence suggests that, at least on the surface, satellite television has managed to unite a pan-Arab audience.

The variety of present media outlets is best seen in its thematizaton and specialization. There are dedicated channels for news, music, movies, sport, dramas, and religion, among others. The race for specialization and differentiation fragments audiences. For instance, Al Jazeera and Al Arabia focus exclusively on news, while LBC and MBC focus on talk shows and variety programs, and Rotana and Melody on music, video clips, and movies. This does not even begin to take account of the many sports and Islamic satellite channels. This fragmentation has made it difficult for broadcasters to fully understand their target market, and such understanding has become even more difficult with the proliferation of the internet and related digital technologies that further fragment audience (Kraidy 2002). This fragmentation has also ensured that all audience segments are catered for, with myriad programs appealing to almost all tastes; this is particularly useful in a market like the pan-Arab one in which populations vary greatly according to religion, age, socioeconomic life standards, education, geographic locations, and tribal differences.

The Arab nation-state

With political environments typically characterized by lack of democracy, dictatorship, tribal affiliations, and limited access to information sources, the Arab region has been politically vulnerable to global media. Globalization has helped to weaken the Arab nation-state. The most important feature of Arab transnational media and also the internet is the fact that they can transcend geographical boundaries and time barriers between the Arab states and the outside world. Arab satellite TV programs, for example, have given Arabs all over the Arab world and in the Diaspora the opportunity not only to receive more credible news and analysis programs, compared to the content of the past, but more important, to view current affairs with a critical perspective. This helps minimize the centrality of the local national state-controlled media, and weakens the influence of state media censorship.

While Masmoudi (1997) claims that the internet has brought about serious positive effects on the Arab world, especially in the political arena, Hamada (2008) argues that satellite television has been critical in determining public agendas, which eventually restrict government dominance. Thus, he notes, the Egyptian government directs, distorts, and constrains local satellite communications. The Egyptian government's lack of control over other Arab satellite channels that deliver different types of political programs enabled a different public sphere to form. Ghareeb (2000), claims that the proliferation of satellite channels, the pan-Arab press, and the internet together provide a forum of free expression that challenges traditional state restrictions on such freedoms. In several Arab countries, audiences have abandoned state media in favor of the transnational, pan-Arab media, which has, in turn, forced state media to think of new ways to regenerate their image, not only to target local audiences but also audiences from Arab Diaspora communities.

This new satellite culture has provided a stimulus to other channels, including government-owned local media, by its breach of social taboos, thus enhancing deliberate dialogue. For instance, a survey of satellite dish owners showed that those owners bought their receivers to gain access to the outside world, to learn about other cultures, and to have access to news and information from outside sources. Their news preferences are Arab independent news channels such as MBC and Al Jazeera, as well as foreign channels such as CNN and the BBC (Youssef 2001). Eickelman (2003) argues that the information revolution, and particularly the daily doses of uncensored information from stations such as Al Jazeera and international coverage by CNN, is shaping Arab public opinion, forcing Arab governments to respond. Lynch (2003) argues that unlike earlier stations, which focused on belly dancing and soap operas, Al Jazeera favors politics, and its talk shows include representatives from across the region, presenting sharp arguments that shock audiences who have been unaccustomed to such controversial content. Such content has infuriated virtually every Arab government because of its critical and at times sarcastic tone. Alterman (1998) also argues that a multitude of information sources available to Arab audiences has made them selective and able to evaluate the credibility of each media outlet.

While Arab regimes maintain various levels of control over their satellite television stations, they are notably permissive when these stations are critical of other (enemy) Arab regimes. In fact, Arab regimes opposed to each other have used satellite television for propaganda purposes, or as a platform for dissidents, critics, and opponents of enemy governments. As a result, transnational broadcasting has intensified or publicized rifts between Arab governments. Al Jazeera remains a constant source of objection and tension between a variety of Arab governments and Qatar's rulers. In September 2002, Egypt, Saudi Arabia, and Jordan's relationships with Qatar became tense because of an Al Jazeera program. Is was not a surprise, therefore, that the Council of Arab Ministers of Information, with the exception of Lebanon and Qatar, issued in 2008 a document that includes organizing principles for satellite transmission of radio and television, which shows an intention to restrict free broadcasters whose programs have produced antagonism to Arab regimes. According to the document, Arab television is obliged to respect the principles of national sovereignty; each state has the right to impose what laws and regulations it deems fit. Finally, the competition between Al Jazeera and Al Arabia is not just competition between two news channels. It also represents the competition between two visions and two states (Qatar and Saudi Arabia). It seems that the new rulers have inherited the tribal tradition in which the tribe's poet hails the chief and smears the rival. Nowadays, channels owned by Gulf rulers or businessmen serve as the modern poets, and television is their stage (Khalil 2006).

Amin (2004) argues that transnational broadcast services were responsible for the creation of a strong pan-Arab public opinion, particularly evident when millions of people demonstrated in the streets of Arab cities in support of the Palestinians' intifada. Transnational media are thus a forum of free public discourse and can set the agenda for public debate on national, regional, and international issues, ranging from political democratization to intellectual freedom to peace in the Arab region. Hamada (2008) argues that the new "quasi-public sphere" created by the eruption of Arab global media has made it possible for Arab audiences to engage in a political debate completely different from the kind that was presented on government-controlled television. Thus, Masmoudi (1997) anticipated that the free flow of information bound to be enhanced by access to the internet would inevitably force Arab leaders to be more open and allow more freedom of speech in their countries. He argues that such free flow of information would inevitably affect public opinion, and eventually, would have an effect on political decision making. Ghareeb (2000) agrees that the creation of greater Arab cultural unity, the accessibility to more credible news sources, the exposure to other Arab cultural traditions, may all help create a common Arab agenda, and may result in a more active and involved citizenry, better informed and engaged in the decision-making process. Abdel-raouf (1998) also points to the potential of the internet in mobilizing Arab civil society and in creating a more democratic atmosphere in which lay citizens would have a bigger say in the political debate. These new media sources provide information about the region and recent conflicts and thus may help shape Arab public opinion, illustrated in recent demonstrations such as those against the US strikes on Iraq or Afghanistan or the Israeli attacks on Lebanon and Gaza.

However, the impact of media technologies in fostering democracy and opening the public sphere is not universal. Although we can accept the assumption made by Manuel Castells (2000) who asserts that "the media have become the essential space of politics," we have to be careful as we ana-lyze whether all types of media and in all conditions and circumstances have the potential to establish such a vibrant public sphere. It is safe to state that the nature of the public sphere depends to a large extent on the nature of the political system in which it exists (Dahlgren 1995). Analysis of the contem-porary political climate must take into account the interaction between the media and political candidates, issues, and citizens. Political participation, citizenship, and the media cannot be separated (Franko 2005).

Ayish (2002), for instance, claims that the emergence of commercial media and the restructuring of government-operated systems are in no way condu-cive to political pluralism and diversity in Arab societies dominated by author-itarian political systems. Hamada (2008) has also argued that in the case of Egypt, where the overwhelming majority is poor, illiterate, and unemployed, and where that majority suffers from lack of resources and from public restric-tions, citizens have felt unmotivated to engage in the public sphere. The role of new communication technologies, especially the internet, in enhancing the public sphere is rather limited. This is also the case in many other Arab coun-tries. Hamada (2008) also argues that despite the fact that satellite television has brought about a new "quasi-liberal public sphere" in Egypt, there is in fact no noticeable improvement in the democratic quality of political institutions and political life there. This is mainly due to the fact that democratic transfor-mation is contingent on a comprehensive political reform that considers the rule of law, free elections, independent media, a real separation between state authorities, especially executive and legislative authorities, independence of the judicial authority, a powerful civil society and public opinion, and absence of emergency law and dominance of principles of good governance. The quali-ties of transparency, accountability, responsibility, and decentralization are necessary to real change. According to Lynch (2006), national Arab public spheres could never really develop, as they are at the mercy of the politics of the carrot and the stick practiced by the ruling elites of authoritarian states. A gradually emerging public sphere in authoritarian systems cannot be understood as the Habermasian ideal of an area of negotiation between the state and civil society – if only because non-state actors have to be able to voice their arguments freely in public in order to break the political and discursive monopoly of authoritarian governments. Lynch affirms that one has to look at the actual public discourses to get an accurate picture of the political potential of an Arab civil society and public sphere. In terms of its political influence, the effects of such a public sphere (which is still in its infancy) may be very limited. Consequently, we should differentiate between the public sphere in an authoritarian setting, and that in liberal democracies. In an authoritarian context, the public sphere is not an open place of contestation, as liberals would have it. The public sphere is structured and the rules of the game can be changed by an intrusive state at any time.

Moreover, Karam (2007) sees the worldview offered by satellite media as one-dimensional. Channels such as Al Jazeera focus on international politics and ignore local and national issues that have a more direct bearing on viewers' lives: unemployment, poverty, or health care. These programs hardly encourage democratic behavior, but rather fill viewers' heads with sensational disasters to dwarf their own suffering. Karam's fieldwork reveals that Arab youth turn to TV not for political guidance but merely to escape their troubled lives. Finally, some argue that most of the Arab satellite channels are state-owned and are far from enhancing the public sphere. At the same time, private channels are owned by wealthy businessmen whose main interest is to maximize revenue from advertising. The tendency toward maximization of profit determines the policy as well as the content of the programs of private channels, which is noninformative, noncontroversial, and mainly cheap entertainment (Fakhreddine 2000).

Finally, one of the most important effects of the transnational pan-Arab media is that it gives Arabs the opportunity to be exposed to each other, to learn more about each others' traditions, music, arts, and even dialect, as well as to be exposed simultaneously to the common problems and challenges that face Arabs as a collective. There is no doubt that the new media have enforced a sense of cultural unity among Arabs, thereby acknowledging their diversity, helping to reflect a mobilized public opinion on issues of common concern, and overcoming some nationalist discourses and hence promoting a pan-Arab identity (Alterman 1998). Rinnawi (2006) argues that one indirect effect of the intensive exposure to Arab transnational media is the emergence of a pan-Arab *imagined community* with converging concerns and a sense of regional belonging. According to Rinnawi, media development in the Arab world since the 1990s has been a function of the interplay between local and global forces in political, cultural, economic, and technological sectors, which results in McArabism, or an instant nationalism shared by Arabs inside the Arab world and also in Diaspora.

The role of Diaspora communities

The relationship between Diaspora communities and the global media is dialectic; on the one hand Arab transnational media erupted first from such Arab Diaspora communities in Europe, where the first satellite stations were launched and pan-Arab newspapers have been printed; these ventures were also run by Arabs in Diaspora. The Arab migrant communities have also been the first beneficiaries of such transnational media (Rinnawi 2010; Abdulla 2007; Miladi 2006). Arab satellite television, by virtue of following the migration patterns of Arabs, has achieved a global reach concentrated in metropolitan areas in the West. These media have allowed the reintegration of Arab emigrants into Arab affairs, society, and religion (Miladi 2006). Rinnawi (2010) emphasizes the vital role of Arab satellite TV channels among the Arab Diaspora, where daily watching of such media beaming from homelands can enforce a sense of belonging to the homeland. Arab émigrés, mostly living in the US and Europe, were the first to bring their cultural, political, and Islamic interests and content to cyberspace and helped to define it. They have adapted the new media to express their own cultural traditions, using it to project their ties to Arab culture and community (Abdulla 2007). Communicating online in Arabic by e-mail, discussion boards, and chat applications (both text and audio) provides a valuable link to "home." Arabs in Diaspora have created mailing lists, news groups, and websites around topics ranging from Arabic music to searching for cheap tickets to the Middle East, from looking for wives to finding *halal* grocers and the nearest mosque or church (Ghareeb 2000). Also, the internet is bound to be of a more direct religious benefit to Muslims living in Western countries (Abdulla 2007). Arab Muslims in Diaspora, who constitute a small minority in the West, attempt to be linked online with people who share the same linguistic and cultural background. Transnational media is valuable as a tool for dialogue for Arab Muslim Diasporas, as it is much easier to have face-to-face access to an Islamic scholar, a sheikh or an Imam, in Muslim countries than it is in Western countries. So the satellite media presents a wonderful alternative, allowing people to ask their questions not necessarily of the Imam who happens to be at the mosque but of a variety of Muslim scholars on the multitude of Islamic websites and TV channels.

These Diaspora communities are also the producers of transnational media content. For instance, the Arab newspapers in London were founded and run mainly by Arab Diaspora journalists who were trained in Western journalistic traditions and in Western media outlets such as the BBC. These journalists help transfer such journalistic practices to Arab media outlets (see Mellor 2011). Al Jazeera is a clear example of a news channel that was built by a group of former BBC journalists who were sacked following the closure of the short-lived BBC-Arabic TV venture in 1994 due to disagreement with the Saudi partner at that time – Orbit TV. Also, Diaspora communities are active consumers of Arab TV who actively participate in live phone-in programs or on the internet as bloggers who are accustomed to more freedom in their host societies.

Conclusion

Arab media have been greatly affected by the globalization of the media landscape, as seen for instance in the accessibility of new communication technologies, economic privatization, the use of Arab petrodollar capital for media investments, and the relative political liberalization. Current developments in the Arab media industries have impinged on the parameters of media production and reception and have spread a sense of pan-Arabism.

In the beginning of the third millennium, the Arab media picture is more complex than ever. Transnational media coexist with domestic media, competing for Arabic-speaking audiences throughout the world; domestic production has become more and more commercial, garish and explicit; new programming formats, indigenized media products, and alternative news and entertainment frames are also developing. While pressures for liberalization of public debate increase, so do the new Islamist trends, creating a complex ground where technology is used to liberate and constrain, unite and fragment, innovate and preserve cultural heritage.

Scholarly analysis of the current Arab media landscape has also brought about contradictory views: a multicultural Arab society that has (finally) come to terms with its own diversity and which can be fully integrated into a global culture exists side by side with a society that is threatened by the domination and hegemony of Western/American culture and whose true identity may be lost in this cultural chaos (McNair 2006). It is also a society that has been unified by a revived pan-Arab identity and yet divided by nationalist trends throughout the region. What is clear, however, is that these contradictions, particularly regarding identity and culture, will be the centre of debate for decades to come.

Conclusion

In 1970, Arab states launched the Arab League Educational, Cultural, and Scientific Organization (ALESCO) with the aim of setting up a common Arab cultural market, through such things as organizing Arab fairs and ensuring that media industries fulfil their role of preserving Arab cultural heritage and promoting unity (ALECSO 2008). Two decades later, UNESCO launched Plan Arabia in acknowledgement of the role of Arab cultural and media industries in the development of the region. The plan was a means to promote Arab culture and to make it less dependent on the industrialized countries' cultural production (UNESDOC 1990). However, Plan Arabia still has not fulfilled its main goals of strengthening Arab media industries, whose contribution to the national GDP is rather modest. In Egypt, for one, media industries (including music, book publishing, and film) contribute no more than 0.5 percent of the annual GDP, and such industries suffer from weak and inefficient government support (Ghoneim 2005). In other Arab countries, media industries suffer from similar conditions, particularly in this era of market-economy-model dominance, which combats any form of state subsidy. This is also an era with unprecedented supply of media content produced on- and offline, which constitutes a huge challenge to state censorship and intervention. The growing demand for cultural products owing to, among other factors, the growing percentage of youth population, coupled with the lack of skilled labor, is yet another challenge facing Arab media industries.

The previous chapters reviewed some of these challenges and discussed the impact of selected media industries on the pan-Arab public sphere. This concluding chapter aims to offer a look ahead to the future of these media industries and the role they are expected to play in the near future.

To start with, the publishing industry will have to deal with one pressing issue: copyright and piracy. This is the most acute challenge facing Arab publishers. This problem also hinders international publishers accessing the Arab market, who fear the consequences of piracy in a place where local publishers can buy and sell books without paying for rights (Arabian Business 2009). The result is that the publishing industry operates in an untapped market with huge potential; this is a market that serves over 340 million people living inside the region in addition to a growing population in Diaspora in the

USA and Europe, where 12 million Arabic-speaking people currently live. A related challenge that the Arab publishing industry has to face in the future is the issue of distribution; at the moment, there are hardly any pan-Arab distribution companies and most publishers depend on book fairs to sell their books. The problems facing the development of printing in the Arab world during the past century were complex: ranging from technical to cultural and political. The escalating progress of communication technology, particularly the development of the computer, facilitated overcoming the technical problems of Arabic printing. The early obstacles raised by religious fundamentalists to the actual process of Arabic printing were initially overcome, but emerged again recently in the form of imposed censorship of printed material that diverged from orthodox religious values. The main obstacle that seems to be insurmountable is political censorship, which is mainly a result of poor systems of governance in the Arab world. In summary, the advance in technology coupled with the spread of internet usage among Arab youths has provided new potential for Arab publishers; however, the challenges remain: lack of strategies as to how to employ this technology, a weak market, and lack of skilled labor capable of studying and strategising the untapped market.

In fact, internet technology will continue playing a vital role in (re-) shaping the pan-Arab public sphere, linking Arabs throughout the world in one online community, which will challenge current state intervention and regulation. For instance, a new project called The Initiative For an Open Arab Internet has been started up by a group called the Arabic Network for Human Rights Information (ANHRI); it calls for the free use of the internet without censorship. Another example is the growing number of Arab bloggers located inside and outside the Arab region, such as a group of Cairo activists whose blogs are seen as an innovative form of dissent and mobilization (Fahmi 2009).

There is no doubt that television broadcasting in the Arab world has come a long way in its development and will continue to experience more progress for years to come. On the other hand, this television abundance, enabled by satellite broadcasting and Web video streaming capabilities, will most likely be shaped by global television competition and accelerating media convergence trends. The most recent Arab Media Outlook Report has painted a rather bleak picture of television broadcasting in the context of the current international financial crisis, with more channels going out of business and others limiting their operations. But the development of television is not only a function of economics but of politics as well. State broadcasters will continue to serve as official mouthpieces for their government policies unless significant democratic reforms are brought to bear on Arab media systems. Private broadcasters, on the other hand, will also continue to reflect a trend toward commercial entrepreneurship rather than political pluralism in the context of stagnated democratic reforms in the region. This suggests that regardless of its institutional affiliation, television broadcasting will remain captive to political and legal inhibitions. It will also continue to be an issue of public debate when it comes to cultural identity, with more television stations carrying Western-style programming that has less relevance for indigenous cultures and social systems.

Despite the dominance of satellite television in the region's broadcast environment, radio is likely to keep its presence in the Arab world. The proliferation of community FM radio services has given great momentum to the development of the medium and its role in national politics and social development. The establishment of Web-based radio services and transmission outlets has also been vital, making radio more accessible to more listeners at national and regional levels. In the long run, of course, the future of radio broadcasting in the region will always depend on both politics and economics. The more radio broadcasters operate in a free and participatory setting, the more likely they will be to attract listeners, especially among the younger generation. Radio stations also would derive sustainability from their engagement in their community's public affairs through the launch of critical and open forums that address issues of concern to society. As for economics, radio broadcasters, especially private ones, will be able to survive only through securing durable funding for their operations. For some reason, advertisers seem to be rather hesitant when it comes to sponsoring local radio shows and programs because they still believe that radio reach has some way to go before the issue of financing can be considered. The problem here is that more advertisers are driven by a bias against radio because they believe the age of radio broadcasting is reaching its end. The issue is complicated by lack of research on radio content and exposure, which leaves discussions defined more by subjective speculations than systematic investigations.

The proliferation of satellite television has provided a new challenge for the Arab cinema and it will continue to have a bearing on the profitability of this industry. Joint production (particularly with Western partners) will continue to provide an alternative for the future generation of Arab filmmakers, which in turn may change the regulations, censorship, and content characterizing this industry. The increasing number of Gulf films will continue to be a crucial element that shapes the future of Arab film. The recent annual Gulf Film Festival (GFF) in 2009 hosted around 75 films from the GCC, with the majority from Emirates and Saudi Arabia, most of which are documentaries and short fiction.

The objectives of the 1990 Plan Arabia are very much still relevant to the current media scene in the Arab world; issues such as dependency on

Western (particularly American) cultural production, lack of skilled labor, lack of homogenous media strategies and regulations across the region have been pressing issues for the Arab media industries ever since. The acute future challenge will be to form global, regional and national communication strategies that address this vast potential market comprising millions of Arabic-speaking audiences inside and outside the region.

References

Abaza, M. (2001). "Shopping malls, consumer culture and the reshaping of public space in Egypt." *Theory, Culture & Society* 18 (5): 97–122.

Abbas, H. (2001). "The gloomy picture of the Syrian press: Ink, paper and eternal slogans." *An-Nahar Cultural Supplement*, June 25.

Abdel-Latif, O. (2001). "The medium is the message." *Al-Ahram Weekly* 526, March: 22–28.

Abdel Nabi, A. F. (1989). *Sociology of News* (in Arabic). Cairo: Al Arabi Books.

Abdel Rahman, A. (2002). *Issues of the Arab region in the press in the 20th century* (in Arabic). Cairo: Al Arabi Press.

Abdel Salam, N. (1998). "The Egyptian and Arab electronic journalism experience: Reality and future perspective." *The Egyptian Journal of Media Research* 4 (in Arabic).

Abdelali, A. (2004). "Localization in modern standard Arabic." *Journal of the American Society of Information Science and Technology* 55 (1): 23–28.

Abdelrahman, A. (1996). al-Sihafah al-<'>Arabiyyah fi muwajahat al-taba'iyyah wa-al-ikhtiraq al-Sihyuni, Cairo, Al-Arabi.

Abdel-raouf, M. (1998). *Egypt and the information society*. Cairo: Dar el-thaqafa (in Arabic).

Abderrezak, H. (2007). "The modern harem in Monknèche's Le Harem de Mme Osmane and Viva Laldjérie." *The Journal of North African Studies* 12 (3): 347–68.

Abdo, I. (1942). *Tarikh alWaqa'e al Misriyyah*. Alexandria: Bulak Press.

Abdo, I. (1951). *Tatawur as Sahafa Al Misriyyah*. Beirut: Dar Al Adab Press. 2nd ed.

Abdulla, A. K. (2006). "Dubai: The journey of an Arab city from localism to globalization." *Al Mustaqbal Al Arabi* 18 (323): 58–84.

Abdulla, R. (2007). *The Internet in the Arab World: Egypt and Beyond*. New York: Peter Land Publishing.

Abu Dhabi Cultural Complex (1996). *Symposium on the History of Arabic Printing until the End of the 19th Century*. Nadwat Tarikh at Tiba'a al Arabiyyah hata 'intiha' al Karn at Tasi' 'Ashar. Abu Dhabi.

Abu Khalil, A. (2008). "The psychological war: Zionism in our bedding (and minds)." *Al-Akhbar* newspaper, January 10, http://www.al-akhbar.com/ar/node/112387

Abu Zeid, F. (1993). *Arab émigré press* (in Arabic). Cairo: Alam Al Kotub.

Abu-Lughod, L. (1993). "Finding a place for Islam: Egyptian television serials and the national interest." *Public Culture* 5 (3), 493–514.

Achilles, Z. & Miege, B. (1994). "The limits to the adaptation strategies of European public service television." *Media, Culture, and Society* 16 (3), 31–46.

Adousry, S. (2008). "Abu Dhabi . . . steps towards cinema." *Al Sharq Al Awsat*, October 9: Culture supplement.

al Bakry, A. (2001). "Media told to exercise freedom." *Gulf News* 24 (October): 3.

Al Faisal, A. Al A. (2005). *Electronic Newspapers in the Arab World*. Amman: Dar Al Shorouq (in Arabic).

al Issah, U. (2005). "as Sahafah al Falastiniyah bayn harbayn 'alamiyatyn," *ash-Sharq al-Awsat*, 12 May.

al Leithy, M. (2007). "Why do we watch only American movies?" *Akbar Al Youm* 64, 3289 (Nov.)

al Shayji, H. (1989). *As Sahafah fi al Kuwait wal Bahrain*. Manama: Gulf Panorama.

Al-Ahram Weekly (2005). http://weekly.ahram.org.eg/2005/762/cu8.htm

Al-Awsteany, S. (2005). "Imposing more restrictions and censorship on the internet in Syria." *Islam Online*, www.islamonline.net/Arabic/news/200505/23/article05.shtml

Al-Ayam e-newspaper (2005). "Ministry of Telecommunication: We support initiatives to facilitate access to the internet," www.alayyam.com/znews/site/template/doc_view.aspx?did=18593&Date=4/5/2005

al-Bustani, F. I. (1948). "Ash-Shammas Abdallah al-Zakher." Unpublished lecture delivered on the centennial of the death of al-Zakher.

Al-Dakhil, M. (2005). "Destructive Academy is harmful to the family." *al-Riyadh*, 27 February.

Al-Hadidi, M. S. 1982. *Documentary Films in Egypt and the Arab World*. Cairo: Dar Al Firk Al Arabi (in Arabic).

Al-Harethy, H. (2006). "Arab Committee to hold internet rules violators accountable." *Al-Hayat* newspaper, www.daralhayat.com/arabnews/gulf_news/09–2006/Article-20060919–c4fbac12–c0a8–10ed-01b6–e338a499fa76/story.html.

Ali, A. (2006). "Arabic E-newspapers: reality and horizons." In *Proceedings of the Conference for Electronic Journalism in the Arab World*. Sahrjah: Sharja University (in Arabic).

Ali, M. L. (2007). "'ameed as-Sahafah al-Iraqieh Fa'ek Batti: as-Sahafa al-Iraqieh tu'tabar min aghna wa aham sahafah 'rafatha al-Bilad al-Arabiyah." *al-Hiwar*, 21 August. http://www.ahewar.org/debat/show.art.asp?aid=106564

Al-Kahtani, S. A. H. (2000). "Globalization or Americanization: A comparative analysis of portrayals of globalization in United States and Arab mainstream newspapers during the 1990s." Unpublished PhD thesis. Washington D.C.: Howard University.

Al-Mazeedi, M. & Ismail, I. (1998). "Educational and social effects on the internet." *Middle East Journal* March.

Al-Menayes, J. (1996). "Television viewing patterns in the State of Kuwait after the Iraqi invasion." *International Communication Gazette* 57: 121–34.

Al-Mostaqbal Newspaper (2007). "A violating internet café owner is fined," www.almustaqbal.com/stories.aspx?StoryID=59111

Al-Saramy, N. (2006). "The story of blocking websites in Saudi Arabia" *Eilaf*, www.elaph.com/ElaphWeb/ElaphWriter/2006/5/149836.htm.

Al Sharq Al Awsat (2008). *Menhai . . .* the beginning of the Saudi Cinema. 10972: 12 December.

Alterman, J. (1998). *New Media, New Politics: From Satellite Television to the Internet in the Arab World.* The Washington Institute for Near East Policy.

Alterman, J. (2005). "The challenge for Al-Jazeera International." *TBS* 14, Spring.

Al-Thawadi, M. (1990). "The sociology of Arabization and nationalization of language in Algeria, Tunisia and Quebec." *Al-Mustaqbal Al Arabi*, December 1990, 13, 142: 40–56.

Al-Umran, H. (1996). "MMDS: The cultural alternative to DTH, Middle East Broadcast and Satellite." *Gazette*, September: 19–24.

Al-Wandi, M. (2008). "Tarikh as-Sahafah al-Iraqiyah," *Saut al-Watan*, 14 June. http://pulpit.alwatanvoice.com/content-136501.html

Al-Watan Newspaper (2005). "Internet crimes legislations and no intent to open new telecommunication markets." www.al-watan.com/data/20050527/index. asp?content=statenews

Al-Watan Newspaper (2008). http://arabic.cnn.com/2008/middle_east/8/25/newspaper.25august/index.html

ALECSO (2008). http://www.alecso.org.tn/lng/index.php?option=com_content&task=view&id=42&Itemid=72&lang=en

Amara, M., & I. Henry (2004). "Between globalization and local 'modernity': The diffusion and modernization of football in Algeria." *Soccer and Society* 5, 1: 1–26.

AME Information (2008a). "Arab FM radio stations in boom." http://www.ame info.com/152536.html

AME Information (2008b). "UAE ad spend to hit $ 2bn by 2010." http://www. ameinfo.com/152614.html

Amin, H. (2001). "Mass media in the Arab states between diversification and stagnation: an overview." In K. Hafez, ed., *Mass Media, Politics & Society in the Middle East.* Cresskill, NJ: Hampton Press.

Amin, H. (2002). "Freedom as a value in Arab media: Perceptions and attitudes among journalists." *Political Communication* 19, April: 125–35.

Amin, H. (2004). "Social engineering: Transnational broadcasting and its impact on peace in the Middle East." *Global Media Journal* 3, 4.

Amin, H. (2008). "The Arab states charter for satellite television: A quest for regulation." Arab Media & Society, http://www.arabmediasociety.com/countries/index. php?c_article=147

AmmanNet (2008). "About AmmanNet," http://www.ammannet.net/look/english/index.tpl

Arab Advisory Group (2006). *An Analysis of FM Radio Advertising Rates in the Arab World.* Amman, Jordan.

Arab Media & Society (2008). "Arab Satellite Broadcasting Charter," February, http://www.arabmediasociety.com/countries/index.php?c_article=146

Arab Media Outlook (2007–2011). "Forecasts and analysis of news and current affairs media in the Middle East." Dubai: PricewaterhouseCoopers. Available at http://www.pwc.com/extweb/pwcpublications.nsf/docid/14D97CB491E2A59B852573

34000B8AAB/$File/Arab_Media_Outlook_2007.pdf (accessed on 16 December 2007).

Arab Media Outlook (2009). *Forecasts and Analysis of Traditional and Digital Media in the Arab World*. Dubai: Dubai Press Club.

Arab States Broadcasting Union (2007). "ASBU Members," http://www.asbu.net/www/en/doc.asp?mcat=2&mrub=6&msrub=41&dev=true

Arab Thought Institute (2008). *The First Arab Report on Cultural Development*, Beirut.

Arabian Business. http://www.arabianbusiness.com/arabic/513353 (accessed on 23 April 2009).

Arabian Business. http://www.arabianbusiness.com/545092–arab-book-trade-is-game-for-growth (accessed on May 10 2009).

Arabic Network for Human Rights Information, (2004). "The Internet in the Arab World: A New Space of Repression", www.hrinfo.net/reports/net2004/libya.shtml

Armbrust, W. (1995). "New cinema, commercial cinema, and the modernist tradition in Egypt." *Alif: The Journal of Comparative Poetics* 15: 81–129.

Ar-Rifa'i, S. (1967). "Tarikh as-Sahafa as-Suriyyah." *History of the Syrian Press*, vols. 1& 2. Cairo: Dar el-Ma'arif bi Masr.

Asheihaby, M. (2005, 2007). "Asking you about the internet." *Gulf News*, www.akhbaralkhaleej.com/arc_Articles.asp?Article=165268&sn=moda&issueID=10286.

Assad, Soraya W. (2007). "The rise of consumerism in Saudi Arabian society." *International Journal of Commerce & Management* 17, 1/2: 73–104.

As-Samara'i, K. (1996). "At-Tiba'a al-'Arabiya fi Oropa." In *Arabic Printing in Europe: Symposium on the History of Arabic Printing until the End of the 19th Century*. Abu Dhabi: Jam'iyat al-Majid lil-thakafah wat-turath.

Atiyeh, G. N., ed. (1995) *The Book in the Islamic World*. New York: SUNY Press.

Ayalon, A. (1994). *The Press in the Arab Middle East: A History*. Oxford: Oxford University Press.

Ayish, M. (1987). "The VOA Arabic Service: A Study of News Practices and Occupational Values." *Gazette* 40: 121–30.

Ayish, M. (1990). "Media Access in the Third World: A Case Study of a Jordanian Radio Program," *Gazette* 45, 3: 173–87.

Ayish, M. (1991). "Foreign voices as peoples' choices: BBC popularity in the Arab world." *Middle Eastern Studies* 3, July: 374–89.

Ayish, M. (1997). "Arab television goes commercial: A case study of the Middle East Broadcasting Center." *Gazette* 59, 6: 473–94.

Ayish, M. (2001a). "The changing face of Arab communications: Media survival in the Information Age." In Kai Hafez, ed., *Mass Media, Politics, & Politics in the Middle East*. New Jersey: Hampton Press, pp. 111–36.

Ayish, M. (2001b). *Effects of Local Television on Children in the Arab World*. Proceedings of the conference on television effects on children, Sharjah, UAE, Higher Family Council and University of Sharjah, 22–23 March.

Ayish, M. (2001). *Arab World Television in the Age of Globalization*. Hamburg: Deutsches Orient-Institut.

Ayish, M. (2002a). "Political Communication on Arab World Television: Evolving Patterns." *Political Communication* 19, 2.

Ayish, M. (2002b). "The impact of Arab satellite television on culture and value systems in Arab countries: Perspectives and issues." *Transnational Broadcast Studies* 9, Fall/Winter, downloaded at: http://www.tbsjournal.com/Archives/Fall02/Ayish. html

Ayish, M. (2003). *Arab World television in the Age of Globalization: Emerging political, economic, cultural and technological trends.* Hamburg: Center for Oriental and Middle Eastern Studies.

Ayish, M. (2005). "Private television broadcasting in the Arab World: Trends and policies." *Journal of Social Affairs* 82, 1.

Ayish, M. (2008). *The New Arab Public Sphere.* Berlin: Frank and Timme.

Ayish, M., and I. Hijab (1988). "International broadcasting in Arabic: A comparative exploratory study of RMCME, VOA, BBC, RM." *Abhath Al Yarmouk* 4, 1: 15–26.

Aziz, S. (1968). *As Sahafa Al Misriyyah.* Cairo: UAR Ministry of Culture, Dar al Kitab al Arabi lil Tiba'a wal Nashr.

Azzam, M. (2007). "Where are the movie houses?" *Al Thawra*: 7 July.

Azzi, A. (1998). "Mass media in the Grand Maghrib," paper presented at the Seminar on Mass Media in the Muslim World, Department of Communication, International University, Malaysia, 11 June. http://www.geo cities.com/Athen/Ithaca/8257/maghrib.htm

Bab Website (2005). "Phone for Each House in Sudan," www.bab.com/articles/ full_article.cfm?id=3707.

Badran, N. A. (1980). "The means of survival: Education and the Palestinian community, 1948–1967." *Journal of Palestine Studies* 9, 4: 44–74.

Bafel, A. (2006). "Internet in Syria between prostitution and politics," on the *Kurd-Roj* website, www.kurdroj.com/meqalat/8–10/bafil.eli-24.09.06.htm

Bagdikian, B. (2004). *The new media monopoly.* Boston, Mass.: Beacon Press.

Batelco (2007). www.batelco. info/portal/news.php.

Batti, R. (1955). *Tarikh as Sahafa fil Iraq* (History of the Press in Iraq). Cairo: Institute for Higher Arab Studies, Arab League of States.

BBC News (2007). Friday, 12 January, http://news.bbc.co.uk/2/hi/middle_ east/6256985.stm

BBC News (2006). "The press in Saudi Arabia." 13 December, 15:04 GMT.

Bencherifa, M. (1996). "History of printing in the Arab Maghreb," "Tarikh at Tiba'a fi al Maghreb al Arabi," in *Symposium on the History of Arabic Printing until the End of the 19th Century.*

Black, I. (2008) "Too racy for Ramadan." *Guardian*, 17 September. Available at http://www.guardian.co.uk/world/2008/sep/17/middleeast/print

Black, J. (2008) "Egypt's Press: More free, still fettered," *Arab Media and Society*, Issue 4, Winter.

Blanke, J. & I. Mia (2007). "Assessing travel and tourism competiveness in the Arab World." In *The Arab World Competitiveness Report 2007.* Geneva: World Economic Forum. Available at: http://www.weforum.org/en/initiatives/

gcp/Arab%20World%20Competitiveness%20Report/index.htm (accessed on 16 December 2007).

Boing Boing (2006). "Banned in UAE", www.boingboing.net/2006/02/27/boing-boing_banned_in.html

Booz & Company (2008). "Trends in Middle Eastern Arabic television series production: Opportunities for broadcasters and producers." Available at http://www.boozallen.com/media/file/Trends_in_Arabic_TV_Series_Production.pdf

Booz & Company (2009). One year after the GCC Region's post-crisis prospects. Available at http://www.booz.com/media/file/One-Year-After_FINAL.pdf

Bosworth, C. E., ed. (1999). *The Encyclopedia of Islam*. Leiden: Brill Publishing, 1999).

Boughanmi, H. (2008). "The trade potential of the Arab Gulf Cooperation Countries (GCC): A gravity model approach." *Journal of Economic Integration* 23, 1: 42–56.

Boukhnoufah, A. (2001). "Does local TV have a place on Arab TV landscape?" *Arab Broadcasting*, vol. 2, pp. 13–22.

Boyd, D. et al. (1989). *Videocassette Recorders in the Third World*. New York: Longman.

Boyd, D. (1993). *Broadcasting in the Arab World: A Survey of Electronic Media in the Middle East*. Ames: Iowa State University Press.

Boyd, D. (1997). "International radio broadcasting in Arabic: A survey of broadcasters and audiences." *Gazette* 59, 6: 445–72.

Boyd, D. (1999). *Broadcasting in the Arab World: A Survey of the Electronic Media in the Middle East*, 3d edition. Ames: Iowa State University Press.

Bozbani, B. (2006). "Rise in the dealing of Morocco communication." *Moroccan* 26 August. http:www.openarab.net/en/node/364

Browna, A. (2006). "Internet cafés, station to journey to outside customs." On Tharwa Project site, http:www.openarab.net/en/node/364

Bulliet, R. W. (1987). "Medieval Arabic tarsh: A forgotten chapter in the history of Arabic printing." *Journal of the American Oriental Society* 107: 427–38.

Bunt, G. (2003). *Islam in the Digital Age: E-Jihad, Online: Fatwas and Cyber Islamic Environments*. Virginia: Pluto Press.

Burwell, C. (2003). "'I want to tell you about my life now': The voice of Palestinian refugees in frontiers of dreams and fears." *Refuge* 21, 2: 32–40. Available at http://pi.library.yorku.ca/ojs/index.php/refuge/issue/view/1261. (accessed on 12 November 2008).

Cairo Center for Human Rights Studies (CCHRS) (2006). *Media in the Arab World between Liberation and Hegemonic Reproduction*. Cairo: Cairo Center for Human Rights Studies.

Camaüer, L. (2003): "Ethnic minorities and their media in Sweden. An overview of the media landscape and state minority media policy." *Nordicom Review* 2.

Castells, M. (2000). "The global economy." In D. Held and A. McGrew, eds., *The Global Transformations Reader*. Cambridge: Polity Press.

Casters, M. (2006). *Le Monde Diplomatique*, August (Arabic version).

Chatterjee, P. (2005). "Whose imagined community?" In Ackbar Abbas & John N Erni, eds., *Internationalizing Cultural Studies: An Anthology.* Oxford: Blackwell.

CIA World Factbook (various dates). https://www.cia.gov/library/publications/the-world-factbook

Colonna, F. (2003). "The nation's 'Unknowing Other': Three intellectuals and the culture(s) of being Algerian, or the impossibility of Subaltern Studies in Algeria." *The Journal of North African Studies* 8, 1: 155–70.

Curtin, P. & T. K. Gaither (2004). "International agenda-building in cyberspace: A study of Middle East government English-language websites." *Public Relations Review* 30: 25–36.

Da Lage, O. (2005). "The politics of Al Jazeera or the diplomacy of Doha." In M. Zayani, ed., *The Al Jazeera Phenomenon: Critical Perspectives on New Arab Media.* London: Pluto Press.

Dabbagh Information Technology (DIT), (2001).

Dabbas, A. K. & N. Risho. (2008). *History of Arabic Printing in the Orient* (Tarikh at Tiba'a al Arabiyyah fi al Mashrik,) Beirut: Dar an Nahar.

Dahlgren, P. (1995). *Television and the Public Sphere: Citizenship, Democracy and the Media.* Thousand Oaks, Calif.: Sage Publications.

Dajani, K. F. (1980). "Cairo: the Hollywood of the Arab World." *International Communication Gazette* 26: 89–98.

Dajani, N. (1989). "The analysis of the press in four Arab countries," in *The Vigilant Press.* Paris: Unesco.

Dajani, N. (1992). *Disoriented Media in a Fragmented Society: The Lebanese Experience.* Beirut: AUB Press.

Dajani, N. (2000). "World news in the Lebanese media" (in Arabic). *Bahithat* 6.

Dajani, N. (2001). "The changing scene of Lebanese television." *Transnational Broadcast Studies (TBS)*, Fall/Winter at: http://www.tbsjournal.com/dajani.html

Dajani, N. (2006). "The re-feudalization of the public sphere: Lebanese television news coverage and the Lebanese political process." *Transnational Broadcasting Studies* 16.

Dajani, N., with O. Najjar (2003). "Status of media in Syria, Jordan, and Lebanon." *Encyclopedia of International Media and Communications.* Academic Press.

Davis, N. Z. (2002). "*Middle Eastern Languages and the Print Revolution: A Cross Cultural Encounter* (review)." Westhoven: WVA-Verlag Skulima. http://web.mit.edu/cis/www/mitejmes/issues/200512/br_nataliedavis.htm

de Tarrazi, P. (1913). *Tarikh as Sahafa Al Arabiyyah,* vols. I–II. Beirut: Al-Matba'a al adabiyyah.

Deane, D. (2009). "Middle East hungry for TV during Ramadan." CNN, 9 September. Available at: http://edition.cnn.com/2009/WORLD/meast/08/31/ramadantv/

Del Castillo, D. (2002). "Arabic publishing scene." *Publishing Research Quarterly* 17: 4.

Delwany, T. (2005). "Internet diamond of the Jordanians." *Islam online.* www.islam-online.net/Arabic/news/2005–05/23/article05.shtml

Digital Studio (2001a). "Super channel facelift for Jordan Television." Vol. 3, No. 2, Feb., p. 6.

Digital Studio (2001b). "JTV claims revamp a 'success.'" Vol. 3, No. 9, Sept., p. 8.

Dubai Press Club and PricewaterhouseCoopers (2007). *Arab Media Outlook 2007–2011: Forecasts and Analysis of News and Current Affairs Media in the Middle East.* Dubai.

Dumont, J.-C. (2006). "Immigrants from Arab countries to the OECD: from the past to the future." United Nations Expert Group Meeting on International Migration and Development in the Arab Region. Beirut: United Nations Secretariat.

Dutta, S., Z. K. Shaloub, & G. Samuels (2007). "Promoting technology and innovation: Recommendations to improve Arab ICT competitiveness." *The Arab World Competitiveness Report 2007.* Geneva: World Economic Forum. Available at: http://www.weforum.org/en/initiatives/gcp/Arab%20World%20Competitiveness%20Report/index.htm (accessed on 16 December 2007).

Dyer, P. & T. Yousef (2007). "Will the current oil boom solve the employment crisis in the Middle East?" In *The Arab World Competitiveness Report 2007.* Geneva: World Economic Forum. Available at: http://www.weforum.org/en/initiatives/gcp/Arab%20World%20Competitiveness%20Report/index.htm (acceseed on 16 December 2007).

Echchaibi, N. (2001). "We are French too, but different. Radio, music and the articulation of difference among young North Africans in France." *International Communication Gazette* 63, 4: 295–310.

Ecumenical Patriarchate of Constantinople, official Site of the Ecumenical Patriarchate of Constantinople, http://www.ecupatriarchate.org/

Eickelman, D. F. (2003). "The public sphere, the Arab street, and the Middle East's democracy deficit," *Global Media Journal* 2, 3.

Eid, G. (2006). *Internet in the Arab World: New Space of Repression.* Arabic Network for Human Rights Information.

El Shaygi, H. (1989). *As Sahafah fi al Kuwait wa al Bahrain.* Panorama al Khalij, al Manama.

El-Bahry, M. (2007a). "Increase in the number of internet subscribers." *Saba News Agency*, www.sabanews.net/view.php?scope=f69b5&dr=&ir=&id=103280

El-Bahry, M. (2007b). "TeleYemen Launches the New Generation of Access to Internet," Saba News Agency, www.sabanews.net/view.php?scope=f69b5&dr=&ir=&id=104571

El-Bahry, M. (2007c). "Yemeni Telecommunications: Huge Unexpected Figures," Saba News Agency, www.sabanews.net/view.php?scope=f69b5&dr=&ir=&id=112165

Elewa, H. (1998). *The Role of the Satellite Stations in Changing Types of Social Behavior in a Sample of Egyptian Public.* Unpublished doctoral dissertation. Zaqazeeq University, Sharqya, Egypt.

el-Ghrayyeb, A. (1970–71). "Memoirs of Aref el-Ghrayyeb," *As-Sayyad* magazine, 27 August 1970 to 18 March 1971.

El-Hasan, M. S. (2004). "al Inkilabat al Mutataliah 'Atalat as Sahafah as Sudaniyah." *Ash Sharq al Awsat*, 15 August.

Elligett, P. (2009). "Advertisers flock to pan-Arab media: PARC." *Digital Production Middle East*, 14 July 2009. Available at: http://www.digitalproductionme.com/article-1530_advertisers_flock_to_pan_arab_media-parc/

Ellingsen, T. (2000). "The New World Order: Global Village or Civilizational Clashes?" Paper presented at the 18th conference of the International Peace Research Association in Tampere, Finland, 5–9 August.

El-Mallah, M. S. (2007). "Outline of Arabic printing in the world until the end of the 19th century." "Mujaz Tarikh at-Tiba'a al-Arabiyyah fil 'alam hata nihayat al-karn at-Tas' 'ashar," *An-Nashiri al-'electroni*, 27 December. http://www.nashiri.net/content/view/3597/10027/

Elmenshawy, M. (2008). "Silencing Arab media." *International Herald Tribune*, 29 February.

El-Nawawy, M. (2006). "US public diplomacy in the Arab world: The news credibility of Radio Sawa and Television Alhurra in five countries." *Global Media and Communication* 2, 2: 183–203.

El-Nawawy, M., and I. Adel (2002). *Al-Jazeera: How the Free Arab News Network Scooped the World and Changed the Middle East*. Washington: Westview Press.

Elwan, K. (2004). "Internet requires curved methods." Institute for War and Peace Press, www.iwpr.net/?apc_state=heniicr2004&l=ar&s=f&o=168575.

Erlich, H. (2000). Youth and Arab politics: The political generation of 1935–36. In Meijer, Roel, ed., *Alienation or Integration of Arab Youth: Between Family, State and Street*. London: Curzon.

Essam El Din, G. (2000). "Cinema under siege." *Al-Ahram Weekly*, 1 - 7 June, No. 484, http://weekly.ahram.org.eg/2000/484/ec2.htm

Essoulami, S. (2009). "The press in the Arab world: 100 years of suppressed freedom." http://www.al-bab.com/media/introduction.htm

Estimate, The (1998). "The Internet in the Arab World: An update as the Saudis go online," *Estimate* 10, 26.

Et Tayyeb, I. M. (2010). "As-Sulta ar Rabi'a: Mahalak Ser," http://www.alhadag.com/investigations1.php?id=373

Fahim, J. (2008). "The reel estate: Egypt's reel sex dilemma." *Daily News Egypt*, 22 October.

Fahmi, W. S. (2009). "Bloggers' street movement and the right to the city: (Re)claiming Cairo's real and virtual 'spaces of freedom'." *Environment and Urbanization* 21, 1: 89–107.

Fakhreddine, J. (2000). "Pan-Arab satellite television: Now the survival part." *TBS* 5.

Fandy, M. (2000). "Information technology, trust, and social change in the Arab world." *The Middle East Journal* 54, Summer: 3.

Fargues, P. (2006). "The demographic benefit of international migration: Hypothesis and application to Middle Eastern and North African contexts." World Bank Policy Research Working Paper 4050, November 2006. Available at: http://www-

wds.worldbank.org/external/default/WDSContentServer/WDSP/IB/2006/10/25
/000016406_20061025142745/Rendered/PDF/wps4050.pdf

Farid, S. (1998). *Al-Cinema Al-Arabiya Al-Mo'assira (Contemporary Arab Cinema)*. Cairo: The Supreme Council for Culture Publications.

Fayez, A. A. (2000). "Electronic newspapers on the internet: A study of the production and consumption of Arab dailies on the World Wide Web." Unpublished PhD thesis, University of Sheffield.

Film City Oman. http://www.filmcityoman.com/about.htm

Finer, J. (2005). "Press in Iraq Gains Rights But No Refuge," *Washington Post*, 6 June.

Flibbert, A. J. (2001). "Commerce in culture: Institutions, markets and competition in the world film trade." Unpublished PhD thesis, Columbia University.

Franda, M. (2002). *Launching into Cyberspace: Internet and Development and Politics in Five World Regimes*. London: Lynne Rienner.

Franko, E. M. (2005). "The democratic ideal and its translation online: The possibility and potentials of the Internet as public sphere." Paper presented at the annual conference of the Association for Education in Journalism and Mass Communication, San Antonio, Texas.

Galal, A. & R. Lawrence (2005). *Anchoring Reform with a US-Egypt Free Trade Agreement*. Institute for International Economics, Washington, D. C.

Galal, E. (2009). "Identiteter og livsstil paa islamisk satellit-tv." Unpublished PhD thesis. Copenhagen: Copenhagen University, Denmark (in Danish).

Galal, I. (2004). "Online dating in Egypt." *Global Media Journal* 3, 4. http://lass.calumet.purdue.edu/cca/gmj/OldSiteBackup/SubmittedDocuments/archivedpapers/spring2004/grad_research/non_refereed/galal.htm

Gerth, J. & Shane, Scott (2005). "US is said to pay to plant articles in Iraqi press." *New York Times*, 1 December.

Ghareeb, E. (2000). "New media and the information revolution in the Arab world: An assessment." *The Middle East Journal* 54, 3.

Ghareeb, S. (1997). "An Overview of Arab Cinema." *Critique* 6, 11: 119–27.

Ghoneim, A. F. (2004). "Competition, cultural variety and global governance: The case of the Egyptian audiovisual system." HWWA report 246. Hamburg: Hamburg Institute of International Economics.

Ghoneim, A. F. (2005). "Performance of cultural industries in Egypt." Paper presented at the World Intellectual Property & the League of Arab States seminar on intellectual property for journalists and members of the media. Cairo, 23–24 May, 2005.

Guaabyess, T. (2001). "Restructuring television in Egypt: The position of the state between regional supply and local demand. In Kai Hafez, ed., *Mass Media, Politics & Society in the Middle East*. New Jersey: Hampton Press.

Habermas, J. (1991). *The Structural Transformation of the Public Sphere: An Inquiry into a Category of Bourgeois Society,* trans. T. Burger. Boston: MIT Press.

Haddad, M. (1994). "The rise of Arab nationalism reconsidered." *International Journal of Middle East Studies* 26, 2: 201–22.

Hale, J. (1975). *Radio Power: Propaganda and International Broadcasting.* Philadelphia: Temple University Press.

Halim, H. (1992). "The signs of Saladin: A modern cinematic rendition of medieval heroism." *Alif: Journal of Comparative Poetics* 12: 78–94.

Hamada, B. (2008). "Satellite television and public sphere in Egypt: Is there a link?" *Global Media Journal*, 7, Issue 12:2 Spring 2008.

Hamdoun, L. "As Sahafah al Masriyah bayn 'Ahd ath al Intidab al Biritani and Kiyam ath Thawra al Misriyah," http://elsohof.com/tawareekh0000002.html

Hammond, A. (2007). *Popular Culture in the Arab World.* Cairo: Cairo University Press.

Hammoud, H. (2005). "Illiteracy in the Arab World." Background paper prepared for the Education for All Global Monitoring Report 2006. UNESCO.

Hamza, A. al-Latif (1960). *As-Sahafa al Misriyyeh fi ma'at 'am.* Al Maktabah atha kafiah.

Hamza, A. al-Latif (1963). *Adab al Makalah as-Sahafiyyah fi Misr* (The Literature of the Journalistic Article in Egypt). Cairo: Dar al Fikr al Arabi.

Hamza, A. al-Latif (1965). *Al-I'lam lahu Tarikhuhu wa Mathahibuhu.* Cairo: Dar al-Fikr al-Arabi.

Hancock, M. (2008). "Arab Internet use up by nine million." *Business on Sunday*, 24 September.

Harabi, N. (2004). "Copyright-Based Industries in Arab Countries." MPRA Paper No. 4392. Available at http://mpra.ub.uni-muenchen.de/4392/

Hardy, R. (2005). "Young bloggers in Saudi Arabia." On news.bbc.co.uk/hi/arabic/middle_east_news/newsid_6057000/6057582.stm

Hashimi, H. (2007). "Nahwa Tashih Kitabet Tarikh as-Sahafah al-Iraqieh, 2007–06–23" http://www.al-hasimi.blog.com

Hassan, W. (1996). "The information superhighway: Prospects and concerns for the future of Egyptian mass media." Unpublished master's thesis, The American University in Cairo, Egypt.

Hennebelle, G. (1976). "Arab cinema." *MERIP Reports*, no. 52: 4–12.

Higbee, W. (2007). "Locating the postcolonial in transnational cinema: The place of Algerian émigré directors in contemporary French film." *Modern & Contemporary France* 15, 1: 51–64.

Hillauer, R. (2005). *Encyclopaedia of Arab Women Filmmakers.* Cairo: Cairo University Press.

Hindkær, T. (2001). "Arab discussions and opinions about the cultural dimension of globalization." Unpublished masters thesis, University of Southern Denmark (in Arabic).

Hirsch, D. (2005). "Middle Eastern émigré publishing in Europe." Paper presented at the 2nd International Symposium, History of Printing and Publishing in the Languages and Countries of the Middle East, November 2005, Paris.

Hitti, P. (1942). "The first book printed in Arabic." *Princeton University Library Chronicle* 4, November.

Hopkins, N. S. & Ibrahim, S. E. (2003). *Arab society. Class, gender, power & development* (3rd ed.). Cairo: American University Press.

Hudson, M. (2006). "Washington and al Jazeera: Face to Face. Competitive structures to create Middle East realities." In Emirates Center for Strategic Studies and Research (ECSSR), *Arab Media in the Information Age Conference Proceedings*. Abu Dhabi: ECSSR.

Human Rights Solidarity (2006). "As Sahafah fi Libya, tarikhuha wa abraz mahatatuha," http://www.lhrs.ch/default.asp?page1=v_bayan&id=45 (accessed on 6 August 2006.

Human Rights Watch (2002). "Report on human rights in Yemen." www.raynews.net/index.php?topmenuitem=documents/doc008.

Humphrey, M. (2004). Lebanese identities: Between cities, nations and transnations. *Arab Studies Quarterly* 26, 1: 31–50.

Ibrahim, A. (2009). "The international crisis hits the cinema industry." *Arriyadh* 14837, 6 February.

Ibrahim, B. & H. Wassef (2000). "Caught in between two worlds: Youths in the Egyptian hinterland." In Roel Meijer, ed., *Alienation or Integration of Arab Youth: Between Family, State and Street*. London: Curzon.

Ibrahim, M. (1999). "The use of internet in Egyptian press and its impact on journalistic performance." Paper presented to the 5th Scientific Conference of Media Faculty, Cairo University, Egypt (in Arabic).

Ibrahim, S. E. M. (1975). "Over-urbanization and under-urbanism: The case of the Arab world." *International Journal of Middle East Studies* 6, 1: 29–45.

Ihaddaden, Z. (1992). "As Shafa Al Jazairia Min Bidayatiha Il Al Istiqlal," in Abderrahmane Azzi and others, *Alam Al Itisal*. Algiers: Diwan Matboat al Jamieya.

Ilias, J. (1982). *Development of the Syrian Press in a Hundred Years 1865–1965*, (Tatawur as-Sahafa al Arabiyyah fi Ma'at 'Am 1865–1965), vols. 1 & 2. Beirut: Dar an-Nidal.

Inkeles, A. & D. H. Smith (1974). *Becoming Modern*. Cambridge, Mass.: Harvard University Press.

International Federation of Journalists (2005). "World journalists condemn US campaign of propaganda and 'stooge journalism' in Iraq," 5 December, 2005.

International Migration in the Arab Region (2006). "UN Expert Group meeting on int'l migration and development in the Arab region." Working paper, Beirut, Lebanon, 15–17 May 2006.

Internetworldstats.com (accessed on 1 June 2008).

IREX (2005). *Media Sustainability Index in the Middle East and North Africa* 2005. Washington: IREX.

Islamic News (2007). "Illiterates in the Arab Region rise to 70 million," 7 January, 2007. http://www.islamicnews.net/Document/ShowDoc01.asp?DocID=87420&TypeID=1&TabIndex=1

Izzat, A. A. (1983). *As-Sahafah fi duwal a Khaleej al Arabi*. Baghdad: Gulf States Information Documentation Center, Baghdad.

Jaafar, A. (2008). "Arab TV executives face challenges." *Variety*, 2 October. Available at: http://www.variety.com/index.asp?layout=print_story&articleid=VR1117993 365&categoryid=3264

Jalal, S. *At-Tarjamah fil 'alam al Arabi: al-Waki' wat Tahadi* (Translation in the Arab world: Reality and challenge), Higher Council for Culture, Cairo, 1999.

James, L. (2006). Whose voice? Nasser, the Arabs, and Sawt al-Arab Radio. TBS 16.

Jarrar, F. (1999). *Radio and Television in Jordan*. Amman: Al Mujamma Al Malaki Li-bohouth Al Hadara Al Islamya.

Kahki, A. (2008). "Arab youth exposure to reality television and its impact on identity." Paper presented at the Media and Globalization conference, Sultan Qaboos University, 24–26 October, Muscat, Oman.

Karam, G. (1999). *Arab Media in the 21st Century*. Beirut, Lebanon.

Karam, I. (2007). "Satellite television: A breathing space for Arab youth." In N. Sakr, ed., *Arab Media and Political Renewal: Community, Legitimacy and Public Life*. London: I. B. Tauris.

Kareem, E. H. (2004). "Internet requires curved methods." In *Institute for War and Peace Press*, www.iwpr.net/?apc_state=heniicr2004&l=ar&s=f&o=168575

Karthigesu, R. (1994). "Broadcasting deregulation in developing Asian nations: An examination of nascent tendencies using Malaysia as a case study." *Media, Culture, and Society* 16, 3: 73–90.

Katz, E. and G. Wedell (1977). *Broadcasting in the Third World: Promise and Performance*. Cambridge, Mass.: Harvard University Press.

Khalaf, R. (2005). "Saudi Prince aims to entertain Arab world: Tycoon hopes to tap into youth market with his music and movie channels." *Financial Times*, 5 April, p. 12.

Khalil, J. (2004). "Blending in: Arab television and the search for programming ideas." *TBS* 13, Fall.

Khalil, J. (2006). "Inside Arab reality television: Development definitions and demystification." *TBS* 15, Summer.

Khan, R. (2005). *AlWaleed: Businessman, Billionaire, Prince*. London: Harper Collins.

Khazen, J. (1999). "Censorship and state control of the press in the Arab world." *The Harvard International Journal of Press Politics* 4, 3: 87–92.

King Fahd Complex for Printing the Quran, *History of Printing* (Tarikh at-Tiba'a), http://www.qurancomplex.org/searchsite/arb/simplehits.asp?notmenu=true&wor dtxtsrch=%C7%E1%D8%C8%C7%DA%C9&wordtxtsrchEnc=%26%231575 %3B%26%231604%3B%D8%C8%26%231575%3B%26%231593%3B%C9 &itemselect=0 (accessed on 2 May 2008).

Kobrin, R. & A. Shear. (1996). *From Written to Printed Text: The Transmission of Jewish Tradition*. Exhibition catalogue for the exhibition of the same name at the Van Pelt-Dietrich Library, University of Pennsylvania, 21 April–26 June. Philadelphia: Center for Judaic Studies, University of Pennsylvania. www.library. upenn.edu/exhibits/cajs/exhibit1966/geography.html

Kraidy, M. (1998). "Broadcasting regulation and civil society in postwar Lebanon." *Journal of Broadcasting & Electronic Media, 42*.

Kraidy, M. (2002). "Arab satellite television between regionalism and globalization," *Global Media Journal* 1, 1.

Kraidy, M. (2005). "Reality television and politics in the Arab world: preliminary observations." *Transnational Broadcasting Journal*, 15. At www.tbsjournal.com/kraidy.html (accessed on 2 February 2006).

Krek, M. (1979). "The enigma of the first Arabic book printed from movable type." *Journal of Near Eastern Studies*.

Kriem, M. S. (2009). "Mobile telephony in Morocco: A changing sociality." *Media Culture Society* 31, 4: 617–32.

Kuttab, D. (2008). "Satellite censorship Arab League style." *Arab Media & Society*. At http://www.arabmediasociety.com/countries/index.php?c_article=148

Kuwait: Press, Media, TV, Radio, Newspapers. http://www.pressreference.com/Gu-Ku/Kuwait.html

Labib, S. (2000). "Arab satellite television channels: Politics or trade?" *Al Khaleej*, June 9, p. 11.

Leibes, T. & E. Katz (1990). *The Export of Meaning*. Oxford: Oxford University Press.

Lerner, D. (1958). *The Passing of Traditional Society*. New York: Macmillan Press.

Lloyd, C. (2002). "Thinking about the local and the global in the Algerian context." *Oxford Development Studies* 30, 2: 151–63.

Lucas, C. J. (1981). "Arab illiteracy and the mass literacy campaign in Iraq." *Comparative Education Review* 25, 1: 74–84.

Lunde, P. (1981). "Arabic and the art of printing." *Saudi Aramco World*, March/April, http://www.saudiaramcoworld.com/issue/198102/arabic.and.the.art.of.printing-a.special.section.htm

Lynch, M. (2003). "Taking Arabs seriously." *TBS* 1, 1.

Lynch, M. (2004). "Shattering the politics of silence: Satellite television talk shows and the transformation of Arab political culture." *Arab Reform Bulletin*, http://www.carnegieendowment.org/publications/index.cfm?fa=view&id=16242

Lynch, M. (2006). *Voices of the New Arab Public: Iraq, Al-Jazeera, and Middle East Politics Today*. New York: Columbia University Press.

Maddison, J. (1971). Adult Basic Education; Disadvantaged; Educational Radio; Educational Television; Functional Literacy; Independent Study; Literacy Education; Mass Media; Non Western Civilization; Questionnaires; Surveys; Western Civilization. New York: Unesco Publications Center.

Majed, A. (2007). "A Study of the Past and Present of Arab Press (Dirsah hawl madi wa hader as-sahafa al-Arabiyyah)," http://www.al-watan.com/data/200704004/index.asp?content=report

Maktoob Moheet Network, (2007). "Sudan eliminates telecommunication monopoly." http://www.openarab.net/en/node/354.

Mara'i, M. (2006). "Jordan veil site fighting normalization," in *Islam online*, 25 May.

Marghalani, K., P. Palmgreen, & D. A. Boyd (1998). "The utilization of Direct Satellite Broadcasting (DBS) in Saudi Arabia." *Journal of Broadcasting & Electronic Media* 42, 3: 297– 315.

Margy, A. (2006). "Terrestrial phone lines of Orascom next November." *El-Bilad*, www.el-bilad.com/article.php?codear=10052

Marmarita Forum (2006). "How internet hackers skip the control of the intelligence." www.marmarita.com/vb/showthread.php?t=6557

Martin, J. (2006). "Arab journalism comes of age." *The Middle East*, IC Publications, May. http://findarticles.com/p/articles/mi_m2742/is_367/ai_n249 87378/print?tag=artBody;col1

Masmoudi, M. (1997). *The Gateways of New Age of Communication*. Tunis, Tunisia: Metamedia (In Arabic).

Massad, J. (2003). "Liberating songs: Palestine put to music. *Journal of Palestine Studies* 32, 3: 21–38.

McLuhan, M. (1964). *Understanding Media: The Extensions of Man*. New York: McGraw Hill.

McLuhan, M. (2006). "The medium is the massage." In M. G. Durham & D. Kellner, eds., *Media and Cultural Studies*. New York: Wiley-Blackwell (3rd ed.).

McNair, B. (2006). *Cultural chaos*. London: Routledge.

Mdanat, P. (2008). "Impact of community media on social and political life in Jordan." Paper presented at the Workshop on Dynamics of Arab Broadcasting, Florence, Italy, 12–14 March.

Meijer, R., ed. (2000). *Alienation or Integration of Arab Youth: Between Family, State and Street*. London: Curzon.

Mellor, N. (2005). *The Making of Arab News*. Lanham, Md.: Rowman & Littlefield.

Mellor, N. (2007). *Modern Arab Journalism: Problems & Prospects*. Edinburgh: Edinburgh University Press.

Mellor, N. (2008). "Bedouinisation or liberalisation of culture? The paradox in the Saudi monopoly of the Arab media." In Madawi Al Rashid, ed., *Kingdom Without Borders*. London: Hurst & Company.

Mellor, N. (2011). *Arab Journalist in Transnational Media*. Cresskill, NJ: Hampton Press.

Mermier, F. (2006). *Le livre et la ville*. Paris: Actes Sud. Translated into Arabic by Yusuf Doumit as *al-Kitab wal Madinah* (Mukhtarat, 2006).

Middle East Online (2005). "French company dominates Jordan communication market." www.Middeast-online.Jordon/com/?id=392224

Miladi, N. (2006). "Satellite TV news and the Arab Diaspora in Britain: Comparing Al-Jazeera, the BBC and CNN." *Journal of Ethnic and Migration Studies* 32, 6: 947–60.

Miles, H. (2003). *Al-Jazeera: The Inside Story of the Arab News Channel That Is Challenging the West*. New York: Grove Press.

Morgan, M. (2005). "Women and sexuality in Egyptian cinema." *Sexuality in Africa Magazine* 2, 3: 3–6. Available at http://www.arsrc.org/publications/sia/sep05/feature.htm (accessed on 12 November 2008).

Mrowa, A. (1961). *The Arab Press: Its Origin and Development* (As-Sahafa al Arabiyah: nash'atuha wa tatawuriha). Beirut: Maktabat al Hayat Press

Muñoz, G. M. (2000). "Arab youth today: The generation gap, identity crisis and democratic deficit." In Roel Meijer, ed., *Alienation or Integration of Arab Youth: Between Family, State and Street.* London: Curzon.

Munro, J. (1981). "Facing the Future." *Saudi Aramco World*, March/April, http://www.saudiaramcoworld.com/issue/198102/arabic.and.the.art.of.printing-a.special.section.htm

Nafadi, A. (1996). *Sahafat al Emiarat.* Abu Dhabi: Cultural Foundation Publications.

Nagib, M. (2000). "Arabization of the Internet: Assessment and impact." Unpublished master's thesis, The American University in Cairo, Egypt.

Naím, M. (2005). "Arabs in foreign lands. What the success of Arab Americans tells us about Europe, the Middle East, and the power of culture." Foreign Policy, 5 May 2005. At www.foreignpolicy.com/articles/2005/05/05/arabs_in_foreign_lands

Nasser, R. & K. Abouchedid (2001). "Problems and the epistemology of electronic publishing in the Arab world: The case of Lebanon." *First Monday* 6, 9, http://www.firstmonday.org/Issues/issue6_9/nasser/

National Commission for Childhood (2008). "Arab illiteracy rate is 40% and 2/3 of world's illiterates are women," January 29. http://childhood.gov.sa/vb/archive/index.php?t-2432.html

Nehmeh, J. (2008). "Lebanon, the printing press of the East," http://phoenicia.org/zakhir.html (accessed on 30 April 2009).

Neidhardt, I. (2005). "Palestinian society as reflected in its cinema." In Rebecca Hillauer, *Encyclopaedia of Arab Women Filmmakers.* Cairo: Cairo University Press.

Noor Al-Deen, H. (2005). "The evolution of Rai music." *Journal of Black Studies* 35, 5: 597–611.

Ohibuka Watani (2007). "Increase in the Arab illiteracy rate," January 8, http://arec34.jeeran.com/archive/2007/1/140431.html

Olof Palme International Center (2001). *A Comparative Study on the Media Situation in Algeria, Egypt, Jordan, Lebanon, Morocco, Syria and Tunisia.* Stockholm, May.

Omar, N. (2005). The new trend in Egyptian cinema. *Al Thawra*, 13 September: Culture Supplement.

Orthodox Patriarchs of Antioch, http://www.mb-soft.com/believe/txw/antioch2.htm

Osava, M. (1990). *Orality and Literacy.* London: Methuen.

Othman, H. (1997). *As-Sahafa as-Souriyeh: 1877–1970.* Damascus: Syrian Ministry of Culture Press.

Page, J. (2006). "From boom to bust and back? The crisis of growth in the Middle East and North Africa." In Nemat Shafik, ed., *Prospects for Middle Eastern and North African Economies: From Boom to Bust and Back.* London: Macmillan.

Pan Arab Research Center (PARC) (2006). "Advertising Markets," at http://www.arabmediasociety.com/UserFiles/DOCUMENTS%20PARC%20data.pdf

Pan Arab Research Center (PARC) (2009). "Advertising Markets 2009" [Jan.–Dec.], at http://arabiandemographics.iniquus. com/knowledgebase.aspx

Pan Arab Web Awards (2004). http://www.panarabwebawards.org/index.shtml

PANOS Institute (2006). *Restructuring radio broadcasting in Arab countries.* Paris: Institut PANOS.

Parnell, J. (2009a) Arabic IPTV service set for North American launch. *Digital Production Middle East,* 12 May. Available at http://www.digitalproductionme. com/article-1275-arabic-iptv-service-set-for-north-american-launch/

Parnell, J. (2009b). Bucking the trend. *Digital Production Middle East,* 22 December. Available at http://www.digitalproductionme.com/article-2090-buck ing-the-trend/

Pedersen, J. (1984). *The Arabic Book,* trans. G. French. Princeton, N.J.: Princeton University Press.

Peterson, M. A. (2005). "The Jinn and the computer: Consumption and identity in Arabic children's magazines." *Childhood* 12, 2: 177–200.

Piecowye, J. (2003). "Habitus in transition? CMC use and impacts among young women in the United Arab Emirates." *Journal of Computer-Mediated Communication* 8, 2.

Pinto, O. (1929). "The libraries of the Arabs during the time of the Abbasids." *Islamic Culture* 3: 211–43.

Press Reference, Algeria. http://www.pressreference.com/A-Be/Algeria.html

Press Reference, Kuwait. http://www.pressreference.com/Gu-Ku/Kuwait.html

Press Reference, Morocco. http://www.pressreference.com/Ma-No/Morocco.html

Press Reference, Tunisia. http://www.pressreference.com/Sw-Ur/Tunisia.html

Qulaini, S. (1997). "The effects of watching satellite television on social trends among Egyptian youth." *Humanitarian Sciences and Arts Journal* 25: 71–144.

Rachty, G. & K. Sabat (1987). *Importation of Films for Cinema and Television in Egypt.* Paris: UNESCO.

Rayashi, I. (1953). *Kabl wa B'ad.* Beirut: Matabi' al-Hayat.

Rayashi, I. (1957). *Al-Ayam al-Lubnaniyah.* Beirut: Sharikat at-Tab' wan-Nashr al-Lubnaniyah.

Reporters without Borders (2006). "Internet under censorship," Qatar, www.rsf.org/ article.php3?id_article=10765 . 2 June.

Rifai, S. (1969). *Tarikh as-Sahafa as-Suriyya* (History of the Syrian Press) vols. 1, 2. Cairo: Dar al Maárif bi Masr.

Rinnawi, K. (2003). *The internet and the Arab World as Virtual Public Sphere.* Burda Research Center, Ben-Gurion University.

Rinnawi, K. (2004). "The Internet and the Arab World as virtual public sphere." Burda Research Center, Ben-Gurion University.

Rinnawi, K. (2006). *Instant Nationalism: McArabism and Al-Jazeera: Transnational Media in the Arab World.* Latham, Md. and Oxford, UK: University Press of America.

Rinnawi, K. (2009). "The Iranian nuclear project through the eyes of the Israeli and the Arab media." In Z. Zeraoui, *Irán: Tribalism and Globalism.* Mexico: Enrique Press.

Rinnawi, K. (2010). "Cybernauts of Diaspora: Electronic Mediation through satellite TV: the case of Arab Diaspora in Europe." In Andoni, A. and P.J. Diarzabal, *Digital Diasporas.* Reno: University of Nevada Press.

Robertson, R. (1992). *Globalization*. London: Sage.

Roper, G. (2008). "Muslim printing before Gutenberg." Islamic Heritage, May. http://muslim-haritage.blogspot.com/2008/05/muslim-printing-before-gutenberg.html

Rosen, M. (1989). "The uprooted cinema: Arab filmmakers abroad." *Middle East Report* 159, July-August: 34–37.

Rossetti, C. (2009). "Kotobarabia's Arabic E-Books extend borders," 18 June. http://publishingperspectives.com/?p=1420

Rugh, W. (1979). *The Arab Press*, New York: Syracuse University Press, 1979.

Rugh, W. (1987). *The Arab Press: News Media and Political Process in the Arab World*, 2d edition. Syracuse, N.Y.: Syracuse University Press, 1987.

Rugh, W. (2004a). "Washington and the Challenge of Arab Press Freedom," *Arab Reform Bulletin* 2, 11. http://www.mafhoum.com/press7/219529.html

Rugh, W. (2004b). *Arab Mass Media*. London: Praeger.

Rugh, W. (2005). Origins and development of radio and television broadcasting in the Arab world

Sabat, K. (1966). *Tarikh at-Tiba'a fish-Shark al-Arabi* (History of Printing in the Arab East). Cairo: Dar al-Ma'arif bi-masr.

Sabra, M. (2005). "Morocco discovers its cinema culture." In Rebecca Hillauer, *Encyclopaedia of Arab Women Filmmakers*. Cairo: Cairo University Press.

Sadiki, L. (2000). "Popular uprisings and Arab democratization." *International Journal of Middle East Studies* 32, 1: 71–95.

Saghiya, H. (2006). "The Arab press and various sources of repression." In *Arab Media in the Information Age*. Dubai: The Emirates Center for Strategic Studies and Research.

Sakr, N. (1999). "Satellite television and development in the Middle East." *Middle East Report*, Spring: 6–8.

Sakr, N. (2000). "Optical illusions: Television and censorship in the Arab world." *TBS* 5, Fall/Winter.

Sakr, N. (2006). "Commercial interests in Arab media." In Emirates Center for Strategic Studies and Research (ECSSR), *Arab Media in the Information Age Conference Proceedings*. Abu Dhabi: ECSSR.

Sardar, Z. and M. W. Davies. "Knowledge, learning institutions and libraries in Islam: Book publishing and paper making." http://www.muslimheritage.com/topics/default.cfm?ArticleID=642

Sarhan, H. http://arab2.arabtube.tv/videos/Shows/_Political_shows/eXclusive_The_1st_Interview_with_Hala_Sarhan_Part_2_and_emar_problem

Saudi Gazette (2009). "Saudi cinema to rub shoulders with world at Gulf Film Festival." Available at: http://www.saudigazette.com.sa/index.cfm?method=home.regcon&contentID=2009040934525 (accessed on 1 July 2009).

Schleifer, A. (2000). "A dialogue with Mohammed Jasim Al-Ali, Managing Director, Al-Jazeera," *TBS* 5: Fall/Winter.

Schramm, W., F. S. Siebert, and T. Peterson (1963). *Four Theories of the Press*. University of Illinois Press.

Scott, S. P. (1904). *History of the Moorish Empire in Europe*, vol. 3. Philadelphia and London: J. B. Lippincott.

Seib, P. (2009). *The Al-Jazeera Effect: How the New Global Media Are Reshaping World Politics*. New York: Barnes and Noble.

Shafik, V. (2001). "Prostitute for a good reason: Stars and morality in Egypt." *Women's Studies International Forum* 24, 6: 711–725.

Shafik, V. (2007). *Popular Egyptian Cinema: Gender, Class and Nation*. Cairo: Cairo University Press.

Shaheen, M. (1957). *Shari' as-Sahafa'* (The Press Street). Cairo: Dar al-Ma'arif bi Masr. 2nd ed.

Shalaby, A. (1954). *History of Muslim Education*. Beirut: Dar Al Kashaf.

Shamounki, N. & W. Orme (2003). "Mass media, press freedom and publishing in the Arab world: Arab intellectuals speak out." http://www.undp.org/arabstates/ ahdr/press_kits2003/2_AHDR03E2_FINAL...pdf

Siebert, F., T. Peterson, and W. Schramm (1963). *Four Theories of the Press*. Champaign: University of Illinois Press.

Singh, N. S. (2000). "Dilemmas of a free media." Paper presented to the International Press Institute's seminar on Media and Democracy in the Arab World, Amman, Jordan, 3–4 February.

Smith, C. G. (1968). The emergence of the Middle East. *Journal of Contemporary History* 3, 3: 3–17.

Springborg, R. (2008). "Arab Gulf States in the Arab World: Providing new leadership or decoupling?" *The Middle East in London* 4, 8: 3–4.

Sreberny-Mohammadi, A. (1998). "The media and democratization in the Middle East: the strange case of television." *Democratization and the Media* 5, 2: 179–199.

Stanton, A. (2007a). "A little radio is a dangerous thing: State broadcasting in mandate Palestine, 1936–1949." Columbia University.

Stanton, A. (2007b). "Exporting Arab TV: Overseas audiences prove to be a lucrative market." *MEB journal*, September/October. Available at www.mebjournal.com (accessed on 4 October 2007).

Steinberg, S. H. (1996). *Five Hundred Years of Printing*. London: British Library.

Sudanet Website, (2006). www.sudanet.net/new/arabic/about_sudanet.htm.

Suleiman, M. (1997). "Tunis & the world: The Tunisian youths' attitude to other countries." *Al-Mustaqbal Al Arabi* 20, 220: 69–86 (in Arabic).

Suleiman, M. (2009). "Early printing presses in Palestine: A historical note." *Jerusalem Quarterly*, Winter. http://www.jerusalemquarterly.org/ViewArticle. aspx?id=15

Suleiman, Y. (2003). *The Arabic Language and National Identity. A Study in Ideology*. Edinburgh: Edinburgh University Press.

Sullivan, S. (2001). "Private-sector media city launched in Amman." *TBS* 7, Fall.

Sultan, H. (2006). "Ministry of Telecommunications imposes an entertainment tax on cellular phones." *SyriaNews*, www.syria-news.com/readnews.php?sy_seq=5496.

Sutherland, N. (2007). "The role of French-Arab women in constructing a postcolonial France." *Al Raida* 24, 116–17 (Winter/Spring): 10–15.

Tarrazi, P. (1913). *History of the Arab Press* (Tarikh as-Sahafa al Arabiyyah), vols. 1–4. Beirut: Al-Matba'a al 'Adabiyyah.

Tawella, W. (2002). *New Media in the Arab World: The Social and Cultural Aspect.* Paper presented to the Conference on New Media and Change in the Arab World. Amman, Jordan, 27 February through 1 March.

The Middle East Magazine (1997). "France: The rise and fall of the Arab Press." April. Available at http://www.chris-kutschera.com/A/arab_press.htm

Thompson, J. W. (1957). *The Medieval Library.* New York: Hafner Publishing Co.

Tibi, B. (1997). *Arab Nationalism: Between Islam and the Nation-State.* 3rd ed. Basingstoke: Macmillan.

Times of India (2005). "Egypt's Amitabh Bachchan mania." Dec. 2. At http://timesofindia.indiatimes.com/india/Egypts-Amitabh-bachchan-mania/articleshow/1315446.cms

Tresilian, D., "Publish or Perish," *Al-Ahram Weekly*, Cairo, 8/04/2006 http://weekly.ahram.org.eg/2006/804/cu2.htm

Tunstall, J. (1977). *The media are American.* Columbia University Press.

UAE Interact (2007). "Media and Culture." at: http://www.uaeinteract.com/uaeint_misc/pdf_2007/English_2007/eyb8.pdf

UN/Dept of economic & Social Affairs (2006). *International Migration in the Arab Region.* UN expert group meeting on international migration and development in the Arab region, Beirut, Lebanon, 15–17 May 2006.

UNDP (2004). *Arab Human Development Report: Towards Freedom in the Arab World.* New York: UNDP Press.

UNDP, *Arab Human Development Report 2003* http://www.zu.ac.ae/library/html/UAEInfo/documents/ArabHumanDevReport2003.pdf

UNESCO (1994). *Television Transnationalization: Europe and Asia* (P. Sepstrup and A. Goonesekera). Reports and Papers, No. 109, Paris: UNESCO.

UNESCO (2005). *International Flows of Selected Cultural Goods and Services, 1994–2003.* Paris: UNESCO.

UNESDOC (1990). http://unesdoc.unesco.org/Ulis/cgi-bin/ulis.pl?catno=85606&set=4A426A69_3_61&gp=0&lin=1&ll=1

Wajihuddin, M. (2005). "Egypt's Amitabh Bachchan mania." *Times of India,* Dec. 2. Available at http://timesofindia.indiatimes.com/articleshow/1315446.cms

Walters, T. & S. Quinn (2003). *Bridging the Gulf: Communications Law in the United Arab Emirates.* Dubai, the United Arab Emirates: Ideas Lab.

Watani, O. (2007). "Increase in the Arab illiteracy rate," Jan. 8. At http://arec34.jeeran.com/archive/2007/1/140431.html

Waters, M. (2001). *Globalization.* 2nd ed. London: Routledge.

Wessler, H. & M. Adolphsen (2008). "Contra-flow from the Arab world? How Arab television coverage of the 2003 Iraq war was used and framed on Western international news channels." *Media, Culture & Society* 4: 439–61.

Wheeler, D. (1998). "Global culture or culture clash: New information technologies in the Islamic world – a view from Kuwait." *Communication Research* 25: 359–76.

Wheeler, D. (2000). "New media, globalization and Kuwaiti identity." *Middle East Journal* 54.

Wheeler, D. (2001). "The internet and public culture in Kuwait." *Gazette* 63, 2–3: 187–201.

Wheeler, D. (2003). "The Internet and youth subculture in Kuwait." *Journal of Computer-Mediated Communication* 8, 2.

Wheeler, D. (2004). "Blessing and curses: Women and the Internet revolution in the Arab world." In Sakr, ed., *Women and Media in the Middle East: Power through Self-Expression*. London: I. B. Tauris.

Wilson, K. "Orality, literacy, and the written Arabic language." http://webfoot.com/advice/WrittenArabic.html (accessed on 27 April 2004).

Winegar, J. (2006). "Cultural sovereignty in a global art economy: Egyptian cultural policy and the new Western interest in art from the Middle East." *Cultural Anthropology* 21, 2: 173–204.

Wise, L. (2005). "Whose reality is real? Ethical reality TV trend offers 'culturally authentic' alternative to Western formats." *Transnational Broadcasting Studies Journal* 15, Fall.

World Association of Newspapers (2008). "How the independent Arab press defies restrictive governments," Paris, 6 November.

World Bank (2007). *Economic Developments and Prospects, Middle East and North Africa Region*. Washington, DC: World Bank.

Yamani, M. (2000). *Changed Identities: The Challenge of the New Generation in Saudi Arabia*. London: The Royal Institute of International Affairs.

Youssef, H. (2001). "Arab issues as presented in the news of CNN and Euronews: A comparative study." Unpublished doctoral dissertation, Cairo University, Egypt (in Arabic).

Zamom, K. (2007). *Interactivity in Radio: Forms and Function*. ASBU Studies Series. Tunis: ASBU (in Arabic).

Zayani, M., ed. (2005). *The Al Jazeera Phenomenon: Critical Perspectives on New Arab Media*. New York: Pluto Press.

ZenithOptimedia (2008). "Advertising boom in developing ad markets compensates for credit-crunch gloom in the West," at: http://www.zenithoptimedia.com/about/news/pdf/Advertising%20boom%20in%20developing%20ad%20markets%20compensates%20for%20credit-crunch%20gloom%20in%20the%20West%20-%2031stMar08.pdf

Websites

http://arec34.jeeran.com/archive/2007/1/140431.html
http://childhood.gov.sa/vb/archive/index.php?t-2432.html

Index

Lightning Source UK Ltd.
Milton Keynes UK
UKHW021046150222
398722UK00005B/229

9 780745 645346